Anonymous

A History of the Year 1893

With special Reference to Canadian Affairs

Anonymous

A History of the Year 1893
With special Reference to Canadian Affairs

ISBN/EAN: 9783337186623

Printed in Europe, USA, Canada, Australia, Japan

Cover: Foto ©ninafisch / pixelio.de

More available books at **www.hansebooks.com**

A

History of the Year

1893

WITH ESPECIAL REFERENCE

TO

Canadian Affairs

TORONTO
THE MAIL PRINTING COMPANY
1894

A History of the Year 1893

CANADIAN AFFAIRS.

NOTES OF DOMINION AND PROVINCIAL POLITICAL HISTORY OF THE YEAR 1893.

HE Canadian who desires to pass in panoramic review the striking events of the year 1893 naturally turns his attention, first, to those matters of national concern which come under the general heading of politics. Here we touch upon points of vital interest, subjects affecting our lives and our liberties, our property and our civil rights, our industry and our trade. Nothing within the realm of politics can be truthfully said to be unimportant. The relations of the governing to the governed are so close, and produce so striking an effect upon the happiness and prosperity of the people, that they cannot at any time be too carefully or too critically examined. The year 1893 was not placid, from the political point of view, as was some of its predecessors. It opened with a threatening storm, and continued cloudy to the end. The circumstances which combined to produce the disturbance were varied. Apart from the fact that in nearly all of the provinces the leading men on both sides were engaged in preparing for the local general elections, which fall due during 1894, we had in the Dominion Parliament a practically new administration, with Sir John Thompson at its head. Sir John Abbott, the former Premier, had enjoyed a short and successful reign. It was with expressions of regret that the Conservatives had learned that failing health necessitated not only his immediate departure for sunny Italy, but his permanent withdrawal from the leadership of their party and the activities of official life. Sir John Thompson, the next in command, was a man of great ability and of undoubted probity. To him the sceptre naturally fell. But his acceptance of the Premiership was followed swiftly by evidence that his work, if to be accomplished with satisfaction to himself and with good results to his party, would demand from him the highest qualities of statesmanship.

Prior to his accession, one of the leading Conservatives of the Province of Ontario had shown signs of disaffection. This important politician, Mr. D'Alton McCarthy, now severed his connection with the party, and announced himself as independent of all former political associations. The points in respect of which Mr. McCarthy differed from the Government were, first, its treatment of the Manitoba school question; and secondly, its adherence to the tariff policy in its then existing form. Mr. McCarthy maintained that the Manitoba School Act, which abolishes the separate system, should have been promptly allowed; or, to put his position in another and perhaps fairer form, a second appeal against it should not have been entertained. He also declared that the customs duties should be subject to sweeping reductions. On January 5, just when Mr. McCarthy was engaging the attention of the country, an election took place in the County of L'Islet. This county had been Liberal for many years; but in the contest of 1891 it was carried by Mr. Desjardins, a Conservative. When Mr. Desjardins accepted an office under the Quebec Government, the seat was, of course, vacated. Then came the fight which terminated, on the day mentioned, by the election, with a majority of 36, of Mr. J. Israel Tarte. Mr. Tarte, who was now a Liberal, was also opposed to the policy pursued by the Administration with regard to the Manitoba law; but his complaint differed from that of Mr. McCarthy in that he held that the statute should have been disallowed. While this was the position so far as the difficult school issue was concerned, there was an unusual flurry with reference to the tariff. There had been, for some time, suggestions from within the Conservative party that the scale of duties should be reduced. Mr. O'Brien, of Muskoka; Mr. Cockburn, of Centre Toronto; Mr. Boyd, of Marquette; Mr. Davin, of Assiniboia; Mr. Calvin, of Frontenac; and Mr. McInerney, of Kent, N.B., had all spoken at one time or other in favor of change. Thus the members were faced with the proposition to apply the pruning knife. Besides the school and tariff questions, Sir John had before him the case of those persons who had been accused during the long session of 1891 of electoral offences or of official improprieties. Mr. McGreevy and Mr. Connolly were awaiting trial, and Mr. Arnoldi was in the same position. The atmosphere thus being cloudy, there was a very earnest desire to hear, at the earliest possible opportunity, from the new Premier. The occasion presented itself in Toronto soon after the opening of the new year. Then Sir John Thompson announced, first, with reference to the tariff, that it was the part of the true Conservative to lop the mouldering branches away, and that it was his intention so to treat the subject. He did not regard the tariff, he said, as perfect, and he added: "Both it and our severe customs law require amendment." Turning to the school issue, he asserted that the difficulty had to be met in accordance with the constitution, and in the spirit of toleration, conciliation, and concession. For further information with regard to the tariff, it was necessary to wait until Parliament met; but the school matter was hung up for the time being. The representatives of the minority in Manitoba had asked the Government to consider their case under sub-section 2 of section 22 of the Manitoba Constitutional Act. In virtue of this clause, as understood by the Premier, and in view of the special law passed in the previous year authorizing the reference of difficult points to the Supreme Court for an opinion, the case had been carried to the highest tribunal for advice.

Parliament met on the 26th of January. It was an early session, and was destined to be short, for the Premier had been honored by the Imperial authorities with a seat on the Board of Arbitration appointed to settle the Behring Sea difficulty, and he was due in Paris within two months. The Speech from the Throne pointed to the growth of trade and to the sufficiency of the revenue. It also made reference to our relations with the outside world. The trouble with Newfoundland arising out of the retaliatory measure consequent upon Canada's objection to the Bond-Blaine Reciprocity Treaty was

SIR JOHN THOMPSON,
Premier and Minister of Justice.

reported to be in process of arrangement, and the Sault Ste. Marie Canal difficulty was expected shortly to pass away. On the subject of legislation, the Speech promised amendments to the Franchise Act, improvements in the Civil Service Law, and the ballot for the Northwest. The Speech, as is usually the case, touched upon few of the subjects which were to agitate the legislators during its session. In following the labors of Parliament, it may be convenient to deal with minor questions first, and to leave the greater for consideration afterwards. The facts regarding Newfoundland were laid before the House in due course. It appeared from the papers that the Ministers, having met the representatives of the colony at Halifax, arranged there for a cessation of hostilities. Hostilities is unquestionably the right word to use, for the colony had treated our fishermen as foreigners, and had taxed our goods, while in return we had laid a heavy impost upon Newfoundland fish. When discussing a *modus vivendi*, the question of union was broached. But nothing was done definitely in the way of arranging terms. It was reported, however, at St.

John's afterwards that Sir William Whiteway, the Premier, had obtained all the information he needed with respect to confederation. "Whether it be the intention of the Government to take a plebiscite on the question, leave it for an issue at the general election, or exclude it from their programme altogether," said one of the colonial papers, "certain it is that no difficulty now exists in ascertaining the terms Canada is prepared to offer." The same journal added: "The present Government will do nothing without consulting the electorate, and this assurance we give on the authority of the Premier and his lieutenants. Should it be decided to submit the question to the people next spring, it will go before them in the shape of a plebiscite, and they will have the greatest freedom in rendering their verdict." No reference, however, was made to the question in the Newfoundland elections, which took place six months later. The difficulties between Canada and the colony were, however, settled. Of the Sault Ste. Marie Canal trouble, the same report can be made. President Harrison had, in the previous summer, laid an impost upon Canadian shipping passing through that canal, in retaliation for what was termed the discriminatory tolls on the Welland Canal. When the season opened, all suspicion of discrimination on the Welland Canal was removed, and the Sault Ste. Marie Canal was once more opened to our use free of charge. The legislation of the session, owing probably to the haste with which the proceedings had to be brought to a close, was not heavy. As a matter of fact, the bills to modify the Franchise Law and to amend the Civil Service Act were dropped. But a very important alteration was made in the Criminal Law. This change had relation to the law of evidence, which is so amended as to render accused persons compellable witnesses, and to admit to the witness-box the wife or husband of the prisoner. An important experiment was made by this provision, and there were not a few experts who doubted its wisdom. But it is of interest to note that the Imperial House of Commons has, on several occasions, passed a similar bill, and that the Lord Chancellor has had such a measure before the House of Lords. Some years ago accused persons were admitted in assault cases to the witness-box to testify on their own behalf. Many of the legal gentlemen who opposed that step have since concluded that it was wise. It is quite possible that those of us who are doubtful of the value of the more radical change may yet admit that it has its advantage.

Passing from the smaller to the more exciting topics, it may be as well to deal at the outset with the treatment accorded by Parliament to the Manitoba school legislation. On March 6, Mr. Tarte, the newly-elected member for L'Islet, fulfilled the promise made to his constituents that he would bring this subject up in the House. He presented an argument favorable to Federal interference with the local statute, charged the Ministers with having neglected to fulfil a pledge solemnly given that they would veto the law, and concluded with a resolution reading thus: "That this House desires to express its disapproval of the action of the Government in dealing with the Manitoba school question in assuming to be possessed of judicial functions conflicting with their duty as constitutional advisers to the Crown, which assumption is wholly unknown to law, and if now acquiesced in would be entirely subversive of the principle of Ministerial responsibility."

HON. WILFRID LAURIER,
The Liberal Leader.

This motion was cleverly prepared. The Government had received an appeal from Manitoba against the School Act. It, or at least a committee of the Cabinet, had sat in a judicial capacity to consider the petition, and had finally referred the point raised in the appeal as to constitutionality to the Supreme Court for an opinion. Mr. D'Alton McCarthy, who opposed Federal intervention, necessarily opposed, also, the sitting of the Cabinet as a court of law, or the assumption by the Government of judicial functions. Mr.

Tarte, who, with others, wanted disallowance, took the same view as that entertained by Mr. McCarthy with reference to the procedure before the Cabinet. Thus, while the two sides were at issue touching the fate that should have been reserved for the disputed bill, they were at one so far as the conduct of the Government in hearing the appeal with reference to it was concerned. It happened that Mr. McCarthy had written a magazine article in which he combated on constitutional grounds the claim of the Cabinet to act as a court. His last sentence stated his position tersely and pointedly. Mr. Tarte borrowed this concluding sentence and used it as his resolution. The debate on the question was short and sharp. After Mr. Tarte had stated his case, Sir John Thompson outlined the Ministerial position. He declared that the right to refer the petition as to the validity of the disputed law to the judges was conferred by the amendment to the Supreme Court Act passed on the suggestion of Mr. Blake in the session of 1892. He further asserted that, having been petitioned to submit the case for consideration, there was nothing for the Government to do but to comply with the request and with the statute. The judicial attitude assumed by the Government was defended on the ground that on other matters, as, for example, appeals under the Railway Act, for or against projected action on the part of any railway company, a committee of the Cabinet sits and adjudicates as a court of law. This latter position was assailed by Mr. McCarthy, his view being that in no case except such as is provided for by statute can the Ministers exercise judicial functions. An important point in Mr. Tarte's speech, however, was his assertion that the Ministers, having at one time promised to disallow, had withdrawn from their undertaking. This allegation was backed by a letter written by His Grace Archbishop Taché to his nephew in Montreal on August 20, 1892. The point in the letter upon which Mr. Tarte relied read thus : " I may tell you that I have learned that the passage of an explanatory law is in contemplation, which would establish in a clear and positive manner that the intention of our legislators in passing the Manitoba Act guaranteed to us our Separate schools. About this intention I have not the shadow of a doubt. The decision of the Privy Council shamefully violates the constitution, and if a remedy is not applied the Federal power will have one more iniquity registered against it. Orders have also been given, I understand, to give us a share of the school lands in Manitoba, which are administered by the Federal power." His Grace concluded: " Sir John Thompson has pledged himself officially and publicly to give us redress, and others have done the same." It became a question at once as to whether a distinct promise had been given to the Archbishop. Mr. Tarte, for his part, connected Mr. Chapleau's name with the understanding; for that gentleman, being then a Minister, had visited the Archbishop prior to the writing of the letter, and there had followed bye-elections in Quebec, at which the Ministerial candidates pledged themselves to be guided by the bishops in their votes on the burning issue. But Mr. Ouimet maintained that there had been no pledge, and a prolonged correspondence followed between His Grace and Mr. Tarte on the point, in which Mgr. Taché, while adhering to the letter as a repetition by him of reports that had reached his ears, and affirming that he had talked with Mr. Chapleau, declined to endorse the view that a promise had been made. An important feature of the debate was the declaration of Mr. Laurier, the leader of the Opposition, upon the question at issue.

HON. MACKENZIE BOWELL,
Minister of Trade and Commerce.

Mr. Laurier said a complaint had been made that the Public schools of Manitoba were, in reality, a continuation of the " Protestant schools." He had heard this denied, but he had not found in any of the blue books or reports on the subject any denial. " If," said he, " this be indeed true, if under the guise of Public schools the Protestant schools are being continued, and Roman Catholic children are being forced to attend these

Protestant schools, I say, and let my words be heard by friends and foes over the length and breadth of the land, the strongest case has been made out for interference, and, though my life as a political man depended upon it, I would undertake to say on every platform in Ontario and in Manitoba—yes, and in every lodge room—that the Roman Catholics of Manitoba had been put to the most infamous treatment." After three days of debating the division was taken, and the resolution of Mr. Tarte was defeated by a vote of 120 to 71. The opponents and advocates of disallowance helped to make up the minority. After this the discussion was transferred to the arena beyond the walls of Parliament. Between Archbishop Taché and Mr. Tarte it grew warm; but it was much warmer when Mr. Ouimet and Mr. Tarte came into conflict. The latter gentleman accused Mr. Ouimet of duplicity to Mr. Chapleau on the occasion of the Cabinet change of the year previous, under which Mr. Ouimet became Minister of Public Works. He said that, while Mr. Chapleau was demanding the Ministry of Railways, Mr. Ouimet was under pledge not to take office unless that Minister's request was satisfied; but nevertheless Mr. Ouimet accepted the Public Works portfolio. This treason, as Mr. Tarte termed it, resulted in the resignation of Mr. Chapleau, and his acceptance of the governorship of Quebec; thus imperilling the Manitoba minority. Mr. Ouimet, at a public meeting, denied the whole story, and replied in kind. Meanwhile the Manitoba law was on its way to the Supreme Court. Here at the fall session its validity was argued by Mr. S. H. Blake and Mr. Ewart. The Manitoba Government, opposing the proceedings, declined to be heard. The point at issue is of interest. When the Act was before the Judicial Committee of the Privy Council, their lordships were asked to determine whether it invaded any of the rights as to education enjoyed by the minority "prior to the union" of Manitoba with Canada. The reply was that there were no state-aided Separate schools before the union; therefore the abolition of such schools was not an invasion of the rights accorded at that time. In the British North America Act, it is set forth that educational privileges conceded "after the union" are protected, and cannot be withdrawn. It was consequently maintained by the representatives of the minority that if there was no protection for the schools in virtue of the claim that they existed "before the union," protection was to be found under the Confederation Act, which sustained the schools if established "after the union." The point which the Supreme Court is to decide is whether the educational clauses of the British North America Act, containing, as they do, the "after-the-union" provision, really apply to Manitoba as well as to Ontario and Quebec. If they do apply, then, the Manitoba minority claims, the Separate schools must be re-established. It is contended on behalf of Manitoba that the clause of the British North America Act cannot be applicable, because Manitoba has a special charter and a special set of clauses concerning the educational policy. With this issue before the Supreme Court the case is at rest until judgment is given.

HON. G. E. FOSTER,
Minister of Finance.

The next disturbing question was that of the tariff. It has already been pointed out that certain members supporting the Government had evinced a desire for a reduction of the duties, and that Mr. McCarthy had declared for a radical change. Fully supporting Mr. McCarthy was Mr. O'Brien, of Muskoka, who had long been a prominent member of the Conservative party. Mr. McCarthy made his first tariff declaration at Stayner, in his constituency, on January 25. Two points were emphasized by him in laying his project before the people. First, it was asserted that there were combinations which enhance prices; and, next, it was declared that as the Americans are about to lower their tariff it was opportune that we should adopt a similar policy. This clearly meant a reduction all round. But accompanying the proposed reduction was a suggestion that we discriminate to the extent of ten per cent. in favor of British imports. Mr. McCarthy desired a maximum and a minimum tariff, such as obtains in France and Germany, the minimum to apply to Great Britain and those countries in which we have favored treatment, and the maximum to have force as respects the United States. Should it be supposed that such a scheme would be productive of irritation across the line, the discrimination in favor of British imports was to be effected in another way, as, for instance, by the lowering of the duties upon such goods as we are bound to purchase in England. In either case, however, it was suggested that an intimation be given to the Washington authorities that any concessions made by them would be met by concessions from us. This was a wide departure from the National Policy. It created a prolonged, and, in some cases, an angry discussion. Nor can it be said that it did not find favor in unexpected quarters. The people of the United States had declared for tariff reduction, and low tariff was in the air. When Parliament met, there was universal curiosity touching the position the Government, and indeed the Opposition, which had, in the election of 1891, advocated unrestricted reciprocity, would assume towards Mr. McCarthy's programme. The Ministerial attitude was developed when, on February 14, Mr. Foster delivered the Budget speech. It was on all fours with the policy outlined by the Premier in his Toronto deliverance, in that it declared that the scale of duties was not immutable, and that change might be looked for. The Finance Minister, however, guarded himself by the statement that tariff alterations must be in accordance with the principles underlying the National Policy. It was further stated by the Minister that there would be during the recess a thorough examination into the question by himself, the Minister of Trade and Commerce, and the Controllers of Customs and Inland Revenue. This enquiry was to be conducted by personal interviews with the merchants, manufacturers, and farmers, and, as a result of the information thus obtained, a measure of tariff reform was to be brought down in the session of 1894. In the meantime there were to be preliminary decreases in the tariff. The Finance Minister announced a reduction of the duty on binder twine from 25 per cent. to 12½ per cent., and the abolition of certain restrictions on coal oil, estimated at about two cents per gallon. Coal oil may now be imported in bulk in tanks, and the total tax on it is a duty of seven and one-fifth cents pe. gallon. Mr. Foster also intimated that mining machinery, the free entry of which expired in the following month, would be placed on the free list for three years more. The policy was received by different shades of opinion in different moods. To the Ministerialists and many of the advocates of tariff change within the Conservative ranks, it was satisfactory. It was argued that any tariff alterations ought to be duly preceded by a very thorough

Hon. John Haggart,
Minister of Railways and Canals.

examination. The Opposition and Mr. McCarthy, however, were not convinced. Sir Richard Cartwright made a vigorous attack upon the Government for its delay, and moved a resolution declaring that the tariff bears heavily and unjustly on the great consuming classes of the Dominion, and, therefore, should be thoroughly reformed in the direction of freer trade. The debate was continued for two weeks. While in progress an animated discussion arose between Mr. Charlton and the Ministers, notably the Minister of Finance, with respect to the procedure of the Government when reciprocity was under consideration at Washington in 1891. It was maintained by Mr. Charlton that the delegates could have secured, had they been in earnest, a measure of reciprocity which did not call for discrimination against Great Britain. But Mr. Foster held to the report already made that Mr. Blaine, with whom the negotiations were conducted, required free trade, if an arrangement were reached between Canada and the United States, and a common tariff against the world, Great Britain not excepted. There had been previously crossfiring between Mr. Foster, the United States Secretary of State, and Mr. Foster, our Finance Minister, on this very point. The debate was brought to a close on February 28th, when Mr. Laurier made a general attack on the policy of the Government, dwelling particularly upon the results of the tariff, and upon the failure of the Ministers to secure a reciprocity treaty with the United States. He denied emphatically that the Liberal policy implied the adoption of the American tariff by Canada. The Liberals, he said, knew that free trade, such as England enjoyed, would be impracticable for this country for many years to come, but their policy was the imposition of such duties only as were necessary for the purposes of revenue. Mr. Foster made a reply, defending his part in the reciprocity negotiations with the United States, and claiming that those of the Liberal party who had spoken on the subject had misrepresented his position. At the close of his speech he called upon the Conservatives who might be dissatisfied with one or two features of the National Policy to support the Government, as the Liberals had pledged themselves to the destruction of the principle of protection. The vote, which was taken in the early morning of February 29, in the presence of brilliant galleries, stood 126 to 71, leaving the Government's majority 55 on the division. Mr. McCarthy and Mr. O'Brien voted with the Administration and against the amendment proposed by Sir Richard, while Mr. Calvin voted on the Opposition side. Immediately following the division came an amendment by Mr. McCarthy in favor of free binder twine. This motion secured the votes of the Opposition, and of the following Ministerialists: Messrs. O'Brien, Davin, Bryson, and Hodgins. In March Mr. McCarthy came forward with a tariff amendment embodying his views. This amendment is really an excellent summary of his speech, for which reason it is given in full: "That since the introduction of the protective system sufficient time has elapsed for the establishment and development of such manufacturing industries as, under existing conditions, can be successfully carried on in Canada; moreover, many manufacturers, sheltered behind the rampart thus erected, have formed combinations and trusts, which prohibit competition, and create and maintain monopolies. That the existing tariff, defensible only as a protective measure, has proved, in many instances, oppressive and burdensome to the great mass of the consuming classes, and especially to those engaged in agricultural pursuits, is unfair and unequal in its incidence, and has been productive of discontent, verging on disloyalty, among those who suffer from its injustice. That no sufficient reason has been adduced or exists requiring investigation respecting the foregoing facts, which are notorious, nor justifying delay in the passage of remedial legislation, which is imperative. That, in the opinion of this House, the tariff ought to be at once amended in respect of the matters herein indicated, and also by the substantial reduction of customs

HON. J. A. OUIMET,
Minister of Public Works.

duties in favor of the United Kingdom, in whose markets all Canadian products are admitted duty free, and of those nations which under treaty obligations with Great Britain would be entitled to the same advantages, graduated, however, so as not unnecessarily to prejudice the business of the country, nor to do wrong to those who have imported and paid duties in accordance with its provisions. And this House declares its readiness to make a light reduction in favor of such other portions of the Empire, or of such other foreign countries, especially the United States of America, as are willing to reciprocate in matters of trade with Canada on fair and equitable terms." The debate was not long, the question having been very thoroughly dealt with in the former discussion. It terminated with a vote of 61 for the amendment, against 116 in opposition to it.

The Liberals voted with Mr. McCarthy, and, in addition, there were on his side Messrs. Hodgins and O'Brien. After this there were sporadic attacks upon the tariff; but the Government tided the issue on the promise to enquire and to propose changes in the following session. During the recess Mr. Foster and Mr. Bowell commenced their investigations among the manufacturers, while Messrs. Wallace and Wood heard the farmers in various parts of the country. Mr. Bowell was not able to attend the entire series of meetings, as it was decided that he should undertake a trade mission to Australia, to which reference will be made later on. Mr. Angers, therefore, joined Mr. Foster, and journeyed with him through Manitoba, the Northwest, and British Columbia, collecting opinions. An official report of Mr. Foster's enquiries has not been published; but the Controllers, who met so many farmers, have issued a statement as to the result of their investigations.

Of 62 witnesses who mentioned the coal oil duty particularly, it seems the majority, 36, advised the removal of the present duties altogether; 23 asked for a reduction of the present duty, while leaving sufficient to protect the home industry; three wanted the duty on coal oil left as it is.

In the matter of barbed wire, five would be satisfied with a reduction, while 35 wanted the article free.

Binder twine, 25 out of 26 wanted it free.

Fourteen favored retention of duties on agricultural implements as affording fair protection; twenty-four wanted the duty reduced; and twelve wanted agricultural implements to be made free.

Of seven who spoke of "stoves, nails, and hardware," only one professed himself satisfied with present duties. The others wanted them reduced. Nine asked a reduction in iron and steel; four were satisfied with the duties.

The subject of tea and coffee was brought up by 23, who thought a revenue should be raised on these articles, which are now free. The majority, if not all, of these witnesses were people who don't drink tea or coffee, and their testimony was opposed by 37 others, who wanted tea and coffee left on the free list.

Forty spoke of the duties on "farm products" as a whole. Two would be willing to see them wiped out altogether; 37 stood for the protection afforded by the present tariff; one farmer thought it should be increased.

Taking separate items, 77 favored the present duty on foreign pork, 12 did not care if it were taken off, and eight wanted more protection. Six were free traders, so far as beef is concerned, while eight delegates urged increased protection, and 41 testified that at least the present duty was necessary to give the farmer adequate protection against American beef.

Fifty-nine urged the benefit of the present duty on corn from the United States, and two wanted it increased. Thirty-two, mostly large stock-raisers, thought they should be allowed to import corn free. Ten said they would agree to free corn from the States, provided our neighbors would take off the duty on Canadian barley. Thus for protection, as against free trade in corn, the opinion stood 71 to 32.

In the matter of grass seeds and hops, all who mentioned these items favored the present or increased duties. Of those who spoke of fruits, five wanted protection increased, 18 were satisfied, and three favored reduction or abolition. Four asked for a specific duty of so much a barrel on imported plums and pears, while two asked that a duty be put on bananas, as they came into competition with home-grown fruits.

Sixty-three delegates volunteered their opinions on the question of free trade.

SIR JOHN CARLING.

Seven were for free trade, fifty-six were opposed to it.

In the opinion of nine delegates, the country could probably get along under direct taxation; thirty-two others, who spoke on the question, opposed direct taxation. Forty-seven out of the fifty-six who spoke on the subject of "Free Trade" had the development of our trade with the United States in view; the other nine thought we should have freer trade with free-trade England.

Eighty-one witnesses referred in their evidence to the tariff as a whole. Twenty-one of these favored a general reduction of all duties; sixty expressed themselves as satisfied generally with the present tariff, having no complaints or grievances to state concerning its operation.

Meanwhile, discussion on tariff lines proceeded. The Patrons of Industry, a farmers' organization, for example, issued a platform in which they called for a "tariff for revenue only, and so adjusted as to fall, as far as possible, upon the luxuries, and not upon the necessaries of life," together with "reciprocal trade on fair and equitable terms with the world." One Ministerial declaration as to the future policy, which fell from Sir Charles Tupper, at Pictou, N.S., on the occasion of a visit he paid to his constituents, was regarded as of especial importance. It was in these words : " We propose a tariff reform that will be as low as possible to produce the revenue absolutely necessary to carry on the public service of the country, and that will give the preference to Canadian workingmen over foreigners, whether mechanics, or manufacturers, or farmers. Where duties are levied, we will levy them on articles that can and ought to be produced in Canada, and we will lighten the duties on articles that we cannot manufacture or produce, and are obliged to import. There are many manufacturing concerns in Canada clamoring for high protection, but under tariff reform we do not expect they will get it ; but we will give them all the protection we can, consistent with a revenue tariff and a due protection for the labor employed." The Liberal leaders also made statements during the year. The more important were delivered at a convention held in Ottawa on June 20 and 21. These will be referred to when the history of the gathering is related.

March 21 was a memorable day in Parliament. Probably at no time has feeling run so high within the walls of the Legislature as on that occasion. The cause of the commotion was a resolution brought in by Mr. Dawson, the member for Addington, censuring Mr. N. Clarke Wallace, the Controller of Customs, for a speech he had delivered at Kingston two weeks before at an Orange banquet. Mr. Wallace entered the official category as head of the Customs Department when Sir John Thompson's Administration was formed. Though in charge of a distinct branch of the Government, he was not a member of the Privy Council. In that regard he was in the same position as Mr. Wood, the Controller of Inland Revenue, and Mr. Curran, the Solicitor-General. But he stood so close to the Cabinet as to render his utterances on all political matters important from the standpoint of party. When in Kingston Mr. Wallace, as chief of the Orange Order, spoke to his assembled brother Orangemen.

SIR OLIVER MOWAT,
Premier of Ontario.

A report of his speech was published in one of the local papers. It appears from this that he referred to the great agitation then in progress in Ulster in opposition to Mr. Gladstone's Home Rule Bill. Mr. Wallace said that in the old country brethren were threatened with a rule that was antagonistic to freedom there. "What is proposed is not only to shake off their allegiance to Great Britain, the bonds of love that bind them to the Empire, but to put them, forsooth, under an alien and hostile government." "We have their (the Home Rulers') public declaration of what they would do if they obtained power--that they would never cease agitating until the last link that bound Ireland to the British Empire is severed. That is their object to-day. They are trying to take the loyal men with them ; but our friends over there say they will never submit. Britain has cast them out ; but, if she does so, she has no right to say what may be their future allegiance. Our friends in that land are preparing, and have asserted their unalterable determination never to submit to that Home Rule which Mr. Gladstone and his Government have laid out for them. I am sure that in their efforts they shall have the sympathy of the Orangemen of Canada—more than sympathy; they shall have our active aid, if active aid is necessary." When the House met on March 21 Mr. Casey, a Liberal member, rose with the report of this speech in his hand, and charged Mr. Wallace with having talked treason against the Queen. He maintained that armed rebellion against Her Majesty was contemplated in Ulster, and that Mr. Wallace, an officer of the Crown in Canada, had not only given countenance to such rebellion, but had offered to lend the rebels active aid from Canada. Mr. Wallace accepted the report of his speech as correct, and declared that he did not take back one word of the statement he had made. But he repudiated the charge of disloyalty, inasmuch as that the position he had taken was similar to that assumed by Lord Salisbury in a speech delivered on May 6, 1892. Lord Salisbury, who was then Premier, declared that he could not accept, in all their width, the doctrines of unrestricted, passive obedience. Parliament, he said, had a right to govern the people of Ulster, but not sell them into slavery. "I do not believe," added Lord Salisbury, "that the people of Ulster have lost their sturdy love of freedom, or their detestation of arbitrary power." Mr. Wallace added that he was as free to oppose Home Rule as others were to support it, and that he opposed it because he feared it pointed to disintegration. Immediately that the Controller took his seat, Mr. Dawson, of Addington, presented a motion of censure. This motion, after relating the circumstances, proceeded to say "that the action of Mr. Wallace in holding out the hope of active aid in resistance to Her Majesty, to those who threaten to levy war in Ireland against Her Majesty, is deserving the severest censure of the House, and, if allowed to pass unnoticed, must place Canada under the scandalous imputation of being disloyal to Her Majesty; and that it is the duty of Parliament to repudiate the utterances of Mr. Wallace, lest the public might be led to the erroneous conclusion that his views are shared in by this body, and endanger the peace, order, and good government throughout Her Majesty's Dominion." An animated and angry debate followed. Mr. Foster, as leader of the House, in Sir John Thompson's absence, opened with a declaration of the Ministerial position on the question. He asserted, first, that every member of Parliament had a right to express his opinions on matters outside of the jurisdiction of Parliament without being called to account by Parliament; and, secondly, that the statement of Mr. Wallace, for which, however, the Government was not responsible, was not a threat to levy war in Ireland against Her Majesty, or to lend aid to persons levying war against Her Majesty. For these reasons he called upon supporters of the Administration to vote the resolution down, as an assault on free speech and an untruthful representation of what the Controller had said. The House, at the outset,

HON. JOHN COSTIGAN,
Secretary of State.

seemed to view the issue on the basis of old party lines until Mr. McInerney, one of the Ministerial supporters, interpreted the expression "active aid" in the Controller's speech to mean actual warfare, and announced that for this reason he would support the motion. Then Mr. Costigan, the Secretary of State, intimated that he, for his part, would find it necessary to vote for the resolution. This declaration coming from a Minister created consternation, for it divided the Cabinet, and set the Ministerialists who were favorable to Home Rule free to condemn the Controller of Customs. There was a difference of opinion as to whether the votes against the Controller would really, if constituting a majority, cast the Government out of office. On this point Mr. Bergin questioned the leader of the House. The reply he received was that, "if the motion passes, it will not be by the vote of friends of the Government." Mr. Curran, the Solicitor-General, nevertheless, followed Mr. Costigan's example in declaring for the resolution. So, also, did Mr. Bergin, Mr. Davin, Mr. Kenny, Mr. Hearn, and Sir Hector Langevin. At one time it was thought that the French

Canadian members supporting the Government would become disaffected and join with the Irish Canadians; but this danger was ultimately averted. During the debate bitterness was added to bitterness in consequence of an assertion by Mr. Davin that, at a Ministerial caucus some years earlier, Mr. Wallace, while announcing his intention to vote for the disallowance of the Jesuits Estates Act, had advised his brother Orangemen in the House to declare themselves in the opposite way in order to save the Government. Mr. Wallace pronounced this statement untrue, and called upon others who were at the caucus to corroborate it if they could. Mr. Sproule, Mr. McKay, of Hamilton, Mr. Boyle, Mr. Cochrane, and Mr. Guillet responded, stating that they had heard nothing of the kind said at the caucus in question. Great excitement prevailed when the vote was taken. The figures stood 74 for the resolution and 105 against it, thus giving the Government a majority of 31. The Ministerialists who voted for it were Mr Costigan (Secretary of State), Mr. Curran (Solicitor-General), Mr. Adams, Mr. Bergin, Mr. Davin, Mr. Hearn, Mr. Kenny, Sir Hector Langevin, Mr. Macdonald (of King's), Mr. Lepine, and Mr. McInerney. On the other hand, Mr. McCarthy and Mr. O'Brien voted with the Ministerialists. The crisis was thus tided over.

Another matter which created much disturbance was an accusation brought by Mr. Edgar against Sir Adolphe Caron, the Postmaster-General. It will be in the memory of all who follow our political history that in 1891 great excitement reigned in consequence of the charges brought with reference to the conduct of political affairs in the Province of Quebec. As a result of the enquiries then made, Sir Hector Langevin resigned from the Administration, and Mr. Thomas McGreevy; with Mr. N. Connolly, were pursued before the courts and committed for trial. In the following session, that of 1892, Mr. Edgar made the charge that Sir Adolphe Caron had received from the Quebec and Lake St. John Railway Company, and from the Temiscouata Railway Company, corporations subsidized by Parliament, sums of money aggregating $100,000, which money was used in corrupting the electorate during the contest of 1887. Sir Adolphe Caron characterized the charge as false. The accusation having been discussed for some days, it was determined, on motion of Mr. Bowell, that a commission should be appointed to make enquiry. A commission was chosen during the recess, and when Parliament reassembled its report of the evidence it had taken was presented.

It should be said here that, on the Liberal side, objection was offered to the reference of the question to a commission, on the ground that the right of parliamentary enquiry was being interfered with. On March 22, Mr. Edgar reviewed the testimony, and drew from it the conclusion that $25,000 had been paid to Sir Adolphe Caron for corrupt purposes out of the Lake St. John bonuses, and that another sum had been paid out of the subsidies to the Temiscouata road. For this reason he moved an amendment to the supply resolution that the facts revealed "should have prevented the subsequent appointment of Sir Adolphe Caron to be an adviser of the Crown, and also render it highly improper that he should continue to hold such office." Mr. Curran made the reply. He deduced from the evidence this argument: Sir Adolphe Caron was, in 1887, one of a committee attending to elections in the Quebec district. Hon. William Ross was a leading Conservative there. This gentleman, who had always promoted the Conservative cause, was three times a millionaire. Sir Adolphe asked him to subscribe to the election fund, and he gave $25,000. The subscription had

HON. DAVID MILLS.

nothing to do with railway subsidies, and, so far as Sir Adolphe knew and believed, was a personal affair. The receipt of the money was legitimate, and there was nothing to show that it had been corruptly used. On the Opposition side, it was maintained that Hon. Mr. Ross had charged the $25,000 against Mr. Beemer, the contractor for the construction of the railway, and that this gentleman had really paid the money. Mr. McCarthy took part in the debate, and declared against Sir Adolphe on the ground that Mr. Ross financed the Lake St. John Railway, and that money should, therefore, not have been accepted from him. On a division the vote stood 69 to 119, the Government thus scoring a majority of 50. Mr. O'Brien and Mr. McCarthy voted with the Opposition.

While Parliament was in session, the news came that Sir Charles Tupper was negotiating a commercial treaty with France. We had been trying to come to terms with the French ever since 1874. Prior to that year, we enjoyed the advantage of the most-favored-nation clause of the British treaty. But in 1873 the French treated us as a separate people, and placed us under the provisions of the general tariff with non-treaty countries, which made their duties upon our products higher than they were before. In the following year Canada increased the duties on French wines, and immediately proceeded to bargain with a view to effecting a return to freer conditions. It was not until 1879 that the business of negotiating really opened. At that time we were very anxious to secure better terms in France for wooden ships, which had previously found a large market there. Originally, the duty on such vessels bought by France was two francs per ton; but the alteration in our status raised the duty, so far as we were concerned, to forty francs, and killed the trade. Canada offered to remove the *ad valorem* duties on French wines if France would take our ships at the old figure and reduce the duties on agricultural implements, tools, cutlery, and fish. But the French Chambers thought the offer was not good enough. Thereupon, the negotiations ended. In 1882 Sir Alexander Galt tried again. He named a list of articles in respect of which a tariff reduction was required by Canada, and promised that we, for our part, would remove the *ad valorem* wine duty, and refrain from levying a transportation tax upon imports not coming directly from France. Once more the negotiations failed. When Sir Charles Tupper became High Commissioner, namely, in 1883, he promptly took up the question where Sir Alexander Galt had left it; but it was not until he had operated for ten years that he secured the bargain of which report was now made. The French, however, before negotiating with Sir Charles, had raised their tariff to a very high figure. Formerly, there was one scale of duties. Under the new arrangement, which came in force in January, 1892, France had a maximum and a minimum tariff. We were governed by the maximum. When the news came that Sir Charles Tupper was negotiating, great interest was evinced in the outlook. Later on, when the treaty itself arrived, doubts were raised as to its advantages. One objection to it was that it called for a reduction in the wine duties, and thus removed the protection the Canadian wine producer enjoyed not only as against France, but also as against the United States. A second objection was the inclusion in the treaty of a most-favored-nation clause. Under this clause, Canada was required to give France the benefit of all tariff reductions she might make in favor of other countries, while France agreed to give Canada no other reductions than such as might be made by her in the duties upon the articles named in the limited list included in the treaty. The very first objection raised to the bargain came from the Finance Minister on March 13. Mr. Foster then plainly intimated that the convention was not what he had looked for, especially in that it gave little and asked from us a great deal. The Minister cited particularly the most-favored-nation arrangement as unexpected, and concluded by mentioning that the treaty, which was subject to ratifica-

Hon. T. M. Daly,
Minister of the Interior.

tion, could be held over for explanation and consideration. The report of Mr. Foster's speech went to London and to Paris, in both of which cities it created much discussion. On the one hand, it was assumed that the Government was bound to sustain the treaty, as it was negotiated under its instructions; on the other, it was maintained that Ministers were free to oppose it, but at the expense of the negotiator—the High Commissioner. Sir Charles Tupper himself took the ground, in interviews he had with representatives of the press, that the Government ought to take the responsibility for the treaty or resign. It was reported at this time that the relations between Sir Charles and the Ministers were very much strained, and that Mr. C. H. Tupper, Sir Charles' son, was insisting that the treaty be ratified. Further communications were had with Paris, however, and the upshot was a postponement of the Ministerial decision until the session of 1894. Meanwhile, an examination of the correspondence between the Ministers at Ottawa and Sir Charles in Paris showed that the Government had objected to the favored-nation clause, but that Sir Charles Tupper had signed the treaty just before the objection reached him.

Another great question which agitated Parliament had reference to the sale, early in the year, of certain Nova Scotia coal mining properties to a wealthy syndicate composed largely of citizens of the United States. The Government of Nova Scotia had effected this transfer under terms that it held to be especially advantageous to the province But some of the Conservatives opposed the transaction. In the Legislature the opposition was futile. The case was, therefore, carried to Ottawa. Here a delegation of members waited upon the Governor-General, and invited the disallowance of the local law for Imperial as well as for local reasons. It was said that the foreigners might fire or flood the mines in time of war, and that thus the coal supply for the navy would be cut off. Lord Stanley referred his interviewers to the Ministers. But important questions had been raised by the appeal to His Excellency, namely: the point as to the right of members to go to the Governor-General direct, and to ask him to set aside a local law, and a second issue as to the power of the Governor-General to deal with such legislation. Mr. Mills introduced the question, and contended that the proper channel of communication was through the Ministers, and that action could not be taken without their advice. Mr. Weldon, who participated in the interview, however, maintained that all subjects had the right to approach Her Majesty's representative by petition, and that it really did not matter whether the petition was verbal or written. The point as to procedure was not determined, but the action of the Government with regard to the legislation was speedily settled. Sir John Thompson asserted that the mines belonged to the province, and that the Federal authorities were not entitled to interfere with the disposition of them. If the property had been improperly dealt with, it was the privilege of the people of Nova Scotia to say so. The bargain might be bad ; but, nevertheless, the Dominion Government could not veto it.

HON. G. W. ROSS,
Minister of Education for Ontario.

Parliament was prorogued on April 1, after the shortest, and, possibly, the most exciting, session on record. When it opened the Government was faced with difficulties and divisions, and while it was in progress new troubles presented themselves. But the Ministers were able to avoid the rocks and to reach the end in safety. Owing to breaks here and there in the Ministerial ranks, the strength of the party varied at different times. It is important to observe how the figures ran. The following record in the divisions tells the story :

	MINISTERIAL MAJORITY.
On Mr. Laurier's motion to reduce taxation, yeas, 53 ; nays, 103..................	50
On the proposition of Mr. O'Brien to adjourn a debate, yeas, 99 ; nays, 58.....	41
On Mr. Mulock's motion for free binder twine, yeas, 51 ; nays, 91	40
On Mr. Edgar's motion *re* Sir Adolphe Caron, yeas, 69 ; nays, 119..... ...	50
On Mr. Dawson's motion censuring Mr. Wallace's speech, yeas, 74 ; nays, 105..	31
On Mr. Pope's motion for free corn, yeas, 50 ; nays, 90	40
On Mr. Tarte's motion *re* Manitoba schools, yeas, 71 ; nays, 121	50
On Sir Richard Cartwright's tariff resolution, yeas, 64 ; nays, 116.............	52
On Mr. McCarthy's tariff resolution, yeas, 72 ; nays, 126	54

Ten days before Parliament prorogued, Sir John Thompson left for Paris to take part in the Behring Sea Arbitration that was to open on April 4. The Premier's appointment to a seat in the great international court, as one of the judges, was an honor alike to Canada and to himself. With him on the bench was Lord Hannen, as a representative of Great Britain. The United States was represented by Judge John M. Harlan, of the United States Supreme Court, and Senator John P. Morgan. France appointed the Baron de Courcelles; Italy, the Marquis Visconti Venosta; and Norway and Sweden, Mr. Gregers Gram. The tribunal was august and learned. Canada had in charge of the case, as British agent, Mr. Charles H. Tupper, Minister of Marine. There were also on the British side, Sir Richard Webster, Sir Charles Russell, and Mr. Christopher Robinson, of Toronto. The legal argument was attended to for the United States by Mr. E. J. Phelps, Mr. Couderet, Mr. ex-Secretary of State Foster, and Mr. H. W. Blodgett. France made splendid preparations for the remarkable international tournament, and treated the gentlemen who took part in it, either as judges or counsel, with marked consideration. At the opening in March, Baron de Courcelles was elected president. A brief history of the memorable case, so happily treated and so satisfactorily concluded, is necessary to the understanding of the work of the arbitrators. In 1867 the United States bought Alaska from Russia. One of the chief products of the territory, or rather of its seas, is the fur seal. The right to catch the seal was afterwards sold by the United States to a specially-incorporated company, whose operations were conducted on a series of islands in Behring Sea known as the Pribyloff group. To these islands, it seems, the seals journey every summer, remaining there until the fall. While there they are driven inland, and are killed to the number allowed by law. For some years the business of sealing was carried on by the company alone; but Canadian vessels ultimately entered Behring Sea and prosecuted the industry, not on land, nor on the coast, but on the ocean. On August 1, 1886, a revenue cutter of the United States seized two Canadian vessels in the Behring Sea, one seventy and the other seventy-five miles from land. These were the Caroline and the Thornton. On the following day the Onward was captured, 115 miles from land. The vessels were taken to Sitka and were condemned, and their captains fined for intrusion within United States waters. In 1887, and in 1889, other vessels were taken. The captures became the subjects of diplomatic correspondence. On the part of Great Britain, restitution was claimed for the seizure of British vessels on the open ocean. The United States Government replied that Behring Sea was a closed sea, the Aleutian Islands closing it in; that the Canadian sealers had no right there; and that, when there, they were violating the law of the United States. Arguments swiftly followed upon arguments, Lord Salisbury leading on one side, and Mr. James G. Blaine, the United States Secretary of State, on the other. At a particular point in the controversy, Mr. Blaine dropped the *mare clausum* theory as untenable, and set up the claim on behalf of the United States to protect seal life in the North Pacific on the ground that the seals were United States property, for the reason that they first saw the light of day in the immediate neighborhood of the Alaskan islands. In brief, the seals, having been born within American

HON. EDWARD BLAKE.

limits, belonged to the United States, no matter in what part of the ocean they might ultimately be found. This point, when presented to Lord Salisbury, was accompanied by a draft treaty practically conceding to the United States all rights over the seals. Whether or not Lord Salisbury was ready to accept the treaty is not certain. But, in all probability, he simply took it into his consideration while he consulted Canada with regard to it. The Dominion objected to the proposed convention, and so afterwards did Lord Salisbury. Thereupon the

United States charged that just as the Imperial Government was about to capitulate the Canadians, mere colonists that they were, rudely interfered and prevented a wise and friendly settlement. The Imperial Government, however, denied that Canada exceeded her rights, or that England had ever promised to make the concession from which it was said she had, at the instigation of the Dominion, withdrawn. Under the new condition of affairs, a discussion of the issue upon its merits became necessary. Then arose the question as to what really were the rights of the United States in Behring Sea. Such rights as the Americans enjoy must have been derived from Russia with the purchase of Alaska. But the Russian rights were governed by international law, and by treaties made with England and other countries. It was contended, on the British side, that under arrangement with Russia England enjoyed full rights in the sea. This point was about to be sent to arbitration when a difficulty arose. Great Britain had, in 1891, agreed in a friendly way, and pending negotiations, to exclude Canadian vessels from Behring Sea for a year, paying them, of course, the damages they sustained through such exclusion. So long as this arrangement was in force, the United States was slow to come to terms upon the main question. Early in 1892 Mr. Blaine asked for a renewal of the bargain. This Lord Salisbury declined until the actual terms of the arbitration had been reached. Then it happened that the dispute nearly resulted in blows, for the United States declared that Canadian sealers would be seized, and Great Britain replied that British vessels would be sent to protect them. The quarrel, however, was healed by the consent of both countries to the renewal of the temporary agreement on condition that the arbitration should go on at once; and, further, that if the arbitration did not result favorably to the United States, the sealers would be compensated for the suspension of their operations. Great Britain afterwards voted $100,000 to the Canadian sealers as damages for the suspension of their work; but announced later on that this sum would not be asked of the United States, although the treaty set forth that it would have to be paid. This snag having been avoided, the terms of the arbitration were decided upon. The questions submitted to the arbitrators were these:

1. What exclusive jurisdiction in the Behring Sea, and what exclusive rights in the seal fisheries, had Russia, prior and up to the time of the cession of Alaska to the United States?

2. How far were these claims of jurisdiction conceded by Great Britain?

3. Was the body of water now known as the Behring Sea included in the phrase "Pacific Ocean," as used in the treaty of 1825 between Great Britain and Russia; and what rights, if any, in the Behring Sea were held and exclusively exercised by Russia after said treaty?

4. Did not all the rights of Russia in the treaty between the United States and Russia of March 30, 1867, pass unimpaired to the United States under that treaty?

5. Has the United States any right of protection or property in the fur seals frequenting the islands of the United States

SIR CHARLES H. TUPPER,
Minister of Marine and Fisheries.

in Behring Sea when such seals are found outside the ordinary three-mile limit?

In addition, it was stipulated that, if the arbitrators found that the United States had no exclusive rights outside of the three-mile limit, they should say what concurrent regulations, if any, were necessary for the preservation of the fur seal. The question of damages was not submitted; but it was provided that the arbitrators could say whether or not there had been illegal seizures. Before the arbitrators, the United States proposed to contend that Behring Sea belonged originally to Russia, that England acknowledged Russia's exclusive rights in the seal fisheries, that these rights passed to the United States, and that, therefore, the United States owned the sea and the seals, and that the seizure of the Canadian vessels was justifiable. It turned out after the treaty was signed, but before the arbitrators had met, that the claim of the United States, in respect of jurisdiction, rested chiefly on certain Russian documents found at Washington, and translated by a Russian official of the State Department, named Ivan Petroff, for the information of the Government. These documents consisted, for the most part, of proclamations or ukases issued from St. Petersburg, in which exclusive jurisdiction in the Behring Sea was asserted. When the papers were sent forward to Great Britain for examination and reply, they were compared with duplicates there, and it was discovered, to the astonishment not only of the British officials, but also of those of the United States, that every sentence which helped the case of the United States had been forged by Petroff. As a consequence, the most forcible evidence on the United States side had to be withdrawn, and the learned counsel for that country were compelled to base the arguments they addressed to the arbitrators upon the theory advanced by Mr. Blaine, as the lesser branch of his case, that the seals were the property of the United States by birth, and could, therefore, be protected wherever found. The arguments on both sides were long and able. While in progress, Great Britain offered to accept regulations protective of the fur species. On August 15 judgment was given. All the claims of the United States as to exclusive rights were denied, and the seizures were practically declared to have been illegal. But regulations were prescribed. These were, in brief, as follow:

1. No seals are to be taken within a zone of sixty miles of the Pribyloff Islands.
2. No seals are to be taken between May 1 and July 31 north of the 35th degree of latitude.
3. During the period that fur sealing is allowed, sealing vessels only shall be allowed to participate.
4. Each vessel shall have a special license and a distinguishing flag.
5. Each captain shall keep a log of the date and place of sealing, and particulars of the catch.
6. The use of nets and firearms is forbidden. Shotguns, however, may be used outside of Behring Sea during the season.

The result, in so far as the judgment against the United States claim was concerned, was a victory for Canada. But the proposed regulations modified this triumph, and practically rendered the result a compromise. The close season, however, was shorter than the United States desired, and longer than Great Britain proposed. The United States, in the draft treaty submitted by Mr. Blaine and rejected through the non-concurrence of Canada, placed the close season at from April 15 to November 10. England, at the arbitration, offered to accept a season extending from September 15 to July 1. The arbitrators determined that the season should extend from May 1 to July 31. Touching the seizures, the arbitrators reported that they had been effected outside of the territorial limits of the United States. But the question of

HON J. C. PATTERSON,
Minister of Militia.

damages was not dealt with, and this is to be considered later on. The judgment was accepted throughout the world favorably. As marks of distinction for their services in connection with the arbitration, Sir John Thompson was appointed a Privy Councillor of England, in virtue of which he is to be known henceforth as "The Right Honorable"; Mr. Tupper became a Knight of the Order of St. Michael and St. George; and Mr. Christopher Robinson was elevated to the same order, which honor, however, he declined for personal reasons.

There was a brief cessation of political activity after the close of Parliament; but on June 20 business was resumed by the Liberals, who held a great and enthusiastic convention at Ottawa for the purpose of formulating a programme. About 1,500 delegates attended at Mr. Laurier's call, and Sir Oliver Mowat, the veteran Premier of Ontario, was elected to the chair. Marked unanimity prevailed, and inspiring speeches were delivered by all the leaders. The resolutions adopted by the convention form the platform upon which the Liberals will fight the next election. Summarized, the planks are as follow :

1. *The Tariff.*—We declare that the existing tariff has oppressed the masses to the enrichment of the few, and that the highest interests of the people demand its removal; that the tariff should be reduced to the needs of honest, economical, and efficient government; that it should be so adjusted as to make free, or to bear as lightly as possible upon, the necessaries of life, and should be so arranged as to promote free trade with the whole world, more particularly Great Britain and the United States.

2. *Reciprocity.*—The Liberal party is prepared to enter into negotiations with a view to obtaining a fair and liberal treaty, including a well-considered list of manufactured articles.

3. *Corruption.*—The convention deplores the gross corruption in the management and expenditure of the public moneys which for years past has existed under the rule of the Conservative party, and the revelations of which have brought disgrace upon the fair name of Canada.

4. *The Public Debt.*—We cannot but view with alarm the increase of the public debt, and of the controllable annual expenditure, and we demand strict economy in the administration of the government of the country.

5. *Trial of Ministers.*—The convention regret that by the action of Ministers and their supporters in Parliament, in one case in which serious charges were made against a Minister of the Crown, investigation was altogether refused; while in another case the charges preferred were altered, and then referred to the commission appointed upon the advice of the Ministry, contrary to the well-settled practice of Parliament.

6. *Public Lands.*—In the opinion of this convention the sales of public lands of the Dominion should be to actual settlers only, and not to speculators, upon reasonable terms.

7. *The Franchise Act.*—In the opinion of this convention the Act should be repealed, and we should revert to the provincial franchise.

8. *Redistributions.*—In the formation of electoral divisions, county boundaries should be preserved, and in no case should parts of two counties be put in one electoral division.

9. *The Senate.*—The constitution of the Senate should be so amended as to bring it into harmony with the principles of popular government.

10. *Prohibition.*—It is desirable that the minds of the people should be clearly ascertained on the question of prohibition by means of a Dominion plebiscite.

After a two days' session, the convention rose. Mr. Laurier subsequently made a tour of Ontario, during which he expounded the policy. Following the session of Parliament, and prior to the convention, the Liberals scored a victory in Vaudreuil. The county was taken by Mr. Macmillan (Conservative) by a majority of 85 at a former election. On April 12 Mr. Harwood (Liberal) carried it over Mr. Chevrier by 155. November 22 brought the Liberals another victory. Mr. Hugh J. Macdonald, son of Sir John Macdonald, had resigned his seat for Winnipeg, explaining that he could not give attention to political affairs. The candidates for the vacant seat were Mr. Isaac Campbell (Conservative) and Mr. Joseph Martin (Liberal). A very vigorous campaign was fought. The vote stood: Martin, 2,208; Campbell, 1,770. The Liberal majority was thus 438. Great surprise was expressed at the result, owing to the fact that Mr. Macdonald had carried the city in 1891 by a majority of 500.

HONORÉ MERCIER, M.P.

A new scandal presented itself in June, and called for action. The Government this time did not wait for Parliament to commence the enquiry, but proceeded with the investigation itself by Royal Commission. Briefly given, the facts of the case are these: The Federal authorities decided in the previous fall to reconstruct the railway and passenger bridges passing over the Lachine Canal a Montreal. The estimated cost was $175,000. Some changes, however, were made in the plans, and these brought the expected price up to $250,000. When the bills came rolling in, they were added up in the Railways and Canals Department, and it was found that $450,000 had been spent. As a result, the Minister called a halt, and appointed the Commission of Enquiry. The first discovery made by the Commission had reference to the principle upon which the work had been conducted. It had not been let by contract, as is usual; but had been prosecuted by the day labor system. A contractor supplied the labor, and the Government officials utilized it. It was intimated by some of the witnesses that too many men had been employed, and that they had not been all kept diligently at work. The engineers explained, however, that the day labor system had to be resorted to owing to the haste with which the bridges were constructed, for it was essential that traffic and navigation should not be interfered with. Mr. Haggart, according to the documents, was not favorable to the day labor plan. He was guided by his advisers. It was charged further, in the evidence, that there had been waste in the purchases both of stone and lumber. This case awaits the report of the Royal Commissioners. Meanwhile the engineer who conducted the work is under suspension.

While this new scandal was a nine days' wonder, an old scandal was revived in November by the trial of Mr. Thomas McGreevy and Mr. N. Connolly, at Ottawa, on the charge of conspiracy to defraud the Government in connection with the Quebec Harbor contracts. This trial was the culmination of what are known as the Tarte charges. It ought to have taken place earlier; but it was delayed through the absence of witnesses. One of these men, Owen E. Murphy, was the principal figure, and indeed the villain, in the case. He had escaped to New York to avoid punishment for a fraud he had perpetrated in Quebec, and there, when his evidence was sought, he suddenly died. Murphy having gone to his reward, the trial was proceeded with without him. The offence charged against Mr. McGreevy and Mr. Connolly is thus described: Large and valuable contracts were to be awarded for work to be performed in Quebec Harbor. A dock was to be built, and a great deal of dredging was required. As the Dominion Government was advancing the money for all this enterprise, the Department of Public Works saw to the letting of tenders, thus relieving the Harbor Commissioners of some of their responsibilities. Mr. McGreevy was a Harbor Commissioner, and, besides, a member of Parliament and a friend of the Minister of Public Works. It was charged by Mr. Tarte that Mr. McGreevy, although ostensibly protecting the public interest as a Harbor Commissioner and a member, really worked with and for the contractors, getting money from them for elections, and, by way of his brother Robert, sharing personally in their profits. This was the chief count in the indictment laid before Parliament in the memorable season of 1891, and it is the basis of the offence of conspiracy for which Mr. McGreevy and Mr. Connolly, a member of the contracting firm, were tried. The jury found Messrs. McGreevy and Connolly guilty, and they were sentenced to one year's imprisonment each in the county jail.

SIR ADOLPHE CARON,
Postmaster-General.

Late in the year several important events, from the Federal point of view, took place. The New Brunswick Governorship, long held by Sir Leonard Tilley, was on September 24 given to Hon. John Boyd. The appointment was very popular; but Mr. Boyd did not live long to enjoy it, for he died suddenly on December 3. He was succeeded by Mr. Justice Frazer. On November 3, Mr. C. H. Mackintosh was appointed Governor of the Northwest in succession to Governor Royal. He had sat in the Commons for Ottawa. An election being necessary to fill the vacant seat, Sir James Grant was nominated by the Conservatives, and was elected by acclamation. On October 4 Mr. J. V. Ellis, of St. John, was sent to jail for thirty days for contempt of court. He had severely criticized, in his paper, the decisions of one of the judges in the celebrated Queen's County election case.

His comments, made five years ago, were condemned at the time by the court; but he appealed without success, and, on appearing for sentence, was committed to jail for the term mentioned. Objection was taken to the treatment he received, on the ground that contempt of court was an antiquated offence, and that, anyway, he ought to have had the benefit of a trial by jury. Sir Alex. T. Galt died on September 22; and Sir John Abbott, the ex-Premier, died on October 31. Thus two respected statesmen passed away within a few weeks of each other. Late in the fall Mr. Bowell went to Australia on a trade mission, the hope being that he would be able to interest the people of the Antipodes in commerce with Canada, and possibly arrange for a reciprocal treaty. Mr. Bowell was well received, and a convention of colonial delegates was proposed as a result of his visit. On his return, he dropped in at Honolulu. Some of the papers in the United States gave the visit international significance, and credited Mr. Bowell with an attempt to annex Hawaii to Canada. But the Minister was entirely innocent of any project of that kind. The year closed in Dominion politics with a discussion of the Northwest Territories school law, which places the Separate schools on a basis similar to that occupied by the Public schools. The friends of Separate schools had appealed for the disallowance of the ordinance. We have to wait until 1894 is well advanced before we know what the fate of the law is to be.

Having reviewed the larger questions which have arisen in the Federal arena, it is but natural to turn to the points that have disturbed the provinces. But, first, it is to be remembered that there are questions in which the Dominion and the provinces are jointly concerned. These, for the most part, have to do with the finances. One of the issues came before a Board of Arbitrators composed of Chancellor Boyd, for Ontario; Justice Casault, for Quebec; and Justice Burbidge, for the Dominion, on April 18, at Ottawa. The question involved was the outstanding accounts between Ontario and Quebec, and the Federal authorities. At Confederation, the two provinces were authorized to divide certain of the assets of Upper Canada between them; but a difference of opinion arose touching the proportion which belonged to each. This matter was referred to arbitration, and was settled in part. The undecided issues, which include the distribution of money held by Canada for these provinces, the interest that should be allowed by the Dominion upon this sum, together with the claims of the Dominion upon the provinces arising out of payments to Indians within these provinces, remained to be determined, and the new Board of Arbitration was appointed to adjudicate upon them. At the first sitting the point was argued as to the interest the Dominion ought to pay upon the funds it holds in trust. On the part of the Federal authorities, simple interest alone was proposed; whereas the provinces contended for compound interest. The arbitrators examined the case closely, and, on November 2, decided that simple interest was the proper thing. Some other points were reported upon, as, for example, the proportion of the Library Fund that was to go to each province; but larger issues, involving vast sums, and the claims of the provinces, with the counterclaims of the Dominion, were reserved for future consideration. While this matter was before the arbitrators, a claim for $650,000 from the Province of Nova Scotia was receiving the attention of the Government. It appears that the province subsidized a railway known as the Eastern Extension to the tune of $650,000. After the road was built Nova Scotia took it over, and subsequently sold it to the Federal

HON. W. B. IVES,
President of the Privy Council.

authorities to become a branch of the Intercolonial. The price agreed upon was the cost, less the amount of the subsidy. Nova Scotia maintains that the road, being a part of the Intercolonial, which is a Government railway, ought to be entirely paid for by Canada, and for this reason it applied for the payment to it out of the Federal exchequer of the subsidy it had given. The administration at Ottawa decided in October that the bargain would have to be observed, as the railway was in operation, and the province was getting what it had paid for. Thus the appeal for $650,000 was set aside.

Being in the East, it may be convenient at this time, seeing that provincial affairs are next in the order of consideration, to deal with local political matters there. There was an early session of the Nova Scotia House to ratify the coal mining contract made by the Government, to which attention has already been directed. The contract gives to a wealthy syndicate rights in several mines at a royalty higher than that which was formerly paid. Opposition was offered to the project, but it ultimately passed. In New Brunswick the Legislature met as a single House. There had long been agitation against the Legislative Council as useless and expensive. The Legislature abolished this body in the year before, and thus the Assembly was able to meet without it. Abolition was a response to the general cry against over-government. An educational difficulty arose during the New Brunswick session. All the schools are, according to law, non-denominational; but it was charged that in Bathurst, Gloucester County, they were being conducted by the Roman Catholic majority as religious schools. A petition signed by 10,000 people was presented to the Legislature, calling for enquiry. Some objection was taken to an investigation, but during the recess a Royal Commission was appointed and enquiry proceeded. No report had been published at the end of the year. In Prince Edward Island, as well as in New Brunswick, the Upper House was successfully attacked. Formerly there was a Legislative Council elected on the basis of a property qualification, and a House of Assembly elected on the basis of manhood suffrage. Now there is but one chamber, consisting of fifteen Councilmen elected on a reduced property qualification ($348), and fifteen Assemblymen elected by manhood suffrage, all sitting together, with equal rights and powers. A general election took place on the island on December 14. There was a novel feature in the fight. The two parties agreed that no money or other material consideration should be paid or given to any voter. Nor was there to be any hiring for special service on election day, except of livery horses. During the contest the Conservative Opposition took exception to the double plan under which the representatives were elected, and charged that the constituencies had been gerrymandered. A question was also raised as to the conduct of the land office, and the finances were attacked. The struggle was desperate, but Mr. Peters, the Liberal Premier, secured twenty-four out of thirty seats, and thus had a majority of eighteen. In British Columbia there was a spicy session early in the year. The Government proposed to undertake the construction of new Parliamentary and Departmental buildings at Victoria. To this project some of the members from the mainland took exception, on the ground that it was the intention to "anchor" the capital at Victoria, although the population was growing on the mainland, and the capital ought to

MR. W. R. MEREDITH,
Leader of the Ontario Opposition.

be there. The petition was interwoven with a demand from the mainland for larger representation, the granting of which, however, was postponed. In view of the postponement, and of the determination to proceed with the new buildings, there came a cry for separation, Vancouver Island to form one province, and the mainland another. After the prorogation of the Legislature political affairs became dull, and for the moment the agitation was forgotten. The Manitoba Legislature did not present any very serious issue; but the Assembly of the Northwest, sitting in January, threw a disputed question into the arena. The constitution of the Northwest calls for Separate schools, and such had been provided for. But the Assembly proceeded to legislate with regard to these institutions. Its ordinance brought them all under one inspectorate and one Board of Control, and required that they should have certificated teachers, and text-books uniform with those used in the Public schools, and that religious instruction should be given only after hours. This was a wide departure from the original system. His Lordship Bishop Grandin petitioned the Federal authorities to deal with this ordinance, and, at the end of the year, the point was still, so far as public report was concerned, undecided. The case resembles that known as the Manitoba Schools case, in that it raises the question as to whether the Dominion Government can touch a local enactment dealing with the educational question.

The Quebec Legislature sat during November and December. A very long session was held. Necessarily, the financial question occupied a great deal of attention. In order to balance the accounts, the Legislature, at the previous session, had laid taxes upon all engaged in business, and in the professions. These taxes so increased the rev nu as to make both ends meet. Early in the session appeals were received, calling for their abandonment; the Government, however, could not see its way clear to their removal. It therefore changed them somewhat, and promised that in time they would be first reduced, and then struck off altogether. A strong objection entered against them was based on the circumstance that they fell upon the cities and towns, and that the rural districts escaped scot free. The Government, however, was not prepared to levy, as proposed, a rate upon all farming property. One of the principal sources of agitation in the House was a series of Government bills providing for the transfer of the Beauport Lunatic Asylum to the Sisters of Charity. In Quebec the insane are farmed out. One of the asylums, that at Beauport, has been a private institution, the Government paying to the owners $132 per annum for every patient. The contract expired early in the year, and, at once, new arrangements were entered into. The Sisters sought, or were asked, to take the contract and to buy the asylum. They agreed to maintain patients at $100 per annum. Then came the question of the purchase of the building. The proprietors wanted $600,000, and the Sisters were willing to give $275,000. A valuation was made, and the valuers estimated the property as worth all the way from $311,000 to $700,000. After prolonged negotiations the sum of $425,000 was agreed upon, with the condition that it was to be paid at the rate of $18,000 annually for sixty years, the province to take over the property and meet the instalments after the end of ten years, if the Sisters were not willing to proceed with the purchase. Opposition was offered to the transaction on two grounds. First, it was said that the province should abandon the farming-out system altogether, and attend to the insane directly itself. Then it was declared that the terms were exorbitant, and that they were really endorsed by the province, which in the end might have to pay. The contract passed the House, but one of the bills, that relating to the provincial guarantee for the purchase, was rejected in the Legislative Council. It was thought that the Government would be in difficulties owing to its defeat in the Upper House ; but as the main feature of the bargain, namely, the letting of the contract for the care of the insane,

COL. O'BRIEN, M.P.

was endorsed, it was stated that the other part of the arrangement did not matter much.

While referring to the Legislature of Quebec, it may be opportune to point to the fact that religious troubles prevailed in the province during the greater part of the year. These were the results of criticisms of what is known as the policy of the church. There had been in 1892 very free expressions of opinion relating to many points, as, for example, the relations of the priesthood to the people. One paper which took a leading part in the controversy was a weekly known as *The Canada Revue*. This journal, with *The Echo*, of Two Mountains, was placed under the ban by His Grace Archbishop Fabre. His Grace forbade the faithful to read the paper, to print it, buy it, or write for it. The proprietor claimed that he had been injured by this action on the part of the Archbishop, and entered suit for damages. Shortly afterwards a jubilee of Mgr. Fabre's consecration was held, and at this celebration the lawsuit was condemned by leading men. More recently, on September 25, His Grace submitted to examination, in which he maintained that he had the right to warn his flock against papers that it would be to their disadvantage to read. The suit was in charge of Mr. Rudolphe Laflamme, Q.C. The situation was strained once more towards the end of the year, when it was reported that Mr. Papineau, the son of the principal figure in the event of 1837, had determined to withdraw from the Roman Catholic Church and join the Presbyterians. Mr. Papineau lived at Monte Bello, on the Ottawa River, and in the Diocese of Ottawa, which is presided over by His Grace Archbishop Duhamel. At his village there was a church which the ecclesiastical authorities had condemned in order that a new edifice might be erected in its place. Mr. Papineau opposed the building of a new church, his opinion being that the old one was satisfactory, and that the people could not afford to pay the tax the enterprise would involve. But, aside from that, he declared that his children were Presbyterian, and that he would join them. The withdrawal created much excitement, and led to a heated discussion of fabrique assessments, and of the duties of the people in respect of the propositions of the clergy.

Turning to affairs political in Ontario, it is found that February brought with it a local contest in Toronto. Mr. Bigelow (Liberal), who had carried the city the summer before, had died, and a new election was necessary. The candidates were Dr. G. S. Ryerson (Conservative) and Dr. Ogden (Liberal). Voting took place on the 29th of the month. The result was a victory for Dr. Ryerson, the figures being: Ryerson, 9,662; Ogden, 7,039; majority for Ryerson, 623. The session, however, did not open until April 20. Pomp and circumstance attended the proceedings, for the legislators were meeting for the first time in their new building, and Ontario was commencing her second century of parliamentary government. The building had been in course of construction since 1886, and it had cost $1,250,000. Of the measures introduced by the Government, the most novel was the bill for the prevention of cruelty to children, and for their better protection. Hereafter the Children's Aid Societies will be recognized by the State, and their operations will be directed by a paid provincial official. Parents who neglect or ill-treat their offspring may be deprived of them, but will be required to pay for their care by some officially-recognized society or other suitable guardian.

To keep young persons off the streets at night, municipalities are empowered to ring a bell at a suitable hour, at sound of which all children unaccompanied by parents or guardians must seek their homes. This measure is known as the Children's Charter. A very noticeable feature of the session was the pronounced opposition exhibited towards everything that had the appearance of a monopoly or a close corporation. This caused several of the bills introduced by private members to be defeated or withdrawn. The request of the milkmen that they be taxed up to twenty dollars was not entertained, because it was suspected that it was prompted by a desire on the part of the larger dealers to monopolize the business. The embalmers likewise were unsuccessful in their endeavors to give their calling the legislative status of a profession. On the suggestion of the Premier, the architects withdrew their request for more exclusive powers. The proposal of the druggists to confine the patent medicine business to registered pharmacists was abandoned in the face of the rising tide of opposition. A measure to prescribe professional examinations for railway engineers, conductors, and brakesmen, was vetoed by the Government.

Dr. Ryerson, M.P.P.

Altogether, the session was more satisfactory to the opponents than to the advocates of close corporations. Considerable public interest was taken in three of the debates of the session. The discussion of Mr. Marter's bill to prohibit the retail sale of intoxicants caused the galleries to be overtaxed on several occasions. The defeat of the measure on a party division was accompanied by a promise on the part of the Government that

D'ALTON McCARTHY, M.P.

the question of prohibition would be submitted to a popular vote. This pledge was redeemed. A plebiscite on the manufacture, importation, and sale of liquors was ordered, and was taken at the succeeding municipal elections, with the result that prohibition was carried. The advocates of female suffrage were exceedingly active. The Government, however, took a stand against the claims of the fair sex. Sir Oliver Mowat objected to them because he believed the country is not ripe for the reform asked, and his colleagues opposed them strictly on Scriptural grounds. The system of minority representation in Toronto came in for the usual condemnation from the Conservative side of the House, which was concurred in by the Ministerialists. The Government committed itself to the abolition of the minority principle, and promised the city another representative. Throughout, the session was fruitful of legislation, and it terminated on May 27, from which date, until death created two vacancies in the House, little was heard of local politics.

During November preparations were made for the refilling of the seats in the Legislature for East Lambton and North Bruce, which had become vacant under the deplorable circumstances already referred to. While the arrangements were in progress, it was discovered by the existing parties that two new organizations had taken the field. One of these was the farmers' association, the Patrons of Industry, and the other an organization the name of which explains its policy—the Protestant Protective Association. The Patrons had a programme covering both Dominion and Local subjects. In the Dominion arena, they called for lower tariff; in the provincial arena, they demanded a change in the mode of appointing sheriffs and registrars, some of them even calling for the election of these officials by popular vote, and the abolition of the system of official remuneration by fees. The Protestant Protective Association, or P.P.A., was a secret society opposed to legislation unduly favorable to Roman Catholics. It was reported of it that its members were sworn to turn Roman Catholics out of office, and even to refuse them private employment. The general opinion was that the two associations were strong, and that if they grew, as they promised to do, they would be disturbing factors, thwarting the calculations of the existing parties. The elections in Lambton and Bruce furnished them an opportunity to show their strength, and they took advantage of it. In North Bruce the Patrons came forward with a candidate, Mr. McNaughton. This gentleman was opposed by a Liberal and a

HON. LIEUTENANT-GOVERNOR KIRKPATRICK.

Conservative. In East Lambton there ran in opposition to the Ministerial nominee (no Conservative candidate having been chosen) Mr. McCallum, who had the P.P.A. support. The two constituencies had been formerly held by friends of the Government.

Both, on the eventful December 3, were carried by the candidates of the new associations. In East Lambton Mr. McCallum succeeded by a majority of 406, and in North Bruce Mr. McNaughton won by over 500. The result was startling, and at once the organizations, with their respective programmes, were brought into prominence, and were eagerly canvassed. They were talked of the more earnestly for the reason that 1894 was to see a general election, and everybody was disposed to speculate touching the influence they would have upon the fortunes of the Government. While the interesting discussion was in progress, the old year was rung out and a new era dawned upon us, the history of which is yet a secret. With the close of 1893 this chapter ends.

DOORWAY, TORONTO UNIVERSITY.

A NEW GOVERNOR-GENERAL.

THE EARL OF ABERDEEN SUCCEEDS LORD STANLEY AT RIDEAU HALL.

 THE position of Governor-General of the Dominion was assumed by Lord Stanley of Preston five years ago last October, and during his tenure of that high office he earned the good opinion and the esteem of those with whom he was brought in contact, both as a genial English gentleman and as the representative in the Dominion of Her Majesty the Queen. His brother, the late Earl of Derby, dying on April 21, Lord Stanley succeeded to his titles and estates, and returned to England; and the Earl of Aberdeen, a personal friend of Mr. Gladstone's, and during a few months of 1886 Lord-Lieutenant of Ireland, was appointed Governor-General of Canada. Lord and Lady Aberdeen were at Chicago for the opening of the great American International Exhibition, but recrossed the Atlantic in time for the Earl to take part in the House of Lords debate on the Irish Home Rule Bill, after which he came direct from home to the seat of his Vice-Regal dignity at Ottawa. This nobleman, the Right Hon. Sir John Campbell Hamilton Gordon, seventh Earl of Aberdeen in the Scottish Peerage and Viscount Gordon in that of the United Kingdom, is forty-six years of age, and is brother to the late Earl George, whose romantic life—choosing to work as a common sailor on board merchant-vessels in remote seas, instead of enjoying the rank and honors that he inherited at his father's death in 1864—ended by accidental drowning in January, 1870. Their grandfather, the fourth Earl of Aberdeen, and Prime Minister in 1853, was an eminent statesman, long associated with Sir Robert Peel. The present Earl is married to a daughter of Dudley Coutts Marjoribanks, Lord Tweedmouth; both husband and wife are esteemed in Scotland, in Ireland, and in London, as liberal patrons and diligent personal promoters of various beneficent works. The Earl's education began at St. Andrews, and he afterwards entered University College, Oxford, where he graduated with honors in 1871, having the previous year succeeded to the title through the death of his brother. He took his seat in the House of Lords as a Conservative, and supported the policy of Lord Beaconsfield until 1878, when, with Lord Derby and Lord Caernarvon, he took exception to the course adopted by the Government in connection with the differences between Russia and Turkey, and seceded from the ranks of the Conservative party. As chairman of the Royal Commission on Railway Accidents, he displayed great ability and untiring zeal in fulfilling the onerous and monotonous duties imposed upon him, and rendered most efficient service while member of the Committee of the Lords on Intemperance. In 1880 he was fully recognized as a member of the Liberal party, and in the same year he was appointed Lord-Lieutenant of Aberdeenshire. The next and the four subsequent years found him in Edinburgh as Lord High Commissioner, presiding over the deliberations of the General Assembly of the Church of Scotland, and gaining the good opinion of all by his courtesy and geniality. But he was brought most prominently into notice in 1886, when he received the appointment of Lord-Lieutenant of Ireland, with the mission of carrying out Mr. Gladstone's Home Rule policy. Although his tenure of office lasted but a few months he completely won the hearts of the Irish, and overcame their prejudices against him as the representative of the English Government. At his departure the regret was intense and universal. All classes of society turned out on the occasion of his leave-taking, and it is said that Dublin never witnessed such a scene since the days of Dan O'Connell.

Since the fall of Mr. Gladstone's Administration in 1886, Lord Aberdeen has been out of office, but his time has been fully occupied in attending to the work of the numerous religious and philanthropic societies with which he is connected. He has paid close attention to the labor problem, and has contributed large sums to the various schemes devised for the amelioration of the condition of the poor. In him the working classes have a zealous supporter, a fearless advocate, and a staunch and faithful friend.

The mental gifts of Lady Aberdeen when a girl attracted the attention of her instructor, Professor Meiklejohn, of St. Andrews University, who predicted for her a great future— a prediction that has been amply realized. With great facility she acquired ancient and modern languages, and in philosophy and literature, contemporaneous and classical, she is deeply read. For many years she has been a voluminous contributor to British and American magazines, and the articles she has published on social subjects, concerning which she is regarded as an authority, have won for her considerable notice. While ably seconding her husband in philanthropic endeavor, Lady Aberdeen has signalized herself by the deep interest she has taken in the cause of factory girls. By her influence and her pen, she has endeavored to evoke public sympathy for their hardships and sufferings. An eloquent speaker, her voice has often been heard pleading in behalf of the working women of England, who have good reason to be grateful to her for many of the privileges they enjoy. She is president of a woman's labor association in Glasgow, and, like the Earl, is a member of many philanthropic institutions. During her brief stay in Dublin, she did everything in her power to improve the condition of the Irish people. Her own means she devoted to relieve the prevailing destitution, and she gave an impetus to Irish manufactures that is felt even now. Lady Aberdeen's special efforts to provide industrial teaching and useful home employment for the wives and daughters of Irish peasantry have gained much success. At Chicago, on May 1, Lord and Lady Aberdeen were in charge of their model Irish village in the Exhibition. They had a pleasant interview with President Cleveland, to whom they presented six pretty Irish girls, with gifts of shamrock, Irish lace, a shillelagh, and specimens of marble.

The Earl and Countess sailed from England in the steamship "Sardinian," arriving at Quebec on September 17, when they took up their temporary home at the citadel, in the morning attending divine service at the English cathedral.

The staff of the new Governor-General consists of the following :—

Secretary to the Governor-General — Mr. Arthur J. Gordon, C.M.G. Mr. Gordon began his colonial experience as one of the staff of Sir Arthur Gordon, now Lord Stanmore, when Governor of New Brunswick. Mr. Gordon went subsequently with Sir Arthur to Fiji as Private Secretary, and later on, in the same capacity, to New Zealand and Ceylon. Mr. Gordon is distantly related to the Earl of Aberdeen, and Mrs. Gordon is a cousin of His Excellency.

Aides-de-Camp—Captain Urquhart, of the Cameron Highlanders. Captain Urquhart is the eldest son of Mr. Urquhart, of Meldrum, Aberdeenshire. He served through the last Egyptian campaign. Captain Kindersley, of the Coldstream Guards.

Extra Aide-de-Camp and Assistant Secretary—Mr. David Erskine, the eldest son of Mr. Erskine, of Linlathen, Forfarshire. Mr. R. M. Ferguson, brother of Mr. Ronald Ferguson, of Nevar, joined the Earl of Aberdeen at Quebec as extra A.D.C.

The ceremony of installation took place on the morning of September 18 in the Red Chamber of the Legislative Council, the escort from the citadel being furnished by the Q.O.C. Hussars, under the command of Captain Baldwin, and the Guard of Honor by the Royal Canadian Artillery, under the command of Lieut.-Colonel Wilson. Lord

THE EARL OF ABERDEEN.

Aberdeen, accompanied by his Countess and three children, and attended by a large suite, entered the Council Chamber shortly after 11.30 a.m. The proceedings were commenced by the reading by Captain Gordon, secretary of the Earl, of Her Majesty's commission to the Earl of Aberdeen, appointing him Governor-General of Canada, and revoking the commission previously issued to Lord Stanley. The oath of office was administered by Sir Henry Strong, Chief Justice of the Supreme Court, surrounded by the Cabinet Ministers in their Windsor uniforms, including Sir C. H. Tupper and Mr. Haggart, and, in fact, the whole Cabinet with the exception of Messrs. Bowell, Daly, and Ives, and Mr. Foster, who was prevented by illness from being present. Cardinal Taschereau and Monsignor Marois were near the throne. Immediately after the installation was complete, a royal salute was fired from the citadel.

After His Excellency had received the congratulations of his Ministers, the Mayor advanced and presented the address of the Council and citizens.

Lord Aberdeen replied as follows: "Mr. Mayor and gentlemen,—To your loyal manifestation of respect and regard towards the representative of Her Most Gracious Majesty the Queen, and to the cordial welcome and greeting extended to myself on my first arrival in that official capacity, I have listened with feelings of profound pleasure and satisfaction, and this gratification is enhanced by your dignified and kindly assurance, and by the surroundings so happy and so auspicious. It is surely appropriate that the first greetings of Her Majesty's Canadian subjects to a new Governor-General, and the first utterance by the occupant of that position, should be upon this historic ground and amidst the inspiring traditions of this ancient and beautiful city. And your demonstration takes place in an eminently opportune manner immediately after I have been duly enrolled and installed in the distinguished office to which I have been appointed. It is indeed an office of high honor, as well as of grave and serious responsibility. But, gentlemen, does the honor and dignity of the position exclude the holder of it from the common lot, the common heritage of service? Nay, it implies, it includes, it conveys, this privilege, this grand principle and purpose of life. If, and because, your Governor-General is in the service of the Crown, he is therefore also, in a literal and absolute sense, in the service of Canada. In other words, aloof though he be from actual executive responsibilities, his attitude must be that of ceaseless and watchful readiness to take part by whatever opportunities may be afforded to him in the fostering of every influence that will sweeten and elevate public life; to observe, study, and join in making known the resources and development of the country; to vindicate, if required, the rights of the people and the ordinances of the constitution; and, lastly, to promote by all means in his power, without reference to class or creed, every movement, and every institution, calculated to forward the social, moral, and religious welfare of all the inhabitants of the Dominion. Such, gentlemen, I assure you, is the aim and purpose which, in dependence on the one ever-effectual source of help and strength, we desire to pursue. I say 'we,' for by your kindly and appreciative allusion to Lady Aberdeen you have shown that you understand why I contemplate these duties only in conjunction with my wife. Let me thank you, on her behalf and my own, for your cordial recognition of her endeavors in the past, and you may be very sure that the confidence and good will which have pervaded your utterances to-day cannot fail to be a stimulus and an incentive in the performance of whatever work may be before us."

On September 26 Lord and Lady Aberdeen formally opened the Canada Central Fair at Ottawa, when they were given a right royal reception, an address being presented by Mayor Durocher, to which His Excellency replied in happy terms. On Sept. 27 the Governor-General and Lady Aberdeen held a public reception at the City Hall, Montreal; and in the evening Lord Aberdeen was the guest of honor at the Board of Trade banquet at the Windsor Hotel. Their Excellencies met with an enthusiastic reception wherever they appeared. The Board of Trade banquet was attended by nearly three hundred members of the board. Mr. W. W. Ogilvie, president of the board, occupied the chair, having on his right Lord Aberdeen, and on his left Sir Adolphe Caron, representing the Dominion Government. Amongst the distinguished guests at the table of honor were Lieutenant-Governor Chapleau, Chief Justice Sir Alexander Lacoste, Mr. T. M. Daly, Minister of the Interior, and Solicitor-General Curran, representing the Dominion Government; Premier Taillon, representing the Quebec Government; Mayor Desjardins, Sir William Dawson, Mr. T. M. Wright, president of the Chicago Board of Trade; and others. After dinner had been partaken of, Lady Aberdeen and the ladies entered the dining hall. Her Excellency's appearance

THE COUNTESS OF ABERDEEN.

was the signal for great applause. The toast of "The Queen" having been honored, the chairman proposed "The Governor-General," which was received with great cheering. The Governor-General, in responding to the toast, said : " With sincere heartiness, I thank you for the courteous and genial terms in which this toast has been proposed, and for the extremely cordial manner in which it has been received. For the personal and indulgent allusions of the chairman I am grateful, but not the less do I recognize that the reception of this toast must be regarded as due to the respect and good will which you, as loyal Canadians, extend towards the occupant of the high and honorable position which I have been called upon to fill. Gentlemen, when thus either directly or through her appointed representatives we show honor to the Sovereign, we do honor to ourselves. They are much mistaken who seem to regard loyalty as a mere sentimental tradition or a relic of bygone times. (Applause.) Loyalty, at least as it exists in Canada, is rational in character as well as warm in expression, because it is founded on principle as well as on feelings. Ours is a constitutional monarchy. We admire and revere the illustrious and gracious occupant of the throne in respect of personal qualities as well as exalted position, while at the same time we recognize in the Sovereign an embodiment of the constitution, and, therefore, of the sacred guardianship of the rights and privileges of the whole people. And so the monarchy and our loyalty to the Crown are entirely consistent with the recognition, the maintenance, and the development of popular and democratic principles and privileges ; and if any ill-informed people are incredulous on this point, let them visit Canada, for there they will find, side by side, and mingled with a prevalent and outspoken loyalty to the throne and the British connection, a free and independent spirit, and a democratic element not surpassed, I am quite sure, at least on this continent. Gentlemen, may this happy and auspicious combination long continue and flourish. Again I thank you." (Cheers.)

On the following day their Excellencies were the recipients of cordial welcomes and congratulations from the various national societies of the city of Montreal, including St. Patrick's Society and St. Andrew's Society, and also of a civic address.

On October 25 they received a brilliant welcome from the people of Toronto. Lord and Lady Aberdeen were the guests of Lieutenant-Governor and Mrs. Kirkpatrick at Government House. In the morning they visited Upper Canada College, and in the afternoon were received by a crowded audience at the Horticultural Pavilion. The day was a perfect one for the ceremony, and the gardens to which the crowds bent their way looked, despite the quickly-falling leaves, very charming. To the tints of autumn were added the colors of a small, but effective, military display, and the lively spectacle of the moving crowd ; while within the Pavilion were hosts of citizens and a large contingent of ladies, not to mention uniforms, clanking scabbards, gilt swords, illuminated addresses, and the sweet music of the Highlanders' Band. The civic reception culminated with considerable success, and did credit to those who had it in hand. It was a hearty and well-mannered welcome to the representative of the Queen. Addresses were presented from the city of Toronto, by Mayor Fleming, from St. Andrew's Society, the Caledonian Society, the Gaelic Society, the Caithness Society, the Orkney and Shetland Society, the St. George's Society, and the Irish Protestant Benevolent Society. In the evening His Excellency was entertained at a banquet at the Toronto Club.

On October 26 a similarly hearty and brilliant reception awaited Lord and Lady Aberdeen in the city of Hamilton, where they were met at the railway station by the City Council and the Board of Education, the Council Chamber being effectively decorated for the occasion. Numerous addresses were the order of the day here also ; and in the afternoon Lady Aberdeen attended the Convention of the Baptist Women's Missionary Association, where she made an address. A reception at the Council Chamber in the evening concluded the ceremonies of the day.

London was the next place of call for the Vice-Regal party, and at this city they visited Hellmuth College, being received by Principal and Mrs. English, and His Lordship the Bishop of Huron.

Returning to Toronto, the Earl and Countess made a tour of various educational and charitable institutions ; and on the 27th Lady Aberdeen attended a meeting of women at the Horticultural Pavilion, and under her auspices the National Council of Women for Canada was inaugurated. In the evening Lord Aberdeen presided at the second annual meeting of the Children's Aid Society, thus concluding a very arduous week, and terminating a series of the heartiest and most unanimously enthusiastic receptions ever given to a representative of the Queen.

Horticultural Gardens and Pavilion, Toronto.

CANADIAN TRADE AND COMMERCE.

SOME SALIENT POINTS IN THE MERCANTILE RECORD OF 1893.

THE year 1893 cannot be spoken of as having a brilliant commercial record; but, in view of the depression prevailing all over the world, Canadians can readily find materials for thankfulness in the review of its various departments of trade. Crops were scarcely up to a moderate average, and a general lowness of prices characterized nearly all markets; but throughout Canada business was but little affected by the severe depression which existed in the United States during the year. The destructive influences that worked havoc among the financial institutions of the great Republic to the south of us did not reach within our borders; and while old financial firms and trusted banks were there going to the wall, with us not a single banking house of any importance had to close its doors. Payments were maintained with tolerable regularity, and, though there were occasional pinches, there was no widespread calamity. No greater proof could have been given of the soundness of Canadian banking principles and practice, and of the good judgment and reliableness of Canadian banking corporations.

A decline in both the number of failures in Canada of trading firms or companies, and the aggregate of their liabilities, is shown by the report of Messrs. R. G. Dun & Co. for 1893. This state of things is in marked contrast with the same firm's report as to the United States in this particular, for there the year has been the worst since 1860. According to the new method of tabulation adopted by Dun & Co., the number of Canadian failures among manufacturing concerns, last year, was 828, with liabilities of $6,686,191; while the number of failed traders or trading companies was 432, with liabilities of $3,356,452; to this add 17 "other failures" of traders, owing $1,156,601, and we have an aggregate of 1,278 failures, with liabilities amounting to $12,456,426. This is a more favorable showing than that of 1892, which was, in turn, the best since 1886 in respect of number and amount of failures. We give a comparison of Canadian failures for twelve years back:

Year.	No. of Failures.	Amount of Liabilities.
1882	788	$ 8,587,000
1883	1,379	15,872,000
1884	1,308	18,939,000
1885	1,247	8,743,000
1886	1,233	10,171,000
1887	1,366	16,070,000
1888	1,667	13,974,000
1889	1,747	14,528,000
1890	1,828	17,858,000
1891	1,861	16,724,000
1892	1,680	13,703,000
1893	1,278	12,456,000

Trade with Britain is an important feature of the yearly record of the Dominion, and, though there were some causes that militated against exports in that direction, it is gratifying to notice that there was an increase as compared with the exports of the previous year. The embargo laid on Canadian cattle by Great Britain was, of course, a serious blow to the live stock industry. On the other hand, the failure of the home hay crop brought an influx of buyers to Canada, which tended not only to make a demand for that commodity, but, further, to bring our resources within the knowledge of old country traders. The following figures are condensed from the usual monthly statement of the London *Canadian Gazette* of January 11, 1894. The information is compiled from the Board of Trade returns, and shows the amount of trade between the United Kingdom and the Dominion of Canada during the month and eleven months ending the 31st of December, 1893. The value of the exports from the United Kingdom to Canada during the month was £244,899, compared with £315,465 in December, 1892, showing a contraction of £70,566, equal to 22.36 per cent., while for the past year the total amounted to £4,754,886, as against £4,816,502 for the previous year, being a reduction of £61,616, or 1.27 per cent. No horses were shipped to the Dominion last month, and in December, 1892, the value was only £250; for the year the total was £16,351 short of that for 1892. The

Scott Street, Toronto—Looking North.

exports of salt during the month fell off £417, but those of spirits increased £1,847. In wool there was a decrease of £523, but for the year the total was £687 higher than for 1892. Amongst manufactured and partly manufactured goods, the shipments last month of cotton piece goods showed a reduction of £31,609; linen, £12,109; articles partly made of silk, £2,991; woollen fabrics, £14,790; worsted fabrics, £12,998; carpets, £721; and hardware and cutlery, £31,959; but jute piece goods were responsible for an increase of £3,909, and silk £1,326. The iron trade has done fairly well. In pig iron there was an increase of £657; in bars, £489; in railroad, £6,463; in galvanized sheets, £109; in tin plates, £3,710; in lead, £248; and in unwrought tin, £4,100. There was, however, a reduction of £605 in hoops and sheets, £1,000 in cast and wrought iron, £1,934 in old iron, and £1,651 in steel. The year's shipments of railroad iron was £503,656, or £130,106 more than in 1892. Coming to miscellaneous articles, earthen and chinaware, and stationery other than paper, showed increases for the month; but exports of apparel and slops, haberdashery, alkali, cement, oil, writing and other paper, were on a reduced scale.

Turning to the other side of the account—namely, to the imports from Canada to the United Kingdom—the total for the past month was £578,751, against £551,672, showing an increase of £27,079, equal to 4.91 per cent.; while, for the year, the aggregate reached £10,164,317, compared with £11,616,075 in 1892, showing a decrease of £1,451,758, or 12.49 per cent. Of oxen and bulls, £2,690 in value came to hand last month, or £3,269 less than in December, 1892; while no cows or calves were received, the value of which, in the corresponding period, was £351. Sheep and lambs to the amount of £375 came to hand, no imports being recorded in the corresponding period. Wheat showed a falling off of £51,411, making for the year a reduction of £420,083, and in flour there was a decrease for the month of £16,159, and for the year of £193,769. Bacon was responsible for an increase last month of £6,725, but in hams there was a decrease of £7,701. In butter there was a falling off of £13,817, the arrivals last month amounting to only £3,270. Nor was the cheese trade as active as in December, 1892, there being a reduction in imports of £33,723, but for the year the total exceeded that of 1892 by £82,268. Of eggs, £2,543 more in value was received last month, and in fish there was an increase of £5,192. Copper ore

was responsible for an increase of £15. The lumber trade was more brisk, imports of hewn timber showing an increase of £6,621, and those of sawn wood an increase of £132,039. No gold was exported from the United Kingdom to Canada during the past month, the total for the year remaining at £100,000. There were no exports in 1892. The sum of £185 was received from the Dominion to December 31, 1893, none, however, in that month; while, during 1892, £166 came to hand. Of silver, none was shipped last month, the total for the year thus being £24,182. In December, 1892, there were no exports to Canada, the total for the year being £47,761. Silver to the value of £740 was received from Canada during the past year, all in September; and, during 1892, £1,332 came to hand; none, however, in December.

The tonnage of vessels entered and cleared at British ports, with cargoes from and to Canada, in the month and twelve months ended December 31, was:

Month of December.	Entered.	Cleared.
1893............	113,599	10,814
1892............	57,797	2,767
Twelve Months.	Entered.	Cleared.
1893............	1,485,661	815,919
1892............	1,592,250	806,539

The Customs House returns for the port of Montreal show a large increase in the export figures for 1893 as compared with 1892, and an advance of nearly nine million dollars over 1891. This improvement is most gratifying, especially as trade throughout the world has been so dull. While the average annual value of the exports for the thirteen years from 1880 to 1892 inclusive was only thirty thousand dollars, last year's exports aggregated over forty-eight thousand dollars, being an increase over that average of sixty-two and one-half per cent. The continuous increase in the value of the exports shows that the produce of the Dominion is steadily gaining ground in the markets of the world, and that the search for other outlets, when the McKinley bill almost closed the States to Canadian merchandise, proved successful. The value also shows an increase, but not so large a one as the exports, owing to the reduced rate of duty on sugar and some other articles. The amount of Customs duty collected, although a little larger than last year, is much smaller than during the previous six years, or the average of the past twelve. While the abnormally low price of wheat has made that cereal unremunerative to farmers, dairy produce has commanded good prices throughout the year. The success of Canadian cheese at the World's Fair, where it came out first in almost every competition, was very gratifying, and it is certain that the exhibit of the natural products of Canada at that Exposition enlightened an enormous number of visitors thereto as to the climate and possibilities of this Dominion. The export of hay from the port of Montreal to Great Britain has been quite an important business during the past year, and that trade seems likely to permanently retain fair proportions. There is encouragement, too, in the circumstance that the export of deals from this port is largely increasing. The export cattle trade has continued to be unfavorably affected by the Atlantic. This report was faithfully circulated by the newspapers, and caused a stampede (so to speak) among men who knew little of the hay trade, which soon extended to the farming community throughout the United States and Canada, causing a scale of prices to be established based on the panic prices of Europe. The extent of the hay-producing area of the United States and Canada not having been accurately measured or fully understood by those entering this new field of speculation, so suddenly brought into prominence by the reported disaster in Europe, caused surprise in the volume of goods that came forward, not only from the States and Canada, but also from Australia, the Argentine, and other countries, which

MAIN ENTRANCE PARLIAMENT BUILDING, TORONTO.

charges of disease among the animals, and the continuance of the British schedule against Canadian and United States cattle renders any improvement unlikely.

Turning once more to the exports of hay, it may be remarked that, although many shipments were made, the year must be regarded as somewhat experimental and peculiar. It certainly had its disappointments for those in the trade whose hopes, based on the failure of the home crop, were too elevated. The year began with good prices and conditions, the outlook for a satisfactory year was favorable, which conditions continued till June, when the report came from Europe to the effect that large quantities of hay would be needed to feed the drought-stricken districts across the quickly satisfied the needs of Europe, causing a break in prices below those ordinarily obtained in years of good crops. While this break occurred in Europe (from which the markets have not fully recovered), panic prices are still prevailing on this side among the farmers, which has, instead of making the year 1893 a favorable one to the dealers, as it promised at its beginning, made it one in which this vast product has been handled with little or no profit and constant uncertainty, and has opened up new territory that probably would not have been developed as hay-producing for market, but which will no doubt continue to a certain extent to put goods upon the markets in the future. This, together with the curtailment of demand in all our cities, owing to electricity superseding horse-power on our street railways, does not give the trade of 1894 a very brilliant outlook, so far as high prices are concerned. The prices going off so rapidly in Europe proves that whatever may occur over there can only be temporary, and that we must depend chiefly upon our markets on this side of the water for our trade in this commodity.

So important a factor in the production of breadstuffs is our Canadian Northwest becoming that reference to a few salient points with respect to it is not out of place in any notice of the trade and commerce of the year. Canada is, above all things, a food-producing country, and on its capacity in this direction its prosperity largely depends. The distant western points. The day must come when agitation in the western territories will force the consideration of railway charges to the front, and the Exchange might have mooted the question in favor of remote points. The relative cost of transporting a bushel of wheat to the eastern seaboard is one of greater moment to the Northwest than tariff reductions on coal oil, binding twine, barbed wire and implements, all put together. As the hub of the Northwest, we should expect to see Winnipeg, through its Board of Trade, initiating the question, and by joint action of the territories bring the relative freight rates in other parts into solid argument for more liberal charges for the west.

Other features of the address are interest-

DOORWAY OF VICTORIA COLLEGE, TORONTO.

annual address of Mr. A. Atkinson, the president of the Winnipeg Grain Exchange, contains many items of interest bearing on this point. The Exchange has been doing a useful work in bringing about a reduction of expenses in handling grain at terminal points, for, be these higher or lower, the dealers' price is governed accordingly. Mr. Atkinson, speaking on this point, claims for Manitoba that it is now in a position to get the benefits of a first-class business system, and to receive the highest possible value for grain at initial shipping points. Nothing that the board has undertaken reflects greater credit on it. It is, however, a marked omission in such an address that no voice is heard as to the heavy cost of the transport of grain from more ing, as showing the development of the Province of Manitoba. Thus the area under wheat increased about 15 per cent. for 1893 over that of 1892. As to the average yield of the province of 15½ bushels to the acre, we are agreeably surprised, and it is to be hoped, and, perhaps, anticipated, with some degree of confidence, that for the stocks in hand, available for market, the farmer may realize a largely-increased price. On the question of quality, 1893 claims to make a good showing—No. 1 hard, 53 per cent.; No. 2 and relatives, 30 per cent.; No. 3 and relatives, 6 per cent.; leaving but 11 per cent. of lower grades. The great feature in this result is the old-fashioned treatment of the seed sown by bluestone enforced on the attention of farmers through the medium of the Grain Exchange. Another admirable feature which Mr. Atkinson mentions is arbitration by a committee on questions of dispute within the trade. It is unfortunate that the actual exports of Manitoba wheat are not distinctly shown in the Trade and Navigation returns of Canada. Most of the exports are accumulated at Fort William, in the Province of Ontario, where the export entries are made ; so that Ontario gets credit for exporting the grain grown in Manitoba and the Territories. As an instance of how this works out, it may be said that for the year ending 30th June, 1893, the wheat exports of Manitoba are given as 401,000 bushels, though probably 6,000,000 actually went to Europe.

Canadian barley has not made a phenomenal showing during the past year as to quantity, but the quality of this cereal has remained unimpaired, as the following extract from an American newspaper adequately shows. Referring to Canadian barley, *The Buffalo Commercial* (Republican) says :

"The barley raised in a small district in the Province of Ontario is distinctly better than any other, and the reason may be found in the peculiar soil found in that region, probably in the underlying limestone. The proof of the superiority of the barley may be found in the testimony of the maltsters and brewers of this State, and also in the decisive fact that Canadian barley fetches in the American market 10 to 15 cents a bushel more than its American rival. Facts are facts, and there is no sense in blinking them."

The provision trade of the year was made somewhat eventful by the extraordinary fluctuations that occurred in the prices of pork. The values of this commodity began to rise early in the year, the causes for the same being variously stated ; but the initial source of the disturbance seems to have been that the cotton-growers of Missouri and the Mississippi valley found it more to their interest to grow cotton than pork, and had consequently neglected to provide for this portion of their food supply. This caused a demand at Chicago, the centre for this meat, and a large amount of speculation was indulged in. From about $12 per barrel, the price gradually rose until no less a figure than $21 was reached. The artificial inflation was, however, only maintained for a short time, though its history comprised the downfall of more than one ambitious speculator who had hoped to make his pile out of the exigencies of buyers. In June and the early part of July the excitation was at its height, and from this time prices gradually declined to a normal standard. The experience was, perhaps, valuable, as showing the field open to the Canadian farmer in this particular line. Hogs can be grown in Canada to advantage, and experience shows that there is a large market for the best breeds.

In his annual review of the lumber trade of the Maritime Provinces, Mr. J. B. Snowball says that the winter of 1892-93 proved the most favorable for log-getting for many years, and, consequently, that a much larger output was secured for the force employed than was anticipated. Spring freshets were poor, and driving expensive. About ten million superficial feet of logs were left in the brooks. Notwithstanding the favorable season, the exports from Chatham, N.B., fell off twelve million superficial feet from last year. And while the exports from St. John were ten millions more than in 1892, still the exports from the province show a decrease of thirteen millions. The increased export from Nova Scotia is caused by the excessive quantity of birch deals shipped from that province. The present winter Mr. Snowball considers to be the most severe experienced in the Maritime Provinces for the past twenty years, the snow being deeper there already than at any time during last year. Operations, too, were only entered into on a limited scale, and with an anticipated production of 25 per cent. less than last year. But this severe weather is likely to reduce the production below this estimate, and next year's export must be small. The total shipments from New Brunswick in 1893 comprised 312,343,485 superficial feet of deals and 5,731 tons of timber, which shows a decrease of 12,906,325 superficial feet of deals, and 5,570 tons of timber, on the totals of the preceding year. From Nova Scotia the shipments were 109,252,930 superficial feet of deals and 5,606 tons of birch timber. Unlike New Brunswick, Nova Scotia's exports of lumber during 1893 show an increase of 21,391,532 feet over those of the preceding year.

A special correspondent of *The St. John Telegraph*, who writes over the signature "L," gives in a recent issue a comprehensive and interesting account of the business of Yarmouth for the year 1893. The year, he says, has been a prosperous one for the town, and this largely by reason of the railway and steamer communications lately secured by this "metropolis of Western Nova Scotia."

The value of Yarmouth's exports for the

year was close upon a million dollars ($952,418), and is made up as follows:

Fish and fish products	$600,000
Field products and shipping	227,318
Forest products	113,000
Manufactures	12,100
Total	$952,418

The manufactures consisted of cotton duck, sail canvas, and woollens. The value of imports for the year was $656,000, which is some $160,000 more than in the previous year; and the lessened aggregate of duty paid last year indicates that an increased amount of free goods, such as the raw material of manufactures, had been imported in 1893.

"The shipping industry has, of course, developed in a manner that has been providing remunerative employment for large numbers of artisans and fishermen. The contiguous market of the United States is a never-failing one for large quantities of fresh fish that have been almost daily sent there from this port. The facilities afforded for this traffic by the splendid Yarmouth line of steamers have, of course, been largely the means of giving quick and profitable returns for these exports."

A lucrative industry, for instance, is the trade in fresh lobsters, which employs many of the shore fishermen. Mackerel, halibut, codfish, haddock, have also found increased demand at satisfactory prices. Indeed, it has been found there that, just as parts of Western Ontario so industriously export their

TORONTO UNIVERSITY LIBRARY.

received a great set-back during the last decade," says the correspondent. "Owing to the competition of steamers, and that of iron sailing vessels as well, the wooden tonnage of the port has been very largely reduced, so that at the close of 1893 the tonnage is not much more than one-third of what it was in 1879; and it is being constantly reduced by sale and loss of vessels, without any building to take their place. Men who owned and built wooden vessels were made painfully aware of the general depression of the shipping industry, and have naturally turned their attention and their money into other channels of investment. The result has been that Yarmouth's manufacturing and fishing interests have been

turkeys, chickens, eggs, and dairy produce to American cities, as to raise the prices of such food products to rates almost prohibitory for their own residents, so the values of fresh fish products in Yarmouth itself were made by the American demand "so buoyant that the Yarmouth fish-eater generally pays a good round price during the export season for any fish delicacy." Three-fourths of the $600,000 worth of fish exported from Yarmouth went to the United States. The remainder represents cured and packed fish sent to more distant markets.

It is very satisfactory to learn that the good people of Yarmouth have taken one of the likeliest steps to attract to themselves a portion of the stream of American summer travel which the salubrity and natural beauty of Nova Scotia induces—to wit, they have built a good hostelry, the Grand Hotel, on Main Street. The American traveller will not long continue to frequent a place that has not good hotel accommodation, and in this particular Yarmouth folk have reasoned shrewdly. The Western Counties railway, from Annapolis to Yarmouth, has had a good year ; and now is heard much promise of a narrow gauge railroad from the latter place eastward to Lockport, some ninety miles.

The annual report of the St. John's, Newfoundland, Chamber of Commerce on last year's fisheries is not a particularly cheering document. It opens with a reference to the seal fishery of last spring, which was the worst ever experienced since the introduction of steamers into the industry. Last year all the steamers sailed from 150 miles north of St. John's, and missed the great body of seals. As a consequence, the total catch was only 129,160 seals, against 348,000 the year before. In addition to this, the price of oil and skins was very low, and the poor catch was rendered doubly unproductive on this account. The Labrador cod fishery was the only one really productive. The catch was very good, and the cure equally so, with the exception of a small quantity taken at the latter part of the season, and which unfavorable weather prevented being properly dried. The shore fishery was only fairly productive, and the bank fishery was very poor—so much so, indeed, that the Chamber fears its early extinguishment, for the return is not by any means commensurate with the capital invested. The catch of pickled fish is indifferent and unsatisfactory, the take of salmon is only fair, and the herring fishery is also poor, especially frozen herring, the unusually mild weather experienced preventing that industry being entered into with the usual vigor.

Full returns of last season's salmon pack in British Columbia show that the combined output of the canneries has indeed been very large. In British Columbia there are at present forty-three canneries. These are located as follow : Twenty-six on the Fraser River, eight on the Skeena, three on the Naas, three at River's Inlet, and one each at Lowe's Inlet, Albert Bay, and Nanoose Bay. The entire pack is estimated at 576,584 cases. The pack of the Fraser River canneries shows an average of 19,000 cases each. The salmon fleet this year consists of ten vessels, and by them something over 400,000 cases have been taken to Liverpool and London. Of the remaining 175,000 or more cases, the greater number went overland to supply the eastern markets and some for reshipment to the old country. Australia took several thousand cases. We have in a previous issue given the cargoes carried by the first seven vessels of the fleet. We now give a complete record of the shipments by vessels for the year :

Vessels.	Cases.	Value.
Brk. Routenbeck.....	38,800	$201,875
Shp. Sirene..........	66;558	282,790
S.S. Grandholm	31,707	158,535
Brk. Jessie Stowe....	30,000	136,112
" Ladstock........	35,773	178,865
" Formosa	38,126	191,880
" City of Carlisle..	37,381	185,905
Shp. Candia........	50,318	249,523
Brk. Primera	24,666	128,350
" Harold (appr)...	56,000	275,000

An exceedingly interesting report of the output of canned tomatoes, in 1893, by the factories of the United States and Canada is published in the last issue of *The American Grocer*. The pack of American canneries is given at 4,300,443 cases. To this output New Jersey contributed 977,242 cases ; Maryland, 1,417,626 cases ; Indiana, 347,260 cases ; California, 451,547 cases ; Delaware, 271,277 cases; and New York, 160,887 cases. The output of Canada is estimated at 156,000 cases, as compared with a pack of 143,627 cases last year. The combined pack represents 4,456,443 cases, or 1,089,651 cases in excess of last year's pack. The total output in 1893 is, compared with that of previous years, as follows :

Year.	Cases of 2 doz. tins each.
1893.............................	4,456,443
1892.............................	3,366,792
1891.............................	3,405,365
1890.............................	3,166,177
1889.............................	2,976,765
1888.............................	3,343,137
1887.............................	2,817,048
Total for seven years......	23,531,727
Average per year...........	3,361,675
Average per years 1891-1893...	3,742,867

"The result of the pack of 1893," our exchange remarks, "will prove a surprise, and be a warning to the trade. It is apparent from the records of the past five years that the average annual requirement of the United States is about 3,300,000 cases, which quantity could be sold at fair prices and avoid a carry over. Fortunately for the packer, the bulk of the season's output is in possession of distributors."

The annual report of the Toronto Harbor Trust for 1893 gives particulars of the shipping trade of Toronto, and shows that, by the comparative statement of goods arrived by water during that year and the year before, while there is an increase in 1893 of general merchandise received, an increase in fruit and grain, there is a decrease in bricks, lumber, stone, and sand, the result of the decline in building operations, and a marked decline in coal imports (from 161,000 to 126,000 tons), probably by reason of the failure of a large coal house. An increased number of steamboat arrivals is noted and a decrease in sailing vessels, the total arrivals being 2,577. The bay was clear of ice for eight months—April 7 to December 8.

The report of the shipping operations carried on by the Maritime Province owners the past year is not a particularly pleasing one. The total number of new vessels registered during the year is 298, an increase of some thirty-eight vessels over those struck off from the registration. The combined tonnage of these 298 vessels, however, amounts to but 24,400 tons, while the tonnage of the 260 vessels struck off is 91,439 tons. The tonnage lost this year by disaster has been far from inconsiderable, for, as the vessels of the maritime fleet grow older, they become more subject to loss. The tonnage registered in the different parts of the Maritime Provinces for the years 1892 and 1893 is given in the following table, which we take from *The Halifax Chronicle*:

PORT REGISTRATION.	TOTAL TONNAGE	
	Dec. 31, 1892.	Dec. 31, 1893.
NOVA SCOTIA—		
Amherst................	906	906
Annapolis	9,119	7,268
Brichat	5,414	5,167
Barrington	1,859	2,061
Digby	12,554	11,537
Guysboro..............	2,057	1,889
Carried forward......	83248	754942
Halifax................	51,339	46,666
Liverpool.............	7,771	7,279
Lunenburg...........	27,576	29,339
Maitland	29,677	29,621
Parrsboro.............	29,507	31,404
Pictou.................	17,064	15,247
Port Hawkesbury...	2,765	2,535
Port Medway........	1,824	1,879
Shelburne............	7,522	6,938
Sydney...............	5,330	5,248
Truro..................	2,390	1,431
Windsor..............	128,926	118,035
Weymouth...........	3,739	3,879
Yarmouth............	79,043	66,532
Total...............	426,436	394,861
	394,861	
Decrease............	31,375	
NEW BRUNSWICK—		
Chatham..............	9,063	9,765
Dorchester...........	6,304	4,921
Moncton..............	2,710	2,700
Richibucto...........	3,584	1,598
Sackville.............	1,734	1,266
St. Andrews.........	3,394	3,486
St. John	163,222	131,909
Total...............	190,011	155,645
	155,645	
Decrease............	34,366	
P. E. ISLAND—		
Charlottetown.......	22,706	19,409
SUMMARY.		
Nova Scotia..........	426,436	394,861
New Brunswick.....	190,011	155,645
P. E. Island..........	22,706	19,403
Grand total.........	639,153	569,915
	569,915	
Total decrease....	69,238	

HURON STREET, BRANTFORD—CHRISTMAS, 1893.

AMONG THE ROCKIES. L. R. O'BRIEN, Pinxt.

CANADIAN FARMING INTERESTS.

A GLANCE AT THE FIELD OF AGRICULTURE, DAIRY FARMING, AND GRAZING.

THOUGHTFUL persons will not lightly esteem the importance to Canada of agricultural pursuits. The country has to be fed, and, in addition, some sixty millions of dollars' worth of produce has to be gathered in and sold abroad to enable us to meet our liabilities, and to pay for what we buy in other lands. While our mining, fishing, lumber, and manufacturing interests are not to be lightly esteemed, the business of agriculture in its influence upon the welfare of the community is more potent than any one of them. These four special departments bring us in forty millions of British or foreign dollars; but the tilling of the soil produces an income, by sales elsewhere, equal to that sum, with twenty millions added to it.

The spring of 1893 opened well. In Ontario there was a severe winter; but the snow and ice disappeared easily and gradually, and by the beginning of May the fields were in tolerable condition. Last year, more than any other, was the value of underdraining vividly felt. The drained lands came early into use. On the other hand, those not similarly treated were flooded and retarded, and in some cases their fall wheat was destroyed. On the whole, however, wheat was not materially damaged, and the outlook at that time was favorable. Commercial and fiscal influences were soon perceived to be affecting the character of agricultural enterprises. For example, barley, owing to the McKinley duty, was very little grown. At the same time, there was a movement into other branches of production. Live stock received more attention, and pigs were regarded as a good investment. While the spring was favorable in Ontario, it was, unfortunately, somewhat late in Manitoba and the Northwest, although by May 25 the news was most satisfactory from this district—grain was going into the ground at a lively rate, and the large bulk of wheat-seeding was completed. Pleasant growing weather had given life to the seed, and at many points it was several inches above the soil.

The annual meeting of the Ontario Agriculture and Arts Association, was held in Toronto, on March 16, when the report of the secretary showed that during the year 445 Clydesdale horses had been registered, 19 Shires, 71 draught horses, and 24 hackneys. The number of cattle registered was 343 Ayrshires, 25 Herefords, 12 Devons, and 85 Polled Angus. The sheep registered were 112 Dorset horned and 12 Suffolk horned, while in swine there were 613 Berkshires, 545 Yorkshires, 29 Suffolks, 39 Tamworths, 275 Chester whites, and 411 Poland Chinas. From the sale of herd books, the receipts amounted for the year to $3,142. The expenditure for the seventh Provincial Spring Stallion Show was $1,887, and the receipts from all sources $1,032. The amount paid out on account of the ninth annual Fat Stock Show was $1,722, and the receipts amounted to $1,095. The judges of the farms in Leeds and Stormont had incurred expenses amounting to $392. The report further pointed out that at the World's Fair there would be entered 257 horses (75 being passed conditionally), 259 cattle (175 being passed upon), 523 sheep (350 being approved of), 152 swine (150 being approved of). Reference was made to the scheduling of Canadian cattle by the American Government. Diplomas were also granted by the association to graduates of the Ontario Veterinary College.

The Spring Stallion Show, which opened at the Drill Shed, Toronto, on March 8, was attended by a big crowd of spectators. The number of entries was about equal to that of the previous year, while in some of the classes the exhibits were superior. The thoroughbred class was particularly good, but the competition in the hackneys was somewhat limited. The judging gave general satisfaction, the judges for the various classes being as follows : Thoroughbreds, R. Pringle, Toronto; carriage or coach stallions, W. H. Gibson, Buffalo ; standard-bred roadsters, Dr. Willoughby, Colborne ; Suffolk Punch, J. F. Quinn, Brampton ; hackneys, A. Wilson, Paris.

One of the agricultural events of the early

spring was the publication of the reports of the Ottawa Experimental Farm. The Director of this institution, Mr. William Saunders, says:

"Six years have passed since the initial steps were taken towards establishing a system of Experimental Farms for the Dominion of Canada. Prior to this, during the session of the House of Commons in 1884, a select committee was appointed to inquire into the best means of encouraging and developing the agricultural interests of Canada, and this committee made a report in favor of the establishment of an experimental farm. No further steps, however, were taken in this direction until November, 1885, when an investigation was undertaken for the purpose of ascertaining the condition of experimental work in agriculture in the United States, Great Britain, and other countries, and a report was prepared on this subject under date of February 20, 1886, which was submitted to the House of Commons during the session of that year. 'The Experimental Farm Station Act,' which was based on the recommendations embodied in that report, was introduced shortly after, and passed with the concurrence of both sides of the House; and on the 16th of October following the organization was begun by the appointment of a Director to undertake the work.

"One of the provisions of the Act required that the Central Experimental Farm, which was to serve the provinces of Ontario and Quebec, should be located near the capital, and prior to my appointment I had been instructed by the Minister of Agriculture to inspect those farms near Ottawa, some twenty in all, which had been offered for sale to the Government as sites for the Central Experimental Farm. After spending several weeks on this work, it was found that none of the farms offered possessed the combined features desired in the Central Experimental Farm, when instructions were received to visit and inspect other farms not offered in the neighborhood of the capital, when, among others, the present site was examined. Finding that this land, although in a very rough condition and parts of it very swampy, presented advantages greater than those of any other farm in the neighborhood in its variety of soil, contiguity to the city, commanding position as to elevation, facilities for drainage, etc., which made it eminently desirable for the purpose, a report was prepared recommending that this farm be chosen. Shortly after this, a portion of the land was purchased at private sale, and the remaining area required was expropriated under the Act, and the prices to be paid for the several portions subsequently fixed by the Dominion arbitrators.

"The day following that of my appointment as Director of Experimental Farms, I left for the Maritime Provinces to enter on a systematic inquiry into the conditions of agriculture in all the settled portions of the Dominion from the Atlantic to the Pacific, for the purpose of ascertaining where the

HON. JOHN DRYDEN,
Ontario Minister of Agriculture.

experimental farms which it was designed to establish in the several provinces could be best located so as to confer the greatest benefit on the farmers of the Dominion.

"During the interval which had elapsed between the passing of 'The Experimental Farms Act' and the appointment of the Director, many offers of land had been made to the Government in all the provinces and territories, and, in justice to the parties concerned, it seemed necessary that all those farms offered, which were in central or promising localities, should be inspected and reported on, and to accomplish this involved much time and labor.

"Since it was designed that the Experimental Farm to be established in the Maritime Provinces should serve the requirements of the three provinces, namely, Nova Scotia, New Brunswick, and Prince Edward Island, there were many reasons why it was desirable that this farm should be located not far from the boundary line between Nova Scotia and New Brunswick, so that it might be almost equally accessible to the farmers of these two provinces, and at the same time convenient for the farmers of

OTTAWA EXPERIMENTAL FARM REPORT.

Prince Edward Island. While all the farms offered to the Government in the Maritime Provinces were inspected and reported on, the greater care was given to the examination of those situated in the border counties of Cumberland and Colchester, in Nova Scotia, and of Westmoreland and Albert, in New Brunswick.

"As soon as this preliminary survey of the sites offered in the Maritime Provinces was completed, the work was extended to Manitoba, the Northwest Territories, and British Columbia, and, after nearly three months of continuous travel and inspection, I returned to Ottawa to report progress.

"By the appointment on November 1, 1886, of Mr. W. W. Hilborn, of Arkona, Ont., as horticulturist of the Central Experimental Farm, the services of a practical farmer, also those of a man of extended knowledge in fruit-growing, were secured; and during my absence, under his supervision, work was begun on the Central Farm, and nearly twenty acres of the land ploughed before the winter set in. During the winter, Mr. William M. Blair, of Truro, N.S., was selected as superintendent of the Experimental Farm for the Maritime Provinces; and as it had been arranged that each superintendent of the branch farms should, after appointment, spend several months with the Director at Ottawa to gain fuller information as to the aims and objects of the work, the practical knowledge of farming which Mr. Blair possessed was made use of at the Central Farm when the spring opened. Mr. S. A. Bedford, of Moosomin, N.W.T., who was selected in May, 1887, as superintenden, of the Experimental Farm for Manitoba, also joined the staff at Ottawa, which was further reinforced about the same time by the engagement of Mr. John Fixter, of London, Ont., as farm foreman. These all entered heartily into the undertaking, and, bringing their practical knowledge to bear on the difficulties to be overcome, all branches of the work made rapid headway. On the 2nd of May the work of clearing, removal of stone, extracting of stumps, and ploughing, was vigorously begun; and before the season closed a considerable area of land was cleared and brought under cultivation, the system of drainage to be carried out fully planned, some of the preliminary work done, and other improvements made. The contract for the fencing was let early in the spring, and completed before winter came.

"During the summer, the Maritime Provinces were again visited in company with Mr. William M. Blair, whose intimate and practical acquaintance with the agriculture of these provinces, acquired by a life-long experience there, was of great assistance; and, after a second careful survey, the advantages offered by the present site of the Experimental Farm at Nappan, N.S., were recognized, and its purchase recommended. Subsequently, the recommendation was adopted, and the negotiations for the purchase completed during the following winter. This site is within half a mile of Nappan Station on the Intercolonial Railway, about eight miles from the boundary line between Nova Scotia and New Brunswick, and is easily accessible from Prince Edward Island. About three hundred acres were purchased, about two hundred of which were cleared and almost free from stumps; the other one hundred acres were wooded with spruce, larch, beech, maple, and other useful trees. The advantages embodied in this site were variety of soil, partial shelter from prevailing winds, a central location, and proximity to the main line of travel. The soil of this farm fairly represents the better class of farms on the border line of the two provinces, and for a long distance on either side. It is chiefly clay loam, more or less mixed with sand, becoming heavy or light as clay or

WILLIAM SAUNDERS,
Director, Experimental Farm, Ottawa.

sand predominates, with some parts gravelly, and with a subsoil varying from clay to gravelly clay. The cleared land may be classified approximately as follows: Marsh or dyke land, valuable for the growth of hay, about fifty acres; lower upland, fifty acres; and higher upland, one hundred acres. The higher land faces the west and overlooks the inlet from the Bay of Fundy, and commands a good view of the Maccan River and the surrounding country.

"Under the judicious management of Mr. Blair, this farm has been greatly improved, underdraining has effected remarkable changes in the relative fertility of portions of the land, valuable experimental work has been conducted with grain, fodder plants, roots, etc., orchards and belts of ornamental trees have been planted, the necessary buildings have been erected, and the barns and stables provided with useful breeds of animals. The details of the work accomplished will be found in the reports of the superintendent, embodied in the annual reports of the Experimental Farms.

"Later, in the summer of 1887, another tour was made through the west in company with Mr. S. A. Bedford, who had resided for many years in Manitoba and the Northwest Territories, and whose experience of farm life on the plains made him a valuable adviser. The investigations extended from Selkirk, twenty-one miles east of Winnipeg, along the line of the Canadian Pacific Railway, to the western boundary of Manitoba. North of Brandon, the country was examined as far as Binscarth, and from this point along the line of the Manitoba and Northwestern Railway to Portage la Prairie. Many journeys were taken north and south of the lines of railway, which involved over 500 miles of driving, and afforded an excellent opportunity of ascertaining the character of the soil and the condition of the settlers over a large portion of the province.

"After much consideration a site near Brandon was recommended, and finally chosen, a farm of about 625 acres, situated partly in the valley of the Assiniboine, and partly on the higher land adjoining. This farm combines the advantages of variety of soil, fertile valley land for pasture, extending to the river; a rich sandy loam on the rise towards the bluffs which form the margin of the valley, on the sloping sides of which, and in the ravines, the soil is lighter, more sandy and gravelly; while on the heights the land is good, and fairly represents the soil in most of the great wheat-growing districts of Manitoba. It adjoins the city of Brandon, and is near the centre of one of the best agricultural sections in the province. It has an abundant supply of spring water of excellent quality, is beautifully situated, and in full view of the passing trains of the Canadian Pacific Railway.

"Possession of this farm was had early in July, 1888, and since then, under the superintendence of Mr. Bedford, rapid and satisfactory progress has been made in every department of the work. Particular attention has been devoted to experiments with grain, fodder crops, and the best methods of treating the soil to prepare it for crop. The farm has been greatly beautified by the planting of avenues and groves of trees; commodious buildings have been erected, and some of the most useful breeds of cattle introduced.

PRESIDENT MILLS,
Ontario Agricultural College.

Particulars of the progress made will be found in the annual reports.

"During October, 1887, an extended tour was made through that part of the Northwest Territories extending along the main line of railway, special attention being paid to that portion known as Eastern Assiniboia. The district lying between the Manitoba boundary and Fort Qu'Appelle was driven over, involving journeys in vehicles of over 400 miles, in company with Mr. Bedford and Mr. A. Mackay, of Indian Head. A wide area of country was inspected and examinations made of the character of the soil, and much information gathered regarding the climate, and especially with regard to rainfall. Similar investigations were made in the neighborhood of Regina, Moose Jaw, Medicine Hat, Calgary, and other important stations along the main line of railway.

"Since by far the larger area of land in this part of the country is open prairie, it was thought best to select a section of bare prairie for this farm, with the view of showing what might be done in such case to provide eventually shelter both for crops and buildings by tree-planting. Several excellent sites were seen, but a section of land which was examined near the town of Indian Head was found to combine more advantages than any other farm inspected, and this was finally chosen for the Experimental Farm for the Northwest Territories. This section, No. 19, Township 18, Range 12 west, adjoins the town of Indian Head on the east ; it lies north of the railway, which skirts its boundary for about a mile. The soil is deep and of excellent quality, and varies from a heavy clay to a sandy loam, with a clay subsoil of a yellowish brown color. The farm consists of 680 acres of land, is situated 104 miles west of the Manitoba boundary, 105 miles north of the United States boundary, and forty-four miles east of Regina. It is in the midst of a large and thriving agricultural settlement, is well supplied with water, and its distance from the Indian Head railway station is but little more than half a mile.

"Possession of the farm was had early in the spring of 1888. Mr. A. Mackay, who had received the appointment of superintendent, and had spent some weeks on the Central Farm, in Ottawa, entered on his duties on the 24th of April. During 1888 this farm was partly fenced, and the fencing completed early in 1889, during which year buildings were also erected — dwellings, barns, and stables ; and for the past four years the work of experimenting in all lines of agriculture and horticulture likely to be useful to the farmers of the Northwest has been successfully carried on. A large number of young forest trees have been planted, and the farm is now practically provided with shelter belts, forest clumps, avenues, and hedges, which, although the planting is so recent, are rapidly improving the general appearance of the farm and changing its character. Suitable breeds of dairy and beefing cattle have been supplied for the improvement of stock, also swine and poultry, and all are being utilized for experimental work. The results of tests of grain and fodder crops have been very useful, and have shown that it is of the greatest importance that land, to be cropped in this district, should be fallowed during the previous summer, as this treatment is almost invariably followed with good results. A large number of the hardier varieties of fruits have been tested ; but while some sorts of small fruits, such as gooseberries, currants, and raspberries, do well, no satisfactory results have yet been obtained with apples, pears, plums, or any of the larger fruits. A lively interest is taken in the results of the work at this farm by the settlers in the territories, and especially by those residing near it in Eastern Assiniboia, and the distribution of the annual reports giving the particulars of the practical work carried on by Mr. Mackay has already produced results which are highly gratifying.

"The Experimental Farm for British Columbia was the last selected and put in operation. Two visits were made to this province within a year, the first in December, 1886, to gather preliminary information and acquire some general knowledge of the condition and requirements of the agriculture of the province, and the second in September, 1887, for the special purpose of finding some suitable spot for the establishment of an experimental farm. During the latter visit, I was accompanied by Mr. S. A. Bedford, who gave much valued assistance. During these visits, opportunities were afforded of examining many farms, both on Vancouver Island and on the mainland ; but of all the sites inspected none appeared to unite so many advantages as a part of the land belonging to the Agassiz estate adjoining the railway station known as Agassiz, in the valley of the Fraser, about seventy miles east of Vancouver. The land offered at this place for the purposes of an experimental farm, and which was finally chosen, consists of about 300 acres, opposite and adjoining the railway station, with a frontage along the railway track of about half a mile. Along the western boundary is a road leading to the Harrison Hot Springs, a place of great resort, five and a half miles distant ; and in the rear rise rocky heights, with intervening patches of bench land, from 900 to 1,200 feet in height, more or less covered with shrubbery and heavy timber. About thirty-five acres of the valley land has been under partial cultivation, and about 200 acres more had been cleared of most of the large timber, with the stumps cut close to the ground, but still undecayed, and the surface occupied with brushwood and ferns. The soil varies from a clay loam through different grades of sandy loam to a soil of a gravelly character, with a porous subsoil, some parts sandy, others a sandy clay, under most of which lies a bed of gravel from three to five feet below the surface.

"The land at Agassiz was purchased in 1888 ; but, owing to delay in perfecting the title, it was not taken possession of until the autumn of 1889. Mr. Thomas A. Sharpe, one of the early settlers in Southern Manitoba, was appointed superintendent, in July, 1889 ; and after spending a few weeks at the Central Farm, he left for the coast, taking with him horses and other supplies, and began work on the premises on the 19th of September, and, before spring arrived, the land formerly under cultivation had been thoroughly ploughed and prepared, and enough new land broken up and cleaned to admit of the planting of several

LEAUCHOIL MOUNTAINS AND THE CHANCELLOR ROCKIES.

Engraved by THE MAIL. Bourne & May, Photographers.

orchards, and at the same time carry on a number of experimental tests with grain, fodder, crops, and roots, particulars of which are given in the report of the Experimental Farm for 1890. Under the energetic management of Mr. Sharpe, the clearing of the land has been steadily pushed, and up to the present time one hundred and five acres have been brought under cultivation, and twenty acres more cleaned and stumped and ready for the plough. A dwelling for the superintendent has been erected, and a large combined barn and stable built, which affords accommodation for stock and horses. Several of the best breeds of dairy cattle have been sent there, with swine, sheep, and poultry, all of which are doing well. The climate is mild, much like that of some parts of England, and is well adapted for fruitgrowing. Since this promises to soon become one of the leading industries in that province, special attention has been given to the securing of a large number of varieties, embracing the promising sorts in all classes, the object in view being to establish large test orchards, where the relative value of all varieties suited to the climate will be ascertained, and, from the experience gained, information can be given to those about to plant as to the sorts best adapted to the climate, and those which promise the most profitable returns. Although only three years have elapsed since this enterprise was begun, there are now growing and under test at that farm 887 varieties of fruit, 569 of which are different sorts of large fruits and 318 of small fruits. To bring together this collection, which is probably the largest on the continent, the nurseries of many countries have been laid under tribute ; and whether received from the north or the south the trees seem to grow equally well, and with such rapidity as to astonish those who are accustomed only to the slower growth seen in the east.

"Here also the different varieties of nutbearing trees are being tried—English and Japanese walnuts, hard and soft shelled almonds, Spanish, Japanese, and American chestnuts, Kentish filberts, with pecans and hickory; and they all grow luxuriantly. British Columbia is noted for the wealth of its timber resources, which are practically inexhaustible ; but there are no hard woods of any consequence in that province. Hence, in addition to the plantations of fruit and nut trees, belts of hard woods have been and are being planted in the valley, and scattered also over the hillsides, consisting of black walnut, butternut, elm, ash, hickory, and other valued eastern and northern trees ; and with the relatively rapid growth which trees make in that country, the question as to how valuable these trees may be in that province will soon be determined, and if it can be shown that the so-called bench lands, which are of little use for agricultural purposes, can be gradually transformed into orchards and plantations of valuable hard-wooded timber, these experiments will prove of great value to that country.

"In the meanwhile, rapid progress has also been made at the Central Experimental Farm, where a wilderness has been transformed into a series of well-appointed fields, orchards, and testing plots. Experiments have been carried on in all directions to test the earliness of varieties of cereals, their relative superiority in yield, quality of grain, stiffness of straw, etc. Those which have succeeded best have been scattered broadcast by a free distribution through the mails; and thus about 30,000 samples, of 3 lbs. each, have been placed in the hands of about 12,000 to 15,000 farmers, and these newer sorts are already, in some localities, influencing favorably the general character of the crops. The relative advantages resulting from early as compared with late sowing for the provinces of Ontario and Quebec have been clearly demonstrated by a series of tests extending over a period of three years. A large number of new varieties of grain have been originated here by cross-fertilization, and some of them promise to be of great value. This work has been extended during the past year, and new varieties originated by this method on each of the western farms also, with the hope that new sorts, which have their birthplace in the countries in which they are to be grown, will probably be better adapted to the climatic vicissitudes which they will have to endure. Varieties of fodder plants and roots have been tested in great numbers, and the results of the work published in reports and bulletins, hundreds of thousands of which have found their way into the hands of appreciative readers.

"The horticultural work has also made rapid progress, first under the superintendence of Mr. W. W. Hilborn, and more recently under that of Mr. John Craig. A very large collection of fruits has been accumulated, and the trees are now fast coming into bearing. Of small fruits a multitude has already been reported on ; new varieties of much promise have been originated, while a large number of different sorts of vegetables have been tested as to earliness, quality, and other important points. The diseases which affect fruit trees and vines have been watched, and the remedies which have been recommended thoroughly tested, and the results given to the public in the annual reports.

"With the appointment of Mr. James Fletcher, early in 1887, to the position of entomologist and botanist to the Dominion Experimental Farms, the subjects of insects and plants injurious to crops, and the remedies for their subjugation, have been made matters of special study; much useful experience has been gained, and the results have been given in reports and bulletins. Mr. Fletcher has also brought together a large collection of useful grasses, and has succeeded in establishing a series of experimental plots, with the object of determining their hardiness and relative usefulness as fodder plants. This branch of his work has been much appreciated; the large number of letters of inquiry which have been received from year to year in connection with these several divisions of the work indicate the lively interest which is taken in them.

"In July, 1887, Mr. F. T. Shutt was appointed as chemist to the Dominion Experimental Farms, which prepared the way for supplying some portion of the information needed in connection with the chemistry of agriculture. Shortly after his appointment, Mr. Shutt accompanied the Director in a visit paid to several of the well-known chemical laboratories in the United States; and by this means much useful information was accumulated, and, from the data obtained, the size and form of the present laboratories were determined and the plans for the building prepared. While this structure was in course of erection, Mr. Shutt proceeded to Europe and visited some of the more important laboratories in Great Britain and on the Continent, and selected the necessary apparatus for the laboratory at Ottawa. On his return, plans of the internal fittings were prepared and carried out; and, as a result of this arrangement, the chemical laboratory at the Experimental Farm has been made one of the most convenient and best-fitted establishments for carrying on chemical work in relation to agriculture to be found in this country. The good work since accomplished by Mr. Shutt in the analysis of soils, fodder, plants, natural fertilizers—such as muds, marls, and mucks, from many parts of the Dominion, also grasses, sugar beets, and many other substances, have made his annual reports very valuable to the farming community.

"During 1887 and 1888, the clearing of the land on the Central Experimental Farm was completed; the main drains and many of the branches, measuring over fifteen miles in all, were laid; most of the buildings planned and erected; avenues, ornamental hedges, and clumps of shrubbery were planted, the land adjacent to the buildings graded and sodded, and the whole aspect of the farm greatly improved. Extensive shelter belts and plantations of forest trees have since been planted, which will eventually add much to the beauty of the place.

"In May, 1888, experiments were begun with poultry, and the services of Mr. A. G. Gilbert secured to carry on this work. Later in the season, when the poultry building was ready for occupation, the birds which had been bred served to furnish it with stock, and Mr. Gilbert was selected to fill the position of poultry manager. The annual reports he has given of the work carried on have been of much service to those interested in poultry, and have served as a guide to many in the management of fowls, as well as in the selection of varieties.

"On February 1, 1890, Mr. James W. Robertson was appointed as agriculturist to the Experimental Farm and dairy commissioner for the Dominion. In his capacity as agriculturist he has taken charge of the stock, originated the many important feeding tests which have been made, and supervised the work. The dairy building and piggery were built in accordance with plans prepared by him, and embody modern conveniences which simplify and lessen the work. In these buildings continued experiments have been carried on in connection with the manufacture of butter and the feeding of cattle and swine, and important bulletins and reports published on these subjects. Owing to Mr. Robertson's frequent and unavoidable absence in pursuance of his other duties, a part of the work which usually devolves on the agriculturist has been carried on by the Director, aided by the farm foreman and by Mr. Wm. Macoun, who discharges the duty of foreman of forestry and assistant in experimental work. The important work carried on by Mr. Robertson as dairy commissioner for the Dominion has already influenced most favorably the dairy exports of this country, and the stimulus which he has given to this industry by the establishment of experimental dairy stations and winter creameries, by his personal efforts and those of the assistant dairy commissioner in Quebec, together with those of the instructors under his charge, will doubtless result in a still greater development of this extensive industry in every province of the Dominion.

"In connection with the establishment and supervision of the experimental farms, the writer has travelled since October, 1886, eight times to the Pacific coast, and ten times to the Atlantic, and visited a large proportion of the more important agricultural districts throughout the Dominion. In all branches of the work undertaken, he has been greatly aided by the faithful services of those who have been associated with him, and in charge of special departments, and to the value of their work he desires to bear grateful testimony; and with their help these establishments have been brought to their present position of usefulness and popularity."

As the farming season of 1893 went on, various causes militated against the crops, prominent among them being a long season of drought in July and August. The prospects of the early part of the year were in a large measure overcast; and, as a matter of fact, the yield for the year was disappointing. In September, the *New York Sun* published the following estimate of the wheat requirements and product. The writer says :—
"Official estimates having been published of most of the greater crops of 1893, we are now able to arrive at a fair approximation of the world's wheat supply for the 1893-94 harvest year, by supplementing these official estimates by conservative commercial ones for other countries. Placing such estimates in juxtaposition with the requirements of the augmented populations of the respective countries, as indicated by the consumption of the last ten years, we arrive at the results embodied in the following table, where both requirements and product are stated in terms of Winchester bushels, or bushels of sixty pounds where foreign weights have been reduced.

"As a tabulation, to possess any value whatever, must include all importing and exporting countries, the effort is made here to cover the entire area that either buys or sells wheat.

ESTIMATED WHEAT REQUIREMENTS AND PRODUCT, 1893-94.

	Domestic Requirements, Bushels.	Estimated Product, Bushels.
United Kingdom....	241,300,000	53,600,000
France........	353,400,000	277,900,000
Italy........	147,800,000	120,500,000
Belgium........	40,000,000	16,000,000
Germany........	113,200,000	90,000,000
Netherlands.......	17,800,000	5,000,000
Switzerland........	14,400,000	2,000,000
Spain........	84,600,000	77,000,000
Greece........	11,100,000	5,000,000
Portugal........	11,100,000	6,000,000
Sweden and Norway	8,300,000	4,100,000
Turkey in Europe...	26,000,000	22,000,000
Denmark........	4,750,000	4,250,000
Bosnia, Cyprus, etc..	4,200,000	4,000,000
South Africa.......	6,500,000	3,500,000
Japan........	15,200,000	14,000,000
Mexico........	12,200,000	12,000,000
Islands and Tropics.	35,000,000	......
Russia (all)........	210,000,000	310,000,000
India........	220,000,000	266,900,000
Austria-Hungary....	181,500,000	188,200,000
Roumania........	26,000,000	46,000,000
Bulgaria........	22,000,000	30,000,000
Servia........	4,800,000	7,000,000
Australasia........	32,000,000	39,800,000
Argentina........	25,000,000	55,000,000
Chili........	13,200,000	18,000,000
Uruguay........	3,800,000	5,000,000
Algeria........	19,000,000	19,500,000
Egypt and Tunis....	17,000,000	19,000,000
Southwestern Asia..	76,000,000	80,000,000
Canada........	39,300,000	45,000,000
United States......	378,000,000	371,300,000
Total......	2,414,450,000	2,217,550,000

	Estimated Deficit, Bushels.	Estimated Surplus, Bushels.
United Kingdom ...	187,700,000	....
France..	75,500,000	....
Italy..............	27,300,000	....
Belgium..........	24,000,000	....
Germany..........	23,200,000	....
Netherlands......	12,800,000	....
Switzerland........	12,400,000	......
Spain........	7,600,000	......
Greece........	6,100,000	......
Portugal........	5,100,000	......
Sweden and Norway.	4,200,000	......
Turkey in Europe...	4,000,000	......
Denmark........	500,000	......
Bosnia, Cyprus, etc..	200,000	......
South Africa........	3,000,000	......
Japan........	1,200,000	......
Mexico........	200,000	......
Islands and Tropics..	35,000,000	......
Russia (all)........	......	100,000,000
India........	......	46,900,000
Austria-Hungary....	......	6,700,000
Roumania........	......	20,000,000
Bulgaria........	......	8,000,000
Servia........	......	2,200,000
Australasia........	......	7,800,000
Argentina........	......	30,000,000
Chili........	......	4,800,000
Uruguay........	......	1,200,000
Algeria........	......	500,000
Egypt and Tunis....	......	2,000,000
Southwestern Asia...	......	4,000,000
Canada........	......	5,700,000
United States......	6,700,000	......
United States, from surplus reserves, crops of 1891 and 1892........	......	100,000,000
Total.	436,700,000	339,000,000

"If we are to accept the indications of the Department of Agriculture, the harvest of the United States will give a product below home needs, while the world's product in 1893 appears to be below the world's requirements by some 196,000,000 bushels. This is partially offset by an extraordinary reserve of something near 100,000,000 bushels in the United States."

The Agricultural Department of the Ontario Government was active during last year in its endeavors to forward the interests of the farming community. Circumstances arose in connection with the Guelph Agricultural College and Farm which led to the retirement of Mr. Shaw, the Professor of Agriculture, who took a responsible position in the United States. It was thereupon determined, in some measure, to reorganize the teaching staff, and the following officers were appointed : Farm Superintendent, William Rennie, an experienced farmer of many years' standing; Lecturer on Agriculture and Live Stock, G. E. Day, B.S.A., who is a university graduate, and also a graduate of Ontario Agricultural College ; Lecturer on Horticulture, H. L. Hutt, B.S.A., the son of a fruit farmer in the Niagara District, and who possesses a good practical knowledge of his subject ; Assistant Resident Master, J. B. Reynolds, B.A., whose course in the School of Pedagogy was a brilliant one, and who has since had considerable experience in Public School teaching. The history of the college shows a gradual, but highly satisfactory, development. In 1874, when it opened its doors, about a score of students responded to its invitations. The number increased till 1878, when 146 were enrolled. The following table gives the number of students in the succeeding years, with the country from whence they came:

Year	Ontario	Other Provinces	British Isles	U. States	Other Places	Total
1878	122	18	6	0	0	146
1879	141	18	3	0	0	162
1880	142	25	8	1	0	176
1881	164	33	18	1	1	217
1882	144	27	30	1	4	206
1883	134	34	30	2	2	202
1884	120	32	32	2	2	188
1885	103	28	41	0	3	175
1886	94	20	33	0	2	149
1887	78	12	20	0	0	110
1888	91	9	26	0	5	131
1889	94	10	22	1	7	134
1890	108	15	17	1	5	146
1891	103	9	16	1	3	132
1892	132	9	13	1	4	159
1893	214	12	15	1	5	247

During the summer season of 1893 numerous picnics of farmers and their friends were organized, the college being the point of interest. In 1892, no fewer than 18,000 visitors called at the college grounds, and an even larger number followed their example in 1893.

The Farmers' Institutes promote and engineer these excursions, and the railways give extremely reasonable rates, often considerably below single fare. The trip does not usually take over a day, and so makes a comfortable outing. The station is about a mile and a half from the college, and certain enterprising citizens of Guelph have established a carry-all service, charging ten cents a trip. A large number of the visitors avail themselves of this means of transit, while others, again, prefer to walk, and march on to their destination in a loose and somewhat straggling column. Once at the college, and all expense and care is ended. President Mills, his family, and the whole of the staff meet the picnickers, throw open everything, and place themselves at their disposal. A substantial lunch, sandwiches, biscuits, cheese, and similar staples, is provided in the spacious gymnasium, fitted up for the nonce with seats. Mrs. Mills and the Misses Mills aid in the distribution, and a piano is generally in the room to add to the jollity of the occasion.

The refreshments disposed of, the tour of the place begins. President Mills delivers an address, setting forth the nature of the

JAMES W. ROBERTSON,
Agriculturist, Experimental Farm, Ottawa.

college, and the line upon which it seeks to benefit the farmers. Then each professor takes the visitors in hand and conducts them over his special department. The dairy proves a great point of interest, and Prof. Dean gives practical illustrations of butter and cheese-making, and of the simple and efficacious methods of milk-testing pursued. Prof. Zavitz shows the visitors the plots of ground planted with the various species of grains, exhibiting the advantages and disadvantages of each. Prof. Panton shows his department of geology and practical botany, and, in connection with his demonstrations, the conservatory, with its splendid variety of flowers, proves a great attraction. The fine live stock exhibit awakens great interest, and the attendants are kept busy explaining the various contrivances used in the keeping, stabling, and treatment of the cattle. In addition to this, the students often give exhibition games upon the lawn, and every effort is made by all connected with the institution to entertain, instruct, and please the men who have greatest cause to be interested in anything calculated to advance the interests of agriculture.

The plan of sending the excursions there has proved a great success. It is an undoubted benefit that the farmers should be brought into contact with the scientific pursuit and exposition of agriculture, while the trip to the beautiful city of Guelph, and the college grounds, proves a most agreeable incident in the too often monotonous life of the farmers, Canada's backbone and dependence.

Realizing the prime importance of the agricultural industry in this province, and the necessity of doing something more than has hitherto been attempted to induce the youth of the country to take a real and practical interest in that science, Hon. John Dryden, Minister of Agriculture, with the co-operation of the Minister of Education, arranged for a short summer course at the Ontario Agricultural College, for the benefit of Public school teachers. The object which he had in view was to so equip the teachers as to enable them to impart instruction in agriculture to the children in attendance at the Public schools, and in this way to stimulate a desire for knowledge upon agricultural subjects, and to cultivate among the young a love for rural life. President Mills and the college staff gave their most energetic attention to the furtherance of the scheme, with the result that the course proved highly popular and successful. The teachers who attended numbered thirty-five, of whom seventeen were women and eighteen men.

The subject of agricultural needs more than once occupied the attention of the Ontario Legislature during the 1893 session. In explaining the estimate for agriculture in the Assembly a few days before the close of the session, Hon. John Dryden made a speech of some importance. His remarks were as follow :

" In connection with agricultural societies, associations, farmers' institutes, etc., I have asked for an increased vote of $2,750, one of the principal items being that of $500 additional to the Ontario Creameries' Association, making the grant $2,000, the same as is given to the Dairymen's Associations east and west. The necessity for this increase is caused by the greater number of creameries which are now being established, necessitating a considerable increase for supervision, instruction, etc. The association had only been organized eight years, and, unlike the Dairymen's Association, it covers the entire province, causing the expenditure of a considerable amount in connection with travelling expenses, as compared with either of the other kindred associations. I would point out that we should now have occupied a better position in the manufacture of butter if this association had been organized earlier. We have increased the quantity and also the quality of the cheese product of this country, while as to butter our exports have decreased largely, and the quality is of that character which will not command the foreign market. This is attributable to the fact that, until recent years, there has been no co-operative effort to control the output by an association of this character. The Dairymen's Associations were organized many years ago, and to that fact is due the exceedingly good position we now occupy as regards our cheese. The quality of this article has improved year by year until now we command the best markets of the world. I am looking forward to the time when, through the instrumentality of the Creameries' Association, the same result may be accomplished in the manufacture of butter. It is perfectly clear that equally good butter can be manufactured in a private dairy ; yet, if we ever expect to take a high position in the foreign market, it must be through co-operative dairying, as undertaken by the creameries that are being organized. Up to the year 1891, we had thirty-five creameries scattered in different portions of the province. During the following year that number was increased by twenty-one, so that, at the end of 1892, there were fifty-six in operation. It is expected that this number will largely increase during the present year, which will certainly increase the expenses of instruction and supervision very largely. To indicate how this expenditure has increased in past years, I may say that in 1890 the travelling expenses incurred amounted to $596.65 ; in 1892, it had reached the sum of $900 ; while in 1893 it is expected that it will reach $1,260.

" I hope that in the near future it may be possible to amalgamate this association with the Dairymen's Associations, for the reason that many of those interested in the manufacture of cheese are likewise interested in the manufacture of butter. In many instances, the cheese factory is now utilized for butter-making during a portion of the year.

"I have reason to know that the association is managed with the utmost economy, and that the money granted by the Legislature is made to go as far as possible. I, therefore, without hesitation, ask the Legislature for this increased vote.

"We are also asking an increase towards the work of the Farmers' Institute. This is occasioned, first, by the increasing number of institutes, and, secondly, by the additional number of meetings that are being held in each of the electoral divisions. I presume it will not be denied that no organization among the farmers has accomplished, in recent years, more good, and has aroused more enthusiasm, or has been the means of disseminating more information, than the Farmers' Institute. I have been exercising my influence, as head of the Department, in suggesting the advisability of holding in every county a series of meetings to cover the entire district. I have pointed out to the officers of these institutes that it is intended not only to hold one or two meetings as the law actually requires, and to secure merely the number of members necessary to draw the provincial grant; what is needed is that farmers, generally, should be interested in this work, that they should be induced to become members of the institute for the reason that in that way, and in that way alone, can they become directly connected with the Agricultural Department, and thus receive the abundant information that is now being scattered by means of the various reports of those societies receiving assistance from the Provincial Treasury. I am glad to be able to say that these institutes, during the past season, have been more largely attended, of increasing interest, and much more enthusiastic, than any series of meetings that have been held in past years. But it will easily be seen that, when a greater number of meetings are held, it means an increased number of speakers required to be sent to the different portions of the country. For these reasons, therefore, we are asking for a slight increase in this grant.

"A further increase is also asked towards the work of the Experimental Union. This union was originally organized in a very small way by a number of ex-students of our Ontario Agricultural College. The idea is to interest these young farmers in carrying forward experiments similar to those carried on at the college at Guelph. But the work is not confined to ex-students; farmers everywhere are invited to co-operate. The plan adopted is to send out from the college samples of grain, seeds, etc., to be experimented with according to the instructions that accompany the samples. The experiments thus conducted are reported upon to the secretary of the union. The report is compiled from the returns received. It will

Mr. J. Fletcher.
Entomologist and Botanist, Ottawa Experimental Farm.

thus be seen that it forms a multiplication of the work done at the college, and the results are considered very valuable. It is in the line of our university extension, which is now spoken of in this country and elsewhere in the work of our universities, and may be called experimental extension. To show the gradual growth of this work, I may point out that in 1890 there were 325 experimental plots among the various members of this union. In 1891 the number had increased to 2,500, and in 1892 to 6,000. It will be seen, therefore, that the extension is increasing more than fifty per cent. each year. I believe that during the past year experimental reports were received from every county of the province but one. The number of experimentalists during that year was 754. The money voted by the Legislature is used almost entirely for printing and for distributing the samples sent out. I have no hesitation in saying that this is one of the most important works undertaken by any of our associations, and I know that the House will cheerfully grant the increase.

"We are asking an additional sum for the printing and distribution of reports, bulletins, etc. The sum voted last year was somewhat overdrawn, and was found to be insufficient. It will be remembered that these bulletins

ONTARIO AGRICULTURAL ESTIMATES. 57

are sent to the individual members of farmers' institutes. We also send them in packages to the various associations of Patrons, as well as distribute them according to application, etc. I have reason to know that the farmers all over the country greatly appreciate the extended distribution of these bulletins and reports. I find that there is an increasing demand for the instruction that is thus afforded. During last year we sent out over half a million bulletins from the Department; and altogether our bulletins, reports, and circulars, reached nearly 800,000. My judgment is that it is economy to scatter these as widely as possible after we have gone to the expense of printing them. I can, therefore, ask with confidence an increased vote for this purpose.

"In the Agricultural College estimates, it will be observed that there is also a slight increase of some $1,200, mostly comprised of one or two items. The first is that of $500 for a librarian and assistant in the Natural History Department. I may say that, in the college library, there are some 6,000 volumes which are not properly catalogued or put in a position to be utilized by the students. There is work sufficient for one man for a full year to put it in proper condition. The museum specimens, which are a valuable collection, need relabelling and rearranging. This assistant will also be required to attend to spraying experiments, to collect insects and plants for class work, as well as to investigate weed pests sent to the institution from various portions of the province.

"A small vote of $500 is being asked for to defray the expenses of the new departure given in the estimates as the summer course of lectures for Public school teachers. It will be necessary to retain during a portion of their vacation some of the professors, to attend to this special work. It is proposed, therefore, to give them a small remuneration for these special lectures. What is proposed will, I hope, be but the beginning of this good work. The object is not to undertake to equip our Public school teachers to teach technical agriculture, or to utilize a text-book on this subject. I am not one of those who believe it is desirable to load up our Public school system by placing additional subjects on the curriculum, but I do think it is possible to induce teachers, say, for an hour each week, to give such talks on agriculture as will prove not only profitable and interesting to the children, but be the means of drawing their attention to the possibilities of rural life. I have never advocated the desirability of retaining on the farm all the children born there; some of them will do better for themselves in other callings; but what I object to is that those who are well fitted to excel in this calling should be induced to leave it and undertake work which is not congenial, and at which they can never excel. Whether we like to face it or not, the statement is true that our Public school system tends to instil into the minds of our young people that the only true road to greatness is to be found away from the country in some town or city. There is no subject more prolific in an educational way than that of agriculture. Short talks on the soil, its composition, how plants grow, are intended to direct attention and interest them in reference to those things with which a child is constantly coming into contact in country life. I believe that nothing will be found of more benefit; and where these children remain to follow the calling of their fathers, or go into other pursuits, they will always be the better for having received some elementary instruction along this line.

"We are also asking a small increase towards the expenses of the boarding-house at the college, partly caused by the presence

MR. WILLIAM RENNIE,
Farming Instructor, Guelph Agricultural College.

of these teachers during the month of July, and also by the exceedingly large number of farmers and others who come to inspect the college and farm during the month of June. I may say that fully 20,000 persons visited the farm last year. These visitors are provided with light refreshments while there.

"It is proposed to make a new departure in the horticultural department. Hitherto we have had no lecturer or instructor in this department, and any instruction given has been given by the head gardener. My judgment is that our Guelph institution is much weaker than it should be in this respect. I hold that it should be so conducted that a young man proposing to direct his attention to any of these specialties, whether horticultural, dairying, grain-growing, or stock-raising, might there be able to secure all the help he needs. The head gardener having resigned, we propose that his place be filled by a lecturer in horticulture; and it is hoped that, with a strong man in this position, we may be able to make a considerable advance in the instruction given. The increase in the expenditure for the present year will be only $100.

"I have to ask for an increase of $100 to the salary of Mr. Zavitz, the experimentalist. Those occupying similar positions on the other side receive much larger salaries. I am not aware that any receive less than $1,500. I am glad to say that any of our people who go to Chicago will be able to see a demonstration of the result of the work in Mr. Zavitz's department. It commands the universal attention and praise of visitors from the States of the Union, as well as from foreign countries. The work of this department has increased considerably during the last few years, and is admired very much by visitors to the college.

"This, with a few additional items in the dairy department, comprises all the increases asked for at the Agricultural College."

One of the remarkable occurrences of the farming year was the great sweep of medals by Canadian cheese at the Chicago Exposition. The Dominion made the remarkable record of getting more than 90 per cent. of the entire awards. The exhibition of dairy products at Chicago was probably the greatest of its kind ever held in the world. The judges appointed by the Exposition Committee on Awards were Messrs. John H. Hodgson, of New York, and A. F. Maclaren, of Windsor, Ont. Both are well known as judges of the highest reputation on the continent. They agreed to recommend that all exhibits of cheese which received a score of 90 and over should be awarded a medal and diploma. The total number of single exhibits of cheese was 667. Of these, Canada sent 162. The plan by which the Dominion Dairy Commissioner collected these from the different provinces is already well known. These 162 exhibits were from 110 different factories, and thus were truly representative of the cheese industry of Canada. Most of the entries at Chicago were in classes for factory cheese. When the judging was completed, it was found that some 135 exhibits in the factory classes were entitled to medals and diplomas. That was evidence that skill and care had been exercised in the selection of the cheese, as well as in its manufacture. If the exhibits from Canada had embraced as many as one-third of the total number which scored high enough to win medals, that result would have been most creditable to our dairymen and dairy commissioner in a World's Fair competition. The facts are that of the total number of some 135 exhibits which won medals in the factory classes, no less than 126 were from Canada. Another strong point in honor of Canada was brought out in the fact that thirty-one exhibits of Canadian cheese scored higher than the highest United States cheese.

The medals went to the several provinces in such a way as to show that Canadian cheeses everywhere are now being made of excellent quality. Of the exhibits which won the honor, sixty-nine came from Ontario, fifty-two from Quebec, one from New Brunswick, two from Nova Scotia, and two from Prince Edward Island. Of the cheese of the make of the present season (1893), twenty lots from Quebec won medals, against one from Ontario. This is, unquestionably the greatest triumph for dairying in Canada which has ever been achieved, and the dairymen of Quebec, particularly, are to be congratulated upon the way in which they have come to the very forefront.

The mammoth cheese which Canada sent to the Chicago Fair attracted more attention and comment, perhaps, than any other single exhibit on the ground. It was surrounded by visitors from morning to night. Some rumors had gone abroad that such an enormous cheese could hardly be good. Prof. Robertson invited the official judges in cheese to examine it. The following is a copy of the certificate they gave:

"Jackson Park, Chicago, Ill., June 14.

"We have examined the mammoth Canadian cheese on the dairy pyramid in the Agricultural Building at the World's Columbian Exposition. For a cheese of such huge size, we pronounce the flavor remarkably good, and the body extraordinarily fine. We found the 1,000-pound cheeses to be of fancy quality, and in a first-rate condition.

"We consider the two-year-old cheese, on exhibition there, to be excellent in flavor, in body and texture, and have never seen cheese which tried better at the same age.

"After examining the cheese, on the dairy pyramid, from the provinces of Ontario, Quebec, New Brunswick, Nova Scotia, and Prince Edward Island, it is our judgment

Engraved by THE MAIL.

ON THE GRAND RIVER, NEAR FLORA.

Photo. by J. R. CONNOR, Elora.

that they are a lot of superior quality, and form a display which is most creditable.
"(Signed) JOHN A. HODGSON,
"(Signed) A. F. MACLAREN."
The judges bored into the mammoth cheese to a depth of two feet, and found it uniformly solid. As it had become a centre of attraction, a display card from the Immigration Department was attached to it. Prof. Robertson had fly-leafs printed by the thousand to give away to those who stopped to make enquiries. These cards gave the facts about the size of the "Canadian mite," and then went on to state : "The exports of cheese from Canada exceed in value the total exports of cheese from the United States. The soil, climate, cattle, and transportation facilities in Canada are admirably adapted for the prosecution of successful dairy farming. The Dominion Government has established experimental dairy stations in different parts of Canada. The Provincial Governments manage travelling dairies and dairy schools for the education of those interested in this branch of agriculture. There are over 1,500 co-operative cheese factories and creameries in Canada. In most of the provinces there are excellent opportunities for intelligent farmers with some means to make dairy farming pay well. There are great areas of unoccupied fertile land in the Canadian Northwest; and in the older provinces of Ontario, Quebec, New Brunswick, Nova Scotia, Prince Edward Island, Manitoba, and British Columbia, improved land can be purchased in neighborhoods where all the snug conveniences of life may be enjoyed."

Of the increasingly important apiarian industry in Canada, an excellent advertisement to the world of Ontario's capabilities as a field for its cultivation was made in the exhibit which the Provincial Government installed at the World's Fair. In glass exhibits twenty-five feet long, five feet wide, and with a showing space seven feet high, more than a dozen States of the Union competed with Ontario. A novice could see with but a cursory examination and comparison of the different exhibits that, in comb honey, Ontario easily excelled. The frames were more completely filled out with evenly-capped honey cells; the surfaces were smoother, and the wax of a more uniformly beautiful white than was to be seen elsewhere. Nor in extracted honey was there any lessening of the splendid success attained by the comb honey from Ontario. Whether or not, and how much, the handsome, variformed jars in which the extracted honey was shown heightened the effect upon the eye in avoiding the tiresome sameness into which the other exhibitors fell in this respect may be exactly determined, there was no question about the superior clearness and brilliantly distinctive coloring of the different varieties. Of these there were shown Linden, Clover, Thistle, Sumach, Golden Red, Boneset, and Buckwheat.

Quite a curiosity in its way was a solid block of 50 lbs. of candied thistle honey shown on a silvered glass platter, and one of the same weight, but covered with a bell-jar, of clover honey. The extracted linden honey was of a lovely light amber hue. Amongst the beeswax was a chunk weighing 50 lbs. Some of the candied honey was as white as the driven snow. Mr. Allen Pringle, of Selby, Lennox County, was the superintendent of the Ontario Apiarian Department.

The export trade during the season of 1893 was, on the whole, unsatisfactory. Shippers were placed on an equal footing with American exporters, and, with all special privileges withdrawn, Canada was subjected to new conditions of competition. That this change should have caused discouragement and loss is not surprising. Early in November the news came that another case of disease had been discovered in a shipment of Canadian cattle landed in England. The lungs of the diseased animal were at once forwarded to the Board of Agriculture, and declared by the board's experts to be infected with contagious pleuropneumonia. The chances of our regaining free entry into Britain for our live stock are, no doubt, lessened by this last case; and if they are ever to be improved, and if our cattle trade is to be put again into the privileged position it occupied up to a year ago, there will have to be more than bald denials furnished to the British Government.

It looks now as though the speediest way to arrive at a happy termination of the disagreement between British and Canadian cattle experts, and between the two Governments, will be for the Dominion Administration to act upon the suggestion endorsed by the Imperial authorities, and make a thorough investigation into the existence of disease among Canadian cattle, paying particular attention to the Northwest country. It appears as though it will be only by furnishing some such evidence as that of the freedom of our herds from disease, as well as evidence with regard to the security afforded by our quarantine precautions, that we can expect a change to be made in the policy of the Imperial authorities.

As a review of the dairying trade of the year 1893, we cannot do better than quote some passages from the address of Mr. Derbyshire, President of the Ontario Creameries' Association, at its ninth annual meeting at Belleville. This address dealt with practical matters, and was eminently suggestive and useful in its tendency. Mr. Derbyshire said :

"That we have made rapid advancement since the formation of this association, no one will deny. The changes that have taken place in the conditions and surroundings of our dairymen during these nine years in Ontario are perhaps greater than have attended any other industry, and I am sure we can do even better work in the future. We have sixty-two regular creameries in this province and twelve winter creameries, a gain of over 50 per cent. We find that where dairying and stock-raising are carried on intelligently the farmers are progressive and well-to-do, which should stimulate us to greater activity in seeing that the proper instructions are placed within the reach of all our friends, so that the best possible work can be done in every section of this Empire Province.

"The past year has been very important to the dairymen of this country, and we should learn many important lessons. We met our neighbors in friendly competition at the World's Columbian Exposition; and, while the results were not so gratifying to us as to our brethren in the cheese industry, still they are full of encouragement and use. Our butter was judged by three eminent experts, two from the United States and one from Canada. The body of our Canadian butter was, on the whole, rated very high, but most of our exhibits lost several points on flavor, which we can remedy by careful attention; and I know our creamery men will cheerfully do anything possible to be leaders in the art of making fancy creamery butter. The circumstances were not favorable to Canadians, by reason of the distant points from which most of our butter had to be sent, taking about ten days in transit, besides the restrictions of the United States customs regulations. It was impossible to have our butter stored in a refrigerator at Chicago, and then brought to the judges, as required, while our American friends were not slow to take advantage of having their butter in the refrigerator until the judges were ready; so I think we did exceptionally well to win twenty-seven awards, and have such a large number of our exhibits come within a point of the minimum fixed for this class. Quite a number of our exhibits failed to score on account of using poor, off-flavored salt. I am sure we will all learn something from this wonderful Exposition, and so improve our creamery buildings, and have them properly equipped with cream-separators and modern machinery, with an educated butter-maker, who has attended our dairy school at Guelph, thoroughly understanding every detail, so that in future perfection will shine forth from every package of butter made.

"In examining some of the fancy creamery butter at Chicago, and talking with the makers, I found that they were only using the latest and most modern apparatus, and were anxious to find out all they could about our methods. In short, these young men were fully alive to the importance of their calling. I found another fancy package, from a central creamery, with several skimming stations, which was nearly perfection, and I think well of this system, especially for winter creameries. After the regular cheese season is over, one central factory can be fitted out properly for making butter, and the neighboring factories can have a separator only, and have the cream taken to this central factory. This will avoid long hauls, and each patron can take his skim-milk home, and enjoy the prestige of having his butter made in a large, influential creamery, where nothing but the finest goods are turned out.

"The past year should also teach us another lesson : to make provision for the dry, hot weather, which is sure to come. In 1893 only a limited number of our farmers were prepared, and our cows decreased in milk nearly 50 per cent. in July and August. If you will allow them to go down, then you can rest assured they will not gain much that season. What a loss to our province! If all our dairymen had been ready, with clean, airy stables, with screens to keep the flies out, and plenty of silage or other green crop, and kept the cows in the stables in the day time, turning them out at night, when the flies would not bother them, making sure they got all they could eat of the best food, plenty of pure water, salting them every morning, treating them kindly, we would have had two millions of money more among our dairymen in this province, which would have meant prosperity to every industry. While so much depends on the success of our dairymen, and no business is so sure and profitable every year, I would urge all to commence the new year with a full determination to keep only profitable cows, in the best way, and give your undivided attention to every detail in connection with the business with which we are identified, so we can swell our exports of butter and cheese from thirteen to twenty millions in 1894.

"This can only be done by all building silos, and having plenty of good, nutritious food, to keep up the flow of the milk throughout the season.

"We have prepared a pamphlet programme, giving the names of the most distinguished speakers on dairy topics on this continent, and the subjects for discussion, and we hope to make this the most important dairy meeting ever held in our country. Anyone desiring information will kindly write their questions, and put them in the question-box, naming the gentlemen you desire to answer, and they will receive careful attention, as we are anxious to obtain for all the exact information they require.

"I desire to especially thank Hon. John Dryden, the Minister of Agriculture, for his kindness and attention to our requirements in every particular during the past year; also Prof. Robertson, Dominion Dairy Commissioner, who has rendered us invaluable service. Our instructor, Mr. Sprague, has been active, and rendered valuable assistance to all our creameries. I specially thank the officers and members of this association for their kindness and co-operation, and I am sure we can all look with pride to the work accomplished by us in 1893. With every member of this association working together in our several localities, and influencing our friends not only to become members, but to improve everything in connection with the dairy, we shall become a power in this province for good."

ENTRANCE TO THE WHIRLPOOL, NIAGARA RIVER.

SIR JOHN ABBOTT.

A SKETCH OF THE EX-PREMIER'S CAREER.

THE Prime Minister of Canada, Sir John Caldwell Abbott, who succeeded Sir John Macdonald, died at his residence in Montreal on Oct. 30. John Joseph Caldwell Abbott was born on March 12, 1821, at St. Andrews, in the County of Argenteuil, in the Province of Quebec. He was the eldest son of the late Rev. Joseph Abbott, who was the first incumbent of that place. The Premier's father, a man of active nature and cultivated tastes, gave to literature many works, of which the best known is " Philip Musgrave ; or, The Adventures of a Missionary in Canada," The Rev. Joseph Abbott was born in the north of England, and, consequently, his son, though of Canadian birth, was of English descent. After spending the first seventeen years of his life under the parental roof, young Abbott entered a mercantile house in Montreal. Unable, through illness caused by the close confinement, to continue office work, he obtained a position in a general establishment at Gananoque, where he remained until, in 1843, he returned to Montreal to study in McGill College. He graduated in due time as a B.C.L., and then turned his attention to the study of law. In 1847, Mr. Abbott was called to the Bar of Quebec. After fifteen years' practice, he was appointed Queen's Counsel, and in 1867 was made a D.C.L.

Mr. Abbott's political life commenced in 1857, when he was elected to represent his native county, Argenteuil, in the Canadian Assembly. In 1862 he was appointed Solicitor-General in the Sandfield Macdonald-Sicotte Cabinet, an office which he held for a short time. Subsequently, while in Opposition, he introduced two bills which added to his fame as a lawyer. One was the Jury Consolidation Act of Lower Canada, and the other an Act providing for the collection of judicial and registration fees by stamps. The main principles of these measures were retained in subsequent legislation. Upon the consummation of Confederation in 1867, Mr. Abbott was elected by Argenteuil to the House of Commons. At the general elections in 1872 he was once more returned for the County of Argenteuil ; and in the following year, as the legal adviser of the late Sir Hugh Allan, he became a prominent figure in connection with the Pacific scandal. Upon being returned again in 1874, his election was disputed and voided. Until 1880 the constituency was held by Liberals, but in that year it was redeemed by Mr. Abbott, who in 1886 retired from the House of Commons to accept, in 1887, the leadership of the Government in the Senate. In June, 1891, on the death of Sir John Macdonald, Mr. Abbott was called upon to form a government, and accepted the task, much against his will. He filled for a time the breach which the old chieftain left, but advancing years called for his retirement, and on November 25, 1892, he made way for Sir John Thompson.

Mr. Abbott's political ideas were not always in unison with the leader of whom he afterwards became a great admirer and devoted follower. Five years after he entered Parliament Mr. John A. Macdonald introduced his Militia bill, which, owing in part to the increased expenditure it involved, brought about his defeat. Among those who opposed the bill was Mr. Abbott. When the future Sir John resigned, Mr. John Sandfield Macdonald, the then leader of the Opposition, formed the Macdonald-Sicotte Administration, and took Mr. Abbott, with Mr. Dorion, who subsequently became Liberal leader, into his Cabinet as Solicitor-General, East. Against this Government, Mr. John A. Macdonald worked with especial energy. But he would not have brought about its destruction had it not been for a division in the Liberal camp, which made Mr. Brown, for the moment, his ally. When the Government did go under, Mr. Sandfield Macdonald essayed a reorganization leaving out of his Cabinet this time Mr. Abbott, and Mr., subsequently Sir, Adam Wilson, and installing in their places Mr. Lucius Seth Huntington, who afterwards exposed the Pacific scandal, and Mr. Mowat. From that date Mr. Abbott drifted towards Sir John Macdonald, with whom he was shortly in close alliance. After the restoration in 1878, Mr. Abbott returned to Parliament to support the National Policy, and in the Commons he remained until 1887, when, on Sir Alexander Campbell's retirement to the Government House at Toronto, he became the representative of the Administration in the Senate.

During his brief term as Premier, which extended over seventeen months, Sir John Abbott showed himself to be equal in every respect, save physically, to the duties of the office. When he assumed the reins, with Sir John Thompson as his right-hand man, it was predicted that he would be the nominal rather than the real head of the Government. But while Sir John Abbott was Premier, he took his full share of responsibilities. His constant and unfailing attention to duty was frequently remarked, and the firmness with which he held to what he believed to be in the interest of the country showed that he had a high conception of his duty. The difficulties which he overcame in the formation of his Cabinet were of no ordinary kind, and the resistance he offered to demands for unnecessary subsidies must have been a severe drain upon his strength. On taking the Premiership, two objections were raised against him. One was that he was a director of the C.P.R., and the other that, in 1849, he had signed an annexation manifesto. In reply to the former, Sir John resigned from the directorate of the company, and sold out all his stock. His answer to the second was as follows: "The annexation manifesto was the outgrowth of an outburst of petulance in a small portion of the population of the Province of Quebec, which is amongst the most loyal of the provinces of Canada. Most of the people who signed the annexation manifesto were more loyal than the English people themselves. There were a few gentlemen of American origin who seized a moment of passion into which these people fell to get some hundreds of people in Montreal to sign this paper. I venture to say that, with the exception of those American gentlemen, there was not a man who signed that manifesto who had any more serious idea of seeking annexation with the United States than a petulant child who strikes his nurse has of deliberately murdering her. They were exasperated by the fact that when 10,000 men, who had suffered distress and disaster in the unfortunate rising before those days, petitioned the Governor, of the time being, to retain for the consideration of Her Majesty a bill which they believed to be passed for paying the men whom they blamed for the trouble, the Governor-General, with an ostentatious disregard, as they believed,

SIR JOHN ABBOTT.

for their feelings, and in contempt of their services and of their loyalty, came down out of the usual time in order to sanction the bill. The people were excited, and under the influence of that excitement a number of them signed this paper. I am often reproached with that. It does not trouble me much. When I raised three hundred volunteers at the time of the Trent affair in a few days, in the loyal and gallant old County of Argenteuil, I received from the representative of my Sovereign a commission of colonel, and I thought that condoned the offence of my youth, and I have twice led that battalion to the frontier to assist in repelling invasions of brigands from within our neighbor's territory."

It was during a serious crisis to the Conservative party, as well as to the country, that Sir John Abbott took and held office. His generally recognized rectitude gave stability to a Government that appeared to be about to be wrecked on a shoal of scandals. The scandal session of 1891 had had a marked effect upon the country. Sir John Abbott managed to turn the adverse tide. To show the reality of his desire for purer administration of the public affairs, he introduced a bill to prohibit Government contractors from contributing to election funds, under severe penalties. The same measure, which became the law of the land, inflicted heavy fines upon civil servants who had any transactions with public contractors, other than those of a purely business and legitimate character.

An outline of his political career does not touch upon many important phases of the life of the late Sir John Abbott. His active interest in the project of a great national highway contributed, in a large measure, to the successful completion of the Canadian Pacific Railway, of which he became a director and solicitor. He was generally credited with having put into legal form the agreement which the C.P.R. Company made with the Government. For a considerable time he was the company's solicitor, and a member of the directorate. As a lawyer, Sir John Abbott won a high place in Quebec. He was especially proficient in corporation law. Sir John was a constant and voluminous reader. When he had time to spare, he devoted it to the study of botany, of which he acquired an extensive knowledge. Sir John Abbott, in short, was a student, and a worker, all his life. He was at all times courteous, and never courted distinction or display. He was a Canadian whom all Canadians, irrespective of party, may admire and emulate.

THE DAM AND WHIRLPOOL ON GRAND RIVER, AT BRANTFORD—HIGHWATER, CHRISTMAS, 1893.

ONTARIO MINERALS.

THE report of the Ontario Bureau of Mines for 1892, which was published in the spring, contains an interesting summary of information as to the present position of the mining interest.

Until recently, gold was supposed to be found in workable quantities only in Hastings, and about the Lake of the Woods. But within the last two years promising leads have been discovered in the valleys of the Thessalon and Vermilion Rivers in Algoma, and near Lake Wahnapitae in Nipissing. An important find of gold has also been made at the Ledyard mine at Belmont, near Peterborough, where a rich vein of ore has been experimentally worked, with very good results. At this mine, there is a large deposit of magnetic iron, its location being Lot 19 in the 1st Concession of Belmont. The iron ore is of first-class Bessemer quality, suited to make the finest steel, being rich in iron and very free from impurities. The Belmont Bessemer Ore Company, of New York, have leased this mine on royalty from T. D. Ledyard, of Toronto, and have built a railway to connect with the Central Ontario Railway, ten miles distant. On the east half of this same Lot 19, several gold veins were discovered last year, and are now being worked under the name of the Ledyard Gold Mines. A shaft has been sunk to the depth of 45 feet on an east and west vein, which is from four to six feet wide, and very clearly defined between walls of talcose schist. This vein is found outcropping in several places, and has been traced for 600 feet west of the shaft. A good deal of honeycomb quartz occurs here, carrying free gold and iron pyrites. These sulphurets are very rich, having assayed at different depths from $117 to $922 in gold to the ton. About two hundred yards west of the shaft is a knoll intersected with quartz veins, also containing visible gold and rich sulphurets, samples of which have assayed $12 in gold to the ton.

Besides these, there are several other gold-bearing veins, which have as yet been only slightly developed. These mines are well situated and easily accessible, being within ten miles both of the Canada Pacific Railway and the Central Ontario Railway, and are situated in a well-settled country, where labor and supplies are cheap, and where even low-grade ores would pay handsomely.

Prospecting has been active in the Algoma and Nipissing regions, and not a few locations have been taken up. Important discoveries of silver, copper, and antimony ores have also been reported in the Township of Barrie, in Frontenac, and of steatite (soapstone) in Grimthorpe, and in both townships prospectors were busy last year. So says Mr. Blue's mining report for 1892.

According to the same authority, the mineral production of Ontario in 1892 was valued at $5,374,139, and the sum of $2,591,344 was paid in wages. In order to form a notion of the importance of industries, many of which are in their infancy, note that this sum would give $500 a year each to nearly 5,200 workmen, or $400 to more than 6,000. The greatest amount of wages was paid in quarrying building stone, $730,000; the next largest being the petroleum industry, $650,000, with drain tile and common brick manufacture, a good third, at $445,000. The wage-bill for copper and nickel mining was $339,821. The increase over last year in value of production is $668,466, to which nickel and copper contributed the greatest amount.

An interesting part of Mr. Blue's report has reference to iron-making. With respect to Ontario the report, in one sense, is not unlike the famous essay on snakes in Ireland; but if there is at present no iron made within the limits of the province, the report furnishes a good deal of cause of wonder why this should be so. Iron-smelting is carried on with considerable success in Quebec and Nova Scotia, where the industry has no more encouragement than in this province. The report states that the sketch of the iron ores of the province is fragmentary and incomplete, as there are thousands of square miles in the mineral-bearing regions of the province that have never been examined either by the officers of the geological survey or prospectors. Mr. Blue has, nevertheless, collected a surprising amount of information about the matter, and, as such information is usually concretionary, the tendency will be towards growth from year to year, permitting of the classification of facts that will, in all likelihood, eventually lead to important results.

The furnaces in the Province of Quebec are those situated at Radnor, fifteen miles from Three Rivers, and at Drummondville. The Radnor forges began operations in 1860, but have not been steadily in operation. Indeed, it is only since the property has been in the hands of Drummond, McCall & Co., of Montreal, that matters have settled down to a business-like basis. In 1891 this firm erected a new furnace, capable of turning out some fifty tons a day, but at the time of which the report treats twenty-five tons a day was the output. The ore used is bog ore or brown hematite. The company owns large quantities of land containing the deposits, but it also purchases from neighboring farmers who have deposits on their own lands. Charcoal is the fuel used, and for the supply the company owns large tracts of forest lands. The product of this furnace is largely used by Ontario manufacturers, and is declared to be equal to Salisbury iron.

The Drummondville furnaces, two in number, also treat bog ore, and use coke as fuel. They are operated by John McDougall & Co., of Montreal, the whole output, which is said to be of high quality, being used in their car-wheel works at Montreal. About 200 men are employed in smelting, procuring ore, chopping in the bush, and converting logs into charcoal.

The bounty granted by the Dominion Government for the production of pig iron is $2 per ton. A bounty was first given in 1883 of $1.50 a ton. This was paid until the end of the fiscal year 1888-89, when for the next three years it was reduced to $1 a ton. Beginning with July 1, 1892, the bounty was doubled, and during the first eight months of that fiscal year the sum of $57,952 was paid in bounties. Up to February 3, 1893, the sum of $388,578 had been paid in the ten years in which the bounty system has prevailed; $309,886 of this has been received by the Londonderry Iron Co., or an average of $30,575 per year. Besides the Londonderry Company, which is the largest concern in the Dominion, there are two other furnaces in Nova Scotia. Besides the bounty, the iron smelters enjoy a protection of $6.72 on the long ton. Speaking of the case of Ontario, the report says that with a protection against competition of $8.72 the business in this province should require no further protection.

The chapter on the iron ores of Ontario is that which best displays the industry and research of the officers of the new department. Every considerable deposit of iron in the province is mentioned, together with speculations as to the probable quantities and the estimated quality. The chapters on copper and nickel are equally interesting. It is altogether a valuable contribution to the subject of the mineral wealth of Ontario, and gives promise of amply justifying the creation of this new branch of the public service.

THE NEW STEAM YACHT, THE CLEOPATRA, ON TORONTO BAY.

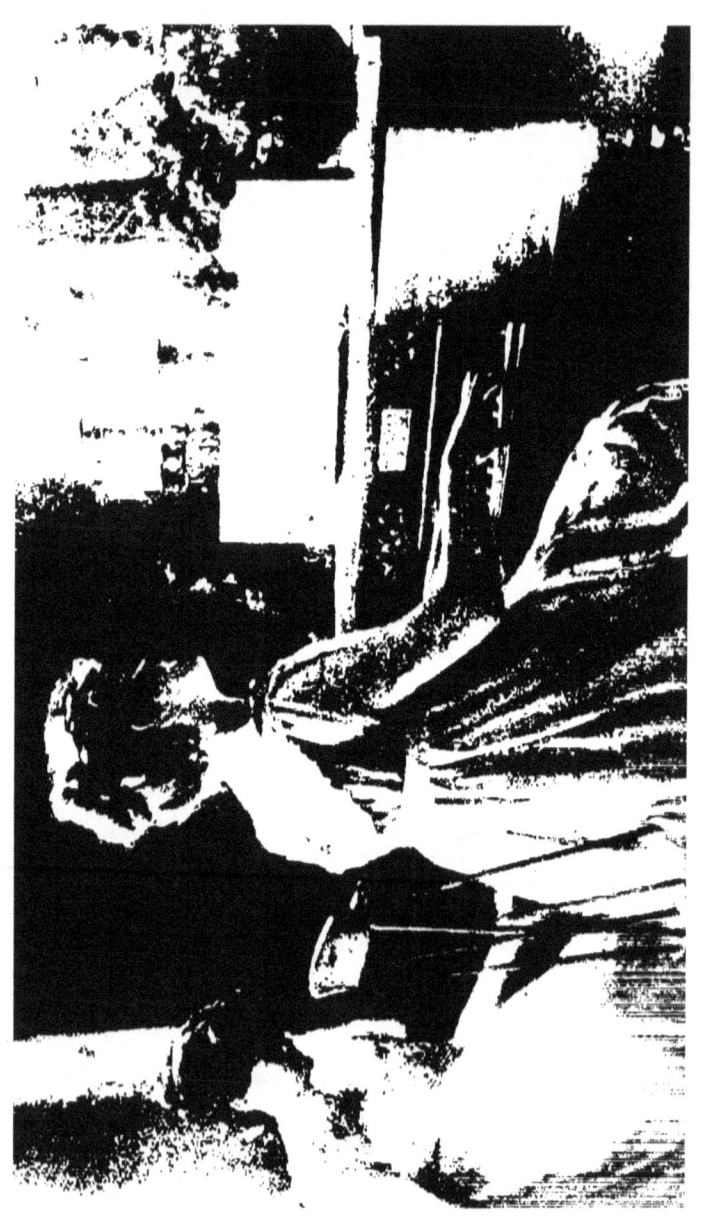

THE SPORTS OF 1893.

A GENERAL REVIEW OF THE WORLD OF RACING, ATHLETICISM, AND RECREATION.

THE TURF.

HE English turf last year was marked by the success of Isonomy's son, Isinglass, in securing the Two Thousand Guineas, Derby, and St. Leger, and adding one more to the small list of "triple-crowned heroes." Though Mr. McCalmont's great horse met one reverse at the back end of the season, it detracted little from his reputation, as Isinglass was admittedly not at his best. Several of the big races fell to horses that had been little fancied, even by their owners; for example, the Duke of Portland's Mrs. Butterwick in the Oaks. In the Cesarewitch, the cast-off Red Eyes ran a dead heat with the outsider Cypria; and Lord Dunraven's Molly Morgan landed the Cambridgeshire Stakes. The two-year-old racing developed some promising material for the classic races of 1894. Lord Rosebery's Ladas, that ran most of the season as the Hampton Illuminata colt, retired with an unbeaten certificate, and now stands a prime favorite for the Two Thousand and the Derby. Matchbox, Son o' Mine, Delphos, and Bullingdon, also showed very high class; while Jocasta and Glare seemed to be the best fillies of the year. In cross-country racing, the past season was made notable by the victory of Cloister in the Grand National Steeplechase. The old horse carried 175 pounds, the highest weight ever successful in this race, and ran the four miles and a half in the fastest time on record for the course. The American turf season saw the abolition of winter racing in the north, and a fairly successful summer on the big tracks, Monmouth Park being a partial failure. The richest event of the year was the American Derby at Washington Park, Chicago, when, after a delay of an hour and twenty minutes at the post, Boundless galloped home in front and earned a cheque for $50,000. The racing at Washington Park throughout was of a high class. In the fall, the Washington meeting was a success for a couple of weeks; but an attempt to open another track there for winter racing was suppressed by law.

The Canadian racing season opened, as usual, with the Ontario Jockey Club's meeting at Woodbine Park, where the club distributed $20,000 in five days. First and second places in the Queen's Plate fell to Mr. J. E. Seagram, of Waterloo, an honor that had never before been secured by one owner. The opening of the Hamilton Jockey Club's new track, a mile and a furlong in circumference, and with appointments unsurpassed anywhere, was an evidence of the prosperity of the Canadian turf. Several new Canadian records were established at this meeting. A feature of the year among Canadian horsemen was their success on foreign tracks. At Chicago, Mr. Hendrie's Versatile set up a new world's record for a mile and three furlongs; while at Saratoga and Morris Park Mr. Seagram's Martyrdom and Victorious won a good many thousand dollars. Victorious placed to his credit the fastest mile ever run by a Canadian-bred, and proved himself the equal of any of the handicap horses over a good distance of ground.

YACHTING.

The year 1893 will pass into history as one of great interest in the sport of yachting, not only on the part of yachtsmen, but of the public generally. Very early in the year, it was known that there would be a race for the America's Cup, a challenge having been accepted by the New York Yacht Club from Lord Dunraven, on behalf of his new cutter "Valkyrie," then building. There were several points about this challenge, and the acceptance of it, which were particularly satisfactory. It came through the Royal Yacht Squadron, the premier yachting organization in England, the same club which had previously failed to come to satisfactory terms with the New York Yacht Club on the occasion of Lord Dunraven's former challenge with the smaller "Valkyrie" of 1889. At that time, the N.Y.Y.C. claimed the right to enforce and interpret in its own manner the new "deed of gift," a document which, the Royal Yacht Squadron maintained, was *ultra vires* in the first place, and, owing to the alleged unfairness of some of its conditions towards a challenger, quite unfit to be made the permanent basis of future challenges, the latter condition being tenaciously insisted on by the N.Y.Y.C., although they were willing to forego some of the more objectionable clauses for the race in question. The Royal Yacht Squadron absolutely declined to risk the possibility of becoming the holders of the America's Cup under conditions so objectionable to them, and the negotiations ended in a very unsatisfactory manner. It was not supposed, at the time, that the Squadron would ever again attempt to renew them, and it looked as though any future challenges for the Cup would have to come through some other foreign yacht club. Time brought changes; among others, a change of sentiment among many members of the New York Yacht Club. They saw that, so long as the club persisted in attaching conditions to the challenge in favor of the holders of the Cup, just so long there would be no challenge, and the venerable mug would come to represent not the "blue ribbon of the sea," or the triumph of yacht architecture and seamanship, but simply a monument to sea-lawyerism. Unofficial hints to Lord Dunraven conveyed the intelligence that the New York Yacht Club would be willing, in the event of a challenge being received, to make concessions under the "mutual arrangement" clause of the new deed of gift that would ensure a fair race. The matter was taken up, and, although the negotiations were lengthy, the terms finally agreed on were thoroughly fair and sportsmanlike, and such as ensured fair play under modern yachting conditions. A common limit of water-line, for both challenger and defender, was agreed on, and the races were to be five in number, if necessary, on open sea courses, the Cup to go to the winner of three of them, and to be held subject to challenge under similar conditions. This latter point was important, because it got over the difficulty over which the New York Yacht Club and the Royal Yacht Squadron had previously failed to come to terms, and enabled the latter club to assume the responsibility of the challenge;

and there was an element of satisfaction in having the precedent for new conditions arranged between such high contracting parties. While some of the details and the method of arriving at the result were criticized by extremists on both sides, there is no doubt that the horizon has been sensibly cleared, and the principle established that international yacht racing must be conducted in a broad spirit of sportsmanship, rather than in that of hair-splitting over technicalities with a view to securing special advantages to the man in possession. The very development of yachting will probably

YACHT ZELMA—PROPERTY OF NORMAN E. DICK.

call for more amendments in future races; but as matters now stand there is less prospect and opportunity than ever of making trouble.

Before the "Valkyrie's" keel was laid, an American yachtsman, Mr. Royal Philps Carrol, had ordered from the Herreshoffs a single-stick racing yacht of about 85 feet water-line, with the definite intention of taking her to British waters to compete in all possible regattas, and to sail for the Gold Cup of the Royal Victoria Yacht Club, and the Brenton's Reef Cup that "Genesta" had carried off to England in

1885. The reputation of the Herreshoffs, gained with "Gloriana" and "Wasp," made it quite certain that the new craft, afterwards known as "Navahoe," would be superior to anything of her size in British waters; and although there was a desire to build a trial horse or two for "Valkyrie," the necessity of meeting "Navahoe" was largely responsible for the production of "Britannia," designed by Mr. Geo. L. Watson for the Prince of Wales; "Calluna," built for a Scotch syndicate by Messrs. William Fife & Son, and the biggest of the lot; "Satinita," a cutter of over 90 feet water-line, owned by Mr. A. D. Clarke, and designed by Mr. Richardson. These made a fine class of racers, to which were added "Iverna," owned by Mr. John Jameson, and "Meteor," late the famous "Thistle," owned by the Emperor of Germany. The half-dozen, including "Navahoe," put in a big season's work, and attracted all the available interest in the sport. "Britannia" made the most starts and most first prizes of any; "Valkyrie" being a good second, especially when it is considered that she had to leave the racing in the middle of the season to fit out and make the Atlantic passage in order to reach New York in ample time to get ready for her matches for the America's Cup. "Calluna" made a worse showing than was expected, and "Satinita" failed in light to moderate weather, but did excellent work in strong winds and heavy seas. A great deal of interest was shown in the performance of "Navahoe," which must, however, have been very disappointing to her owner, after all his trouble. He kept her at it in spite of decisive defeats, and, true to his original intentions, started her in every possible race. In light weather "Navahoe" did not do so badly, frequently making good races with "Britannia" and "Valkyrie," and showing herself superior to the older "Meteor" and "Iverna." In strong winds, however, she was quite overpowered, showing a lack of stability, heeling away over and refusing to steer. Various alterations were tried, and some improvement was noticed towards the end of the season, when she made a good race with "Britannia" for the Brenton Reef Cup, the two racing along in a splendid washing breeze for 120 miles, and never getting more than a mile away from each other, "Navahoe" finally winning by forty seconds. She failed to secure either the Gold Cup or the Cape May Cup, both of which went to "Britannia"; and, on the whole, British yachtsmen formed a much better opinion of Mr. Carrol than of his ship.

The following summary shows the winnings of the larger craft in British waters for the season:

	Starts.	1st.	2nd.	3rd.	Value.
Britannia	43	24	8	1	£1,542

In addition to No. 1, Champion Cup (Dublin), Meteor Shield, Royal Victoria Cup, and Cape May Cup.

	Starts	1st	2nd	3rd	Value
Valkyrie	24	11	4	0	955
Satinita	36	7	6	1	784
Calluna	36	2	6	2	320
Navahoe	18	3	3	0	225

also Brenton Reef Cup.

	Starts	1st	2nd	3rd	Value
Iverna	25	2	3	0	170

and value of private match with Meteor.

	Starts	1st	2nd	3rd	Value
Meteor	2	1	0	0	105
Lais	40	13	14	0	695
Varuna	39	15	9	0	590
Vendetta	32	11	7	0	495
Creole	22	12	4	0	330
Castanet	17	4	5	0	160
Columbine	20	3	5	0	188
Dragon	34	23	7	0	448
Dierdre	34	10	10	0	222
Molly	29	3	7	0	90

"Valkyrie" reached New York, after a protracted and stormy passage, to find no less than four new yachts built expressly for the purpose of defending the America's Cup, out of which "Vigilant" was finally selected as the champion. Of the others, "Colonia," a keel craft built by the Herreshoffs for Mr. Archibald Rogers, was in many respects an enlarged "Wasp," and, although a capable boat, proved decidedly deficient in draft for good windward work. As might have been expected, General Paine could not forego the opportunity of building a cup-defender, and appeared on the scene with "Jubilee," a fin-keel craft, designed by his son, Mr. John B. Paine, who already had some reputation as a designer in smaller classes. In some of the trial races, "Jubilee" showed herself very fast, but was continually in trouble with spars and gear, which spoiled her chances. She is to be thoroughly refitted and raced next season, and is not without friends, who expect great things of her. The third unsuccessful "cup candidate" was "Pilgrim," designed and built by Messrs. Stewart & Burnly, a fin-keel of the most extreme type, in beam and displacement no more than a huge canoe. She turned out a decided failure, and proved pretty conclusively that a bulb of lead hung at the bottom of a deep fin will not produce fair working stability unless beam and displacement are used in proportion. "Pilgrim's" fin has been removed, and she is being turned into a steamer.

The chosen cup-defender, "Vigilant," was built by the Herreshoffs for a syndicate of members of the New York Yacht Club, headed by Commander Morgan and Mr.

"Here They Come!" Thomas Blinks, Pinxt.

C. O. Iselin, the latter gentleman acting as managing owner in all the races.

In design, "Vigilant" showed the long overhangs and convex water-lines of "Wasp" and "Gloriana," a total draft of 14 feet, and a metal centreboard working through the lead keel. In construction and rig, no expense or elaboration was spared to ensure lightness and strength. Tobin Brough was used for the bottom of the hull, and in racing trim this was polished until it rivalled the brass-work on deck, and to such extravagances must be attributed some of the not very large margin by which "Valkyrie" was defeated.

Five races, in all, were started, two not being finished within the time-limit. In the first, "Valkyrie" showed a slight superiority in light winds; but in two decisive races, with good working breezes, "Vigilant" proved the better boat. The final race was fifteen miles to windward and return, in a young gale, which increased in force before the finish. On the windward work "Valkyrie" squarely outsailed "Vigilant"; but, when leading on the run back, unfortunately split her spinnaker, blew a second one to rags, and, although a spare balloon jib topsail was set as quickly as possible, "Vigilant" passed her and won by forty seconds, corrected time. This settled the ownership of the America's Cup for another year, at least ; and the time has now gone by for the receipt of a challenge for 1894. "Valkyrie" wintered in American waters, and will be paced there doing the coming season. It is expected that "Vigilant," "Jubilee," and the old "Volunteer," changed back to a single-sticker, will be prepared to meet her.

Outside of the Cup races, there was nothing of more than local interest in American yachting circles—no new racers, and no attempt to revive either the 40 or 46-foot classes. The World's Fair undoubtedly absorbed much money and interest that would otherwise have been devoted to yachting.

On Lake Ontario there was, decidedly, an off season—no new yachts, except Mr. Jarvis' 21-footer "Thistledown," a short circuit, and a small fleet under the auspices of the Lake Yacht Racing Association, and but few entries in the various classes. The 40-foot class was the most active of any, there being some good racing between "Zelma," "Aggie," and "Dinah," "Zelma" proving herself by all odds the best of the lot in any weather. In addition to club and association races, she secured the Queen's Cup, the Prince of Wales' Cup, the Lansdowne Cup, and went to Charlotte to get the Fisher Cup, sailing two plucky races with "Onward," either of which would have resulted in "Zelma's" favor had not a ridiculous time-limit of six hours for a 30-knot course prevented either of them being finished in time. Neither yacht was able to keep a crew away from business for another race, and the matter is still undecided.

At the annual meeting of the Lake Yacht Racing Association, an important change was made in the rules for the measurement of sail-area, the Seawanhaha system of triangulation being abandoned in favor of a method of obtaining the actual area, a much-needed reform, in view of the great diversity of rigs in use on the lakes, and the heavy tax on sail-area under classification by corrected length.

There will be some new racing craft on Lake Ontario this coming season. Mr. A. G. Cuthbert has orders in hand for two 25-footers for Toronto, and a 30-footer for Hamilton ; and a 30-footer has been ordered from Designer Watson, of Glasgow, by Mr. George H. Gooderham. A new 40-footer is promised by Mr. Monck, of the Royal Hamilton Yacht Club. All this new blood will animate the existing fleet, and produce some interesting racing.

The general yachting prospects in England and the United States are decidedly poor at present. No new craft of any account are reported, and it is almost useless to expect a brisk season without them. The general business depression quickly affects so expensive a sport as yachting, and, what is worse, the elaborate construction demanded in a modern racer has put up the cost to two or three times what it was ten years ago, while adding nothing to the real value of the yacht when used for any other purpose than racing. This is a very serious matter, and one on which it is difficult to legislate, or even to suggest a remedy. Obviously, few men can afford to build a yacht of any size which, if unsuccessful as a racer, can hardly be turned into a cruiser at all, and in any case will involve a heavy loss. The cost of "Vigilant" and her first season's expenses were over $100,000. Sport at this price is only for millionaires, for the possible winnings in money are inconsiderable in any case. One good proposal has come from Admiral Montagu, a prominent English yachtsman, for some international racing with yachts of 40-rating—about 60 feet water-line. Such craft are plenty large enough, and it is to be hoped the experiment will be tried. Something of the sort must be done, or international racing will subside, and its beneficial effect on yachting generally will be lost.

A.C.A. Races—Paddling Out to the Start.

AQUATICS.

The first race of any importance in England during the year occurred on June 30, when George Bubear beat George Hosmer on the Thames, for £2,000 and the championship of England. March 18, the annual eight-oared race between Oxford and Cambridge Universities was decided on the Thames, the former then winning its eleventh victory. July 5-7 the Henley Royal Regatta was held, Guy Nickalls winning the Diamond Sculls. July 19, G. E. B. Kennedy won the Wingfield Sculls at Henley, and amateur championship, V. Nickalls second. September 25, T. Sullivan beat G. Bubear for the English championship.

The season was a busy one in America, both for professionals and amateurs. The Austin, Texas, regatta was held June 7-10. The open scullers' race, three miles with a turn, was won by J. G. Gaudaur; H. G. Peterson, second; James Stanbury, third; Edward Hanlan, fourth; John Teemer, fifth; R. Rogers, sixth. The time was 19.06, the fastest recorded for the distance. At the same regatta, over the same course, Gaudaur and Hosmer won the double sculls, Hanlan and Teemer second, McLean and Ten Eyck third. The consolation sculls were won by Teemer; Ten Eyck, second.

July 24, Jacob Gaudaur defeated Hanlan at Orillia, Ont., in a three-mile with a turn, for $1,000, and the championship of America. The time was 19.53.

Stanbury returned to Australia, September 17, sailing from Vancouver, B.C., on that date.

The regatta of the Canadian Association of Amateur Oarsmen was held at Hamilton, August 4 and 5. A violent rain and wind storm interfered with the concluding day's sport, but the affair was a success, nevertheless. The winners were: Senior double, Vesper, Philadelphia; junior double, Argonaut, Toronto; senior single, E. A. Thompson, Argonaut; junior single, J. Rumohr, Toronto; senior four, Dons, Toronto; junior four, Tecumseh, Walkerville; senior pairs, Toronto.

From Hamilton the oarsmen went to Detroit, where, during the week following, the annual regattas of the N.A.A.O. and the Northwestern Association were held. The first-named association's regatta was held August 10 and 11. The regatta was only fairly successful, as the elements were unfavorable. The winners were: Senior single, J. J. Ryan, Toronto; junior single, W. E. Paine, Toronto; senior double, Star, Buffalo; junior fours, Wyandotte; senior pairs, Detroit; international fours, N.Y.A.C.

The Northwestern's regatta winners were: Senior fours, Argonaut; junior fours, Minnesota; senior pairs, Detroit; junior pairs, Toronto; senior single, E. Hedley, Passaic; junior single, J. Rumohr, Toronto; senior double, Star, Buffalo; tandem canoe, Argonaut; single canoe, R. G. Muntz, Argonaut.

The Lake Geneva regatta was held August 17, 18, and 19. The senior singles were won by E. Hedley, Passaic; senior fours, Argonaut; half-mile canoe race, R. G. Muntz, Argonaut; tandem paddle, H. G. Muntz and F. H. Thompson, Argonaut; senior single, quarter-mile dash, E. Hedley, Passaic.

FOOTBALL—RUGBY RULES.

During the past year, none of the manly games has been the subject of more adverse criticism in the United States than has football, as played under the Intercollegiate rules; while in Canada, during the season of 1893, there was an almost entire absence of unpleasant incidents, or unfavorable comments. The season was, in every respect, a most successful one, and throughout its course the merits of the game were brought more and more into prominence. In an article which appeared in a recent number of the *North American Review*, by two well-known professors of the University of Pennsylvania, the merits of the game are stated, and the benefits that may be got from playing it described, in a concise and interesting manner. The following passage may be appropriately quoted:

"We know that in every position in life which a man can occupy a fairly-developed frame is of great advantage to him; that, *cæteris paribus*, the man who possesses health is able to do better work than his rival who lacks it; that health includes in its very essence the idea of a certain amount of strength; and that, to acquire health and strength and the full development upon which they depend, exercise is essential. We know that, however admirable systems of collegiate gymnastics may be (and we are firm believers in their value), they often fail in supplying the mental stimulus which in competitive athletics react so beneficially on the grosser tissues. Just as certain areas in the brain and spinal cord atrophy after the removal of a limb, so do all the centres presiding over movement grow and develop when varied exercise is taken, and with them the co-ordinate centres that control the higher cerebral functions. The more varied the exercise, and the more it awakens interest and brings into play the mental faculties, the more beneficial it is to the mind and body reciprocally.

The Queen's University Rugby Football Team, Kingston—Champions, 1893.

"We feel sure that these propositions are demonstrably true. Their application to football seems to us obvious. Let us regard intercollegiate athletics as supplementary to a well-devised system of physical education, such as ought to exist at every university and college. The noteworthy contests (exclusive of track athletics which tend to develop specialists in whom one set of muscles is over-developed, but which are of undoubted value to the student body) are those which take place on the river, the baseball field, the tennis court, and cricket ground. Which of them best fulfils the requirements of an ideal exercise?

"Rowing, as practised to-day, develops chiefly the muscles of the back and hips; it does little for the front arm, practically nothing for the pectoral muscles. Baseball makes but little demand on the left arm, or on the left side of the chest. Cricket and tennis are also usually 'right-sided' games. None of them is to be compared with football in the direction of bringing *all* muscles into play. And, moreover, in none of them, except rowing, is the preliminary training, so valuable in strengthening the great involuntary muscles, those of the heart and diaphragm, observed with anything like equal strictness.

"Certainly, whatever physical good can be received from any form of college athletics can be obtained from football; while, above all, the game tends to develop self-control, coolness, fertility of resource, and promptness of execution in sudden emergencies involving, perhaps, personal danger. In other words, no known game compares with football in the development in the individual of those qualities which, while they are sometimes spoken of as the 'military virtues,' are of enormous value to their possessor in all the struggles of life. A further advantage of football over the other forms of college athletics is that it appeals to a much larger proportion of the men. To those who think that bloody noses, torn ears, blackened eyes, bruises or sprains, or an occasional scalp wound, are mighty evils, the game must always be an objectionable one; but to those of us who believe that in the life of a boy the occurrence of injuries not severe enough to leave permanent traces is not necessarily an evil, but often even a positive good, by encouraging fortitude, manliness, and high spirit, the question as to the danger of football in our colleges is only to be answered by absolute statistics."

The above very excellent defence of the much-maligned game is made in reference only to the American development of it, but it applies equally well to football as played under Canadian rules. And it is satisfactory to know that Canadian football has all the merits, and few of the demerits, of the American game. It seems, in fact, as if in Canada a happy medium had been reached, and that both the English game (which, under the influence of conservative ideas, has remained practically unchanged for many years), and the American game (which has undergone a too extensive process of evolution), were both about to be remodelled, and that Canadian methods and rules were going to be taken as the subjects of imitation.

The idea of the game which prevails in some parts of England may be gauged by the fact that not long ago a certain circuit of the United Methodist Free Church assembled and passed the following resolution: "That this meeting deeply deplores the many terrible deaths resulting from the game of football, and urges upon Her Majesty's Government the great importance of so amending the law as to make it a capital offence for one man to kick his fellow to death on the football field."

Even the Muse has not been silent on the subject, and the following lines, from a song entitled "The Half-back's Farewell," may be read seriously, or with a latent smile of amused skepticism:

"When Autumn leaves are falling,
And Nature doth the soul enthrall,
We may not meet again on earth, love,
I'm going to play football.
Farewell, and perhaps forever;
I'm going to play football."

The season of 1893 began under the most favorable conditions, and at its conclusion was put on record as the most successful in the history of the game in Canada. Under the auspices of the two provincial unions, two series of games were played. In Ontario the increasing popularity of the game was marked by the unusually large attendance at matches, by the interest displayed more particularly in the towns, colleges, and cities outside of Toronto, and by the increased number of clubs competing in the ties. The results in Ontario were as follows:

O. R. F. U. TIES.

SENIOR SERIES.

First Round—
Oct. 7—Toronto ....32 Ottawa............. 1
 " 14—Ottawa.....14 Toronto............12
 "   7—Queen's ....13 Ottawa College......23
 " 14—Queen's ....25 Ottawa College...... 3
 "   7—Osgoode....31 R. M. C............11
 " 14—Osgoode....30 R. M. C............10
 " 14—Trinity defaulted to Hamilton.
       'Varsity a bye.

"Gone!" THOMAS BLINKS, Pinxt

Second Round—

Oct. 21—Toronto ....28 Osgoode............34
" 28—Toronto ....21 Osgoode.............13
" 21—Queen's.....27 'Varsity... 7
" 28—Queen's..... 6 'Varsity.............15

Third Round—

Nov. 4—Queen's.....27 Hamilton........... 13
  Toronto a bye.

Finals—

Nov. 11—Queen's.....28 Toronto............. 3
Nov. 18—Queen's.....27 Toronto............. 1

Canadian Championship—

Nov. 23—Queen's.....29 Montreal............11

INTERMEDIATE SERIES.

First Round—

Oct. 7—Trinity II...12 Toronto II........... 6
" 14—Toronto II...47 Trinity II........... 0
" 7—Lornes.....14 St. Catharines....... 5
" 14—St. Cathar's.20 Lornes.............. 3
" 7—London ....16 Petrolea............. 8
" 17—London ....13 Petrolea............13
  K.C.I. defaulted to Queen's II.
  Peterborough defaulted to Osgoode II.
  'Varsity II. a bye.

Second Round—

Oct. 21—Hamilton II. defaulted to London.
" 21—Osgoode II..23 'Varsity II........... 9
" 21—Toronto II.. 2 Queen's II...........10
  St. Catharines a bye.

Third Round—

Oct. 28—Osgoode II..44 Queen's II........... 4
" 28—London.....39 St. Catharines........ 5

Final—

Nov. 4—Osgoode II..22 London.............. 7

JUNIOR SERIES.

First Round—

Oct. 14—'Varsity III..34 Lornes II............ 4
  K.C.I. II. defaulted to Queen's III.
  London II. and Hamilton III. byes.

Second Round—

Oct. 28—'Varsity III..27 Queen's III.......... 4
" 21—London II .. 0 Hamilton III........20

Final—

Nov. 4—'Varsity III..19 Hamilton III 9

The plan of playing home-and-home games in the first, second, and final rounds of the senior series was an innovation which proved to be an excellent one. The fifteen from Queen's University played admirable football throughout, and the congratulations which were tendered them after they had won the provincial championship were in their nature sincere and well deserved. The game in which most interest was displayed was that between the future champions and Toronto, played on November 11, and resulting in the very unexpected defeat of the lafter. In Kingston, on the following Saturday, the Torontos were again beaten, and Queen's on Thanksgiving Day journeyed to Montreal, to win there, before a great mass of shouting and excited humanity, the title to the championship of Canada. The game was played on the grounds of the M.A.A.A. with the Montreal fifteen, the champions of Quebec, and was an excellent exhibition of scientific football. In the evening a banquet was tendered the visitors by the Montreal Athletic Association. The decisive game in Queen's struggle for the championship was undoubtedly that which was played in Toronto on the Rosedale Athletic Ground. The following poetic reference to it, the latter part of which is Queen's Gaelic war-cry, appeared in *The Toronto Mail* on the following Monday :

His cheeks are etched in Rosedale mud,
  His eyes are one too few ;
His nose is warped, his front teeth gone,
  His skull is fractured, both ears torn,
His arms are bandaged, too.
A crutch supports his crippled weight,
  And his anatomy
Subtracts now from the maximum
Two broken ribs, a jointless thumb,
  And fingers—all but three.
And as he limps his sad way out,
Upon the air is borne the shout
That gathers volume on the fly,
And drowns all else save this one cry :
  "Queen's! Queen's! Queen's!
  "Oil-thigh na Banrighinn gu brath !
  "Cha gheill ! cha gheill ! cha gheill !
  "Oil-thigh na Banrighinn gu brath !
  "Cha gheill ! cha gheill ! cha gheill !"

In the intermediate series there were eleven teams entered, and eleven matches played. The Osgoode eleven, which held the junior championship in the preceding year, won the final at London, from the London fifteen, by a score of twenty-two to seven. In the junior series there were six entries, and the 'Varsity III. finished with the coveted honors.

In Quebec the season of 1893 was also an eminently satisfactory one. The greatest interest was evinced over the games between McGill, the Britannias, and the Montrealers. Next season it is probable that the Union will enlarge its membership by the admission of the two Ottawa clubs.

The annual meeting of the Ontario Union was held on December 10, and was, in every respect, a satisfactory one. The officers elected were as follows :

President—H. R. Grant, Queen's University.

First Vice-President—B. P. Dewar, Hamilton.

Second Vice-President—W. J. Moran, Osgoode Hall.

Secretary-Treasurer—R. K. Barker, Osgoode Hall.

Executive Committee — Messrs. Osler Royal Military College ; E. Chadwick, Trinity University ; George Clayes, Toronto

"CHECK."

THOMAS BLINKS, PINXT.

University; N. B. Dick, Toronto; A. F. R. Martin, Osgoode Hall; A. B. Cunningham, Kingston C.I.

The meeting of the Canadian Union followed, and the reports submitted there were equally satisfactory. The officers chosen were:

President—Mr. A. H. Kerr, Toronto.
Vice-President—Gordon McDougall, McGill.
Secretary Treasurer—Alexis Martin, Hamilton.

ASSOCIATION FOOTBALL.

The game of Association football, or, as it has often been termed, the "dribbling code," is not nearly as popular in Canada as the Rugby game, except in a few districts in Western Ontario. In the old country, however, it is essentially the game for the masses; and in many places in England, notably the Midlands, it has usurped to itself a popularity that never was a feature of the Rugby code. For many years Scotland was pre-eminent; but during the last seven or eight years English clubs have more than held their own, chiefly through the instrumentality of professional players from Scotland, many of whom are in receipt of large salaries. The game has now reached a state of perfection in England and Scotland that is not likely to be equalled in Canada. There the season begins in September, and does not close until April, with scarcely a break; while here about two months in the fall and two more in the spring form the playing season. In spite of this great disadvantage, Canadian teams have reached an excellence that is wonderful; and this has been proved in many a field in England and Scotland, some six or seven years ago, when a Canadian team toured through the old country.

For some years, the game in Canada was seen at its best in the town of Berlin and the neighboring district, but now Toronto can hold its own, chiefly because of the University players, many of whom hail from Western Ontario, the great nursery for exponents of the "dribbling code." Berlin has no longer a team that is able to cope successfully with some of the Toronto clubs, its mantle in this respect having fallen on Galt, Windsor, and Essex.

In Toronto, the premier organization is the Senior League, which includes two teams at least, the 'Varsity and Scots, who would be worthy opponents of the Western champions. Last year, the Toronto championship was won by the Scots, an organization largely composed of old countrymen.

Unfortunately, the Toronto champions did not meet the winner of the Western District to settle the championship of Canada; for, though very good clubs are to be found in Montreal, the Dominion championship has always been acknowledged to lie between the winners of the Toronto and Western districts. Galt secured the Western championship last fall after some very hard games.

The coming spring season of 1894 will see some grand games; and as there are no professionals here, nor ever likely to be, the game will always be devoid of those objectionable features which have crept into the old country, and which will in time very injuriously affect its popularity.

CRICKET.

A January thaw, in spite of the disagreeable accompaniments of rain and slush, has its brighter aspects. We instinctively feel that the terrors of winter have been more than half conquered, and that, with a little more patience, we shall once more feel the lovely warmth of a glorious summer sun. And by whom is that time more welcome, more eagerly looked for, than those who participate in the game of games—the game which is played wherever a handful of Englishmen are gathered together?

It is played in Canada, perhaps not yet to that perfection we would have it, but still, when the circumstances surrounding it are fully considered, Canadian cricketers have no reason to be ashamed. Two things are wanting—time and money. We have not much of either, and for this reason we are quite convinced that our success, in the face of our difficulties, is great.

The season of 1893 began early and finished late. British Columbia, in the far west, had a more active season than Nova Scotia or New Brunswick in the east.

The first-named province has a strong club in Vancouver; and the writer hopes the time is not far distant when the crack eleven of that city shall visit Ontario, and measure its strength with our leading clubs. Three members of its team made centuries—Messrs. Campbell, Saunders, and Sewell. The first-named player had the magnificent average of 53.2 runs per innings; Saunders being second with 49.2; and E. Mahon third, with an average of 37.2. One member of the club played for Canada in the international match with the States; and another member, the Rev. H. G. F. Clinton, was one of the spectators. Mr. Hansard made the only century in the Maritime Provinces.

Manitoba and the Northwest had a busy

THE INTERNATIONAL ELEVEN.

F. HARLEY, Umpire. A. F. R. MARTIN. J. F. HALL, Scorer. A. GILLESPIE. T. S. C. SAUNDERS. H. H. HANSARD.
F. CREW. J. M. LAING. G. S. LYONS. F. W. TERRY, Captain. P. C. GOLDINGHAM. M. G. BRISTOWE.
D. W. SAUNDERS.

SPORTS OF 1893—CRICKET.

season; and much good cricket was played in Winnipeg, Portage La Prairie, and other far west cities. Portage La Prairie was strong enough to win two matches from Winnipeg; and the second game was of a sensational nature. Only one innings each was played, Winnipeg going first to bat and making 135, of which H. G. Wilson made 52, and was unfortunately run out; F. W. Sprado made 20, and H. Cameron, 16.

Portage then commenced its innings, and nine wickets were soon down for 43 runs. Messrs. M. H. Gurney and A. C. Corner were the last partners. The former gentleman played a most brilliant game, driving and cutting most determinedly. The bowling was changed and changed, but without effect. Mr. Corner played with excellent judgment and caution. The score rose rapidly; the figures on the telegraph were changed as every ten runs were made. The enthusiasm was intense. Finally, when the excitement was absolutely painful, Corner made the winning hit and the great battle was over. Both men received ovations on their return to the pavilion. Thus ended, as one of the western papers remarks, "one of the best-fought-out matches that ever took place in this province." Winnipeg won the third match by thirty-six runs.

The new association, "Manitoba and the Northwestern," had an opportunity to push forward the game, and we have every reason to believe much good was done.

The Eastern Association was again unable to send an eleven to play against the Ontario Association, and this was generally regretted.

The Montreal club was stronger than in the previous season, and on the 24th of May gained an easy victory over Ottawa. Boyes and Goodwin both distinguished themselves by their capital bowling. The return match on the 18th of August, at Ottawa, was won by the home team, with seven wickets to spare.

A local association was formed at Carleton Place, on the 15th of April, under the name of the "Ottawa Valley Cricket Association." The Rev. R. McNair was elected president, and Mr. Pickup, secretary. Matches were arranged between the clubs of Almonte, Carleton Place, Arnprior, Lanark, and Ottawa. We have not yet heard the result of the series, but have no doubt they were much enjoyed.

Ontario had an exceptionally busy season. One of the most exciting games is always the one between Ottawa and Toronto. On the 20th of June, the first match was played. Toronto won the toss, and made 156 runs in its only innings; Ottawa responded with 46 and 79, thus losing rather badly by an innings and 31 runs. For the winners, Mr. Terry made 63, not out; Fleury, 29; Goldingham, 14; and McLaughlin, 10. In Ottawa's first innings, Laing took 5 wickets for 12 runs. The Ottawa professional, Sheppard, made the second innings rather attractive by a capital display of batting. His score of 30 was well compiled. The return match was played at Ottawa in July, Toronto making 106 and 64 for 6 wickets, while Ottawa made 65, only having one innings. Goldingham played capital cricket for his 44, which was the highest of the match.

The season of 1893 was remarkable for the number of tours taken by the various clubs. Toronto, Rosedale, Hamilton, London Asylum, East Toronto, and Parkdale being particularly prominent, the last-named club coming quite to the front.

School cricket was as interesting as ever, the annual game between Trinity College School and Upper Canada College being won by the eleven from Deer Park, principally owing to Waldie's fine display in the second innings of the College. His 44 were put together by strong, aggressive batting. The prettiest inning of the match, however, in the opinion of many who were present, was Gamble's 16 (run out) for the School. His graceful forward play was, indeed, delightful to look upon, and all were sorry to see him get badly run out.

The Inter-University match was won by Trinity with nine wickets to spare, the score being:

Trinity........102 and 10 for one wicket.
Toronto....... 26 and 85.

Space will not allow the large number of matches played in Ontario to be reviewed in this brief summary of the season's doings. Toronto was, without doubt, the strongest club in the province. London Asylum, Chatham, Hamilton, Rosedale, Parkdale, East Toronto, Toronto Junction, London, Guelph, Peterboro, Paris, Brantford, Galt, Grimsby, Infantry School, Cobourg, Sarnia, Berlin, Brampton, Norway, Riverdale, Forest, Oakville, Aurora, Bishop Ridley College, Barrie, Pickering, Belleville, Picton, Orillia, Kingston, Deseronto, Niagara Falls, Napanee, Port Hope, Bracebridge, Welland, Merritton, Lincoln, W. A. Murray & Co., Gordon Mackay (Toronto), McMaster (Toronto), Campbellford, Stirling, Port Elgin, Owen Sound, Markham, Brantford, Thamesville, Ridgetown, and Millbrook, all participated in the game; and when we look over this list, no one can say the game is dying out in Ontario.

"Found."

Thomas Blinks, Pinxt.

SPORTS OF 1893—CRICKET, LACROSSE.

Centuries were made in the province on the following occasions by the players whose names are given:

Name.	Date.	For what club.	Against whom.	Score.
J. M. Laing	June 7	Toronto	T'r'ntoUniv'rsity	100*
F. W. Terry	July 7	Parkdale	Brantford	100
P. C. Goldingh'm	July 27	Toronto	Rosedale	101
?. W. Terry	Aug. 9	Lond'n Asyl'm	Toronto	101
J. M. Laing	Aug.12	Toronto	Tor'nto Junction	102*
D. L. Thompson	Aug. 12	East Toronto	Murray & Co.	100*
D.W. Saunders	Aug. 18	Guelph	Galt	111*
J. S. Bowbanks	Aug. 23	Rosedale	Chatham	107
D.W. Saunders	Aug. 25	Toronto	Chatham	116*
F. W. Terry	S.11,12	Canada	United States	111

* Signifies not out.

The story of the annual match with the United States hardly needs re-telling. Canada failed lamentably in the first innings, but that grand second will never be forgotten. Never before had a century, or even a half century, figured in the Canadian score-book that chronicles the history of these great games. On this occasion, both these landmarks were reached; and it is earnestly hoped that the ice having thus been most determinedly broken by Terry and Goldingham, Canada's heroes that day, others will make up their minds that the performance shall be repeated at the next match in Philadelphia. Canada was almost in sight of victory, and the Canadian association has no reason to feel ashamed of the eleven men who played at Rosedale in September last.

The same remarks apply to the great match with Australia, when Canada made a very creditable showing indeed. The match was greatly enjoyed, and a new bowler appeared on the Canadian horizon, of whom we expect great things this summer, unless, as is reported, he may be absent from Canada for a time.

Speaking of individual cricketers, no one can doubt that Laing, of Toronto, came rapidly to the front. Many improved, but none so rapidly as he did. We should like to mention other names, but perhaps it would be better not to do so.

During the season Toronto was favored with a visit by that gray-haired and whiskered veteran, Mr. Frederick Gale, perhaps better known the world over as "The Old Buffer." Mr. Gale was much pleased with Canadian cricket, and enjoyed his stay in Canada very much. On his return to England he remarked to a friend that "Canada was the finest country in the world—after England."

The next season will soon be here. Let me advise cricketers all over the Dominion to keep themselves in perfect condition for coming battles, not only by the use of dumb bells and every outside assistance, but by abstinence from, or at least temperance in, the use of all things liable to dim the eye or ruin the nerves.

In conclusion, the writer would wish every cricketer in Canada much prosperity during the year which has just begun.

LACROSSE.

The Canadian Lacrosse Association season was a very successful one, both as regards the game and the attendance. Although the number of clubs competing for the various championships of the association was smaller than in former years, it was a noticeable fact that, of those entered, nearly all stayed in till the last game, and in very many instances two or three extra matches had to be played in order to decide the winner of the districts.

In the Western District, the Beavers, of Seaforth, and Alerts, of St. Marys, were the last in, and it was not until they had met four times that the Beavers were successful in wresting the championship, which they did at Stratford. Orangeville and Fergus had to meet on neutral grounds at Harriston before the winner of the Northwestern could be declared, Fergus succeeding. Walkerton won at home, but lost when at Kincardine. The tie was played off at Listowel, resulting in a victory for the stalwart Kincardinites. In the Central District (the banner district of the association, properly so called, since it produced the champion team of the association), the contests were most keen. The Brampton Excelsiors, and Tecumsehs, of Toronto, winners of their respective sections, played two deciding matches, one in Brampton, the other in Toronto. Many of those who witnessed the match between these clubs at Rosedale, prior to the Toronto-Shamrock match, will remember the splendid effort put forth by the Tecumsehs, the youngest team in the association. The champions, however, won by a close score of 4 to 3. The Brampton game was won by the home club by a score of 4 to 0. In the Northeastern District, Barrie was successful in carrying off the honors against the strong twelves of Orillia, Toronto Second, and Collingwood. In the semi-finals, Seaforth succeeded in defeating Kincardine twice, and Brampton won two hard matches from Barrie. This left Fergus, Seaforth, and Brampton entitled to try for the final, which took place on the 20th of September in Rosedale. Brampton proved too strong for the other competitors; and although having to play two matches—one in the morning against Fergus, the other in the afternoon against Seaforth—won handily. The Excelsiors are, therefore, champions of the C.L.A. Owing to dissension, the Paris,

COBOURG BASEBALL CLUB, CHAMPIONS OF CANADA, 1891.

J. Humphries. W. Muldrew, 2b. J. Fitzsimmonds, l.f. F. Snyder, s.s. R. H. Edmunds, s.s. H. McGuire, Sec'y.
G. F. Grierson, r.f. T. H. Pearce, l.f. G. T. Bickle, Hon.-Pres. C. N. Gill, Mgr. Dr. Fairbanks, Pres. G. H. Brown, c.f. P. Duncan, 3b.
A. Mulhall, 1b. E. J. Malone, c. M. T. Hoinart. P. Mulhall, p. A. Grierson, r.f.
Scores of final games: Dukes of Toronto, Sept. 8—2-0; Alerts, of Lorden, Sept. 27—8-6; Oct. 7—10-5.

Niagara Falls, and St. Catharines clubs did not compete with Stratford for the senior championship; but it is hoped that the big four of the association will form a series for 1894, and thus ensure success to what promises to be the liveliest season in the history of lacrosse.

During the year, a team from Victoria, B.C., travelled east, and met with success in all the larger cities, beating several of the teams in the Senior League series.

BASEBALL.

A revival of interest in this at one time popular game is noticeable in Ontario, and it is due, no doubt, in no small measure to the formation of the Canadian Amateur Baseball Association. This body came into existence at a largely-attended meeting held in Toronto on April 3. With the disruption of the International League, the game suffered from the lack of a guiding hand. This led to steps being taken for the formation of the present league, which has in its membership nearly all the prominent clubs in Ontario. At the initial meeting of the association, some eighteen clubs were represented. These were divided into six districts, and a championship schedule arranged on a basis of not less than twelve and not more than sixteen games. The season opened May 24, and closed August 24. There was a keen struggle for the pennant. Dundas, London, Cobourg, Lindsay, Galt, Guelph, and the "Dukes" of Toronto, being well up in their different districts from the commencement of the fight. London finally disposed of Dundas, and Cobourg defeated the Dukes, one of the games between these teams being a remarkable one, Cobourg winning it in the tenth inning, when the only two runs made in the game were scored. Cobourg then defeated London on the former's grounds, but the western club won the second game on their own grounds, and with the honors even a third and deciding game was played in Toronto on October 7. Cobourg was the winner, after an interesting, but, at times, loosely-played game, the score of which was 10 to 4.

The officers of the Canadian Amateur Baseball Association are: Honorary President, George Sleeman, Guelph; President, J. J. Ward, Toronto; 1st Vice-President, Dr. Brennan, Peterborough; 2nd Vice-President, John Stacey, St. Thomas; Secretary-Treasurer, Cal Davis, Hamilton. Council: M. Kennedy, Toronto; T. E. McLellan, Galt; M. Smith, Hamilton; B. Cummings, Oshawa; M. McBrayne, Chatham; J. Simpson, Lindsay; J. Manley, Toronto; C. N. Gill, Cobourg; B. Sheere, London; J. McGarry, Toronto.

The second championship season of the National League and American Association began April 27, and terminated September 30. As in the year previous, the Boston club was the winner, Pittsburgh was second; Cleveland, third; Philadelphia, fourth; New York, fifth; Cincinnati and Brooklyn, a tie for sixth; Baltimore, eighth; Chicago, ninth; St. Louis, tenth; Louisville, eleventh; and Washington, twelfth.

CYCLING.

The year 1893 was a notable one in cycling the world over. Records on road and track, in competition, and against time, were brought down to figures that, a very few years ago, would have seemed impossible. This has been due to improvement in pneumatic tires; to the lightening, to the greatest possible extent, of racing machines; to the thorough training and intelligent handling of racing men; and, in time contests, to the reduction of pace-making to a science. While record-breaking was in vogue in all countries where cycling is indulged in, to American riders is due the credit of the bulk of the figure-clipping achievements. Long-distance performances were, principally, undertaken by British riders; while, in the United States, short distance or "sprint" records were those most constantly hacked at. Of the Englishmen, F. W. Shorland, G. E. Osmond, A. W. Harris, J. W. Stocks, S. G. Bradbury, and A. V. Linten were more conspicuous for their good work. Meintjes, the South African, while in England, did some record-breaking, which he afterwards eclipsed during his visit to America. Early in the year, Shorland made a new record for 24 hours by covering 426 miles, 440 yards, in the Cuca Cocoa Cup race, and lowered all records from 100 miles to the finish. His 24-hour time was, later, beaten by a Swiss, who, at Paris, completed 433 miles in the day. The latter, however, is the professional record, and has not been generally accepted, even as such. Linton and Wridgeway, respectively, dropped the 100 miles and 12-hour records to 4 hours, 29 mins., 39½ secs., and 240 miles. Of Englishmen, on the road, the best work was done by Edge, Fletcher, and Hale, the last-named making the present road record for 100 miles of 5 hours, 12 mins., 2 secs.

In France, the professionals, Stephane, Dubois, Lesud, and Terront, did the time hewing amongst them. The long-distance feats of Lesud and Terront were most remarkable. The former's 24-hour record has already been referred to, while the latter covered 1,000 kilometers (621 miles, 640 yards) in 41 hours, 58 mins., $52\frac{4}{5}$ secs.

The German champion, Lehr, besides creating a new set of time figures for his country, also dabbled a little in world's records. The records against time for from 4 to 10 kilometers in distance are his.

TORONTO WANDERERS' RACING TEAM, 1893.
W. G. BENDER, G. M. WELLS, J. F. DEEKS, C. McQUILLAN, F. W. YOUNG.

One of the greatest performances of the year was L. D. Meintjes' 100 kilometer (62 miles, 249 yards) race at the World's Fair meet, when he lowered all competition records from 11 to 62 miles, inclusive. Later, in a trial against time, at Springfield, Mass., Meintjes made new records for all distances from 5 to 26 miles, inclusive. In the United States, scarcely a race meet of prominence was held in which one or more records were not battered. John S. Johnson started the ball rolling by riding 2 miles in 4 mins., 47 secs.; then W. C. Sanger put the mile figure in competition at 2 mins., $14\frac{2}{5}$ secs., and, later, at 2 mins., $8\frac{1}{5}$ secs., while he did two miles, in a handicap race, in 4 mins., $31\frac{3}{5}$ secs. In records against time the greatest reductions were made. Windle electrified the world by riding a mile, with flying start, in 1 min., $56\frac{4}{5}$ secs.; and Tyler shared his renown by covering the same distance, from standing start, in 2 mins., $\frac{2}{5}$ secs. Later in the season, Johnson eclipsed both records; but, because he was paced by running horses, his figures were not recognized by the L.A.W. His time from standing start was 1 min., $58\frac{1}{5}$ secs.; and from flying start, 1 min., $55\frac{2}{5}$ secs. These, again, as also Johnson's shorter distance records, were beaten by J. P. Bliss, of Chicago, and W. F. Dirnberger, of Buffalo, in record trials in Alabama, paced by running horses. Zimmerman, while unquestionably the premier bicyclist of the year, did little in the way of record-breaking. In his trip abroad, he cleaned everything before him in France, Scotland, and Ireland, but was debarred from competing in the N.C.A. championships by the refusal of that body to grant him a license. Second to Zimmerman, probably the greatest rider of the year was W. C. Sanger, of Milwaukee. His most important achievements were the capture of the mile, N.C.A. championship; his mile competition record; and his victory over Zimmerman, in Detroit, and, subsequently, at Springfield. Zimmerman's admirers, however, felt that he was not beaten on his merits, so a meeting between the two at the World's Fair tournament was eagerly awaited. Unfortunately, on the first day of the meet, Sanger fell and injured himself so severely as to prevent his meeting with Zimmerman. Following Zimmerman and Sanger, in prominence and accomplishments, came Windle, Tyler, Johnson, Bliss, and Dirnberger, about in the order named. Some idea of the success of the principal American racing men will be gained from the following table:

PRIZES WON.

Name	1st.	2nd.	3rd.	Value of Prizes.
A. A. Zimmerman..	101	8	3	$15,000
W. C. Sanger.....	22	7	4	5,000
H. C. Tyler.......	27	12	4	5,000
W. W. Windle....	16	15	17	3,500
J. S. Johnson.....	82	26	10	10,000
J. P. Bliss........	36	46	41	6,300
G. F. Taylor......	16	23	16	4,200
H. A. Githens	8	21	10	2,000
M. F. Dirnberger.	41	32	13	4,200
F. C. Bald	35	16	12	3,646
G. A. Banker.....	47	24	12	2,000
A. W. Warren	21	18	13	2,650
E. A. Nelson	36	18	15	3,500

On the road few records were lowered. H. H. Wylie made a record from Chicago to New York of 10 days, 3 hours, 35 minutes, and E. C. Yeatnian covered 311 miles on the road in 24 hours. J. W. Linneman twice broke the 100-mile road record, and Frank Waller made a new 25-mile road record.

During the year, the National Cycling Association, a cash prize league, was formed. Amongst the converts to its ranks were H. C. Wheeler, P. J. Berlo, C. W. Dorntge, A. B. Rich, W. W. Taxis, C. M. Murphy, and others. The first year's existence of the association was not a successful one. The attendance at its meetings was not up to expectation, there were not sufficient riders of prominence in its ranks, and the season closed with the association many thousand dollars in arrears.

The year was productive of good results and record-breaking feats in Canadian cycling. The two or three provincial meets of former years were increased to upwards of twenty first-class tournaments, with costly prizes, large fields, and keen racing. Commencing early in August and lasting throughout the month, an Ontario circuit of twelve race meets was the means of bringing to light numerous promising *débutants*, and of giving a much-needed experience to many older riders. Road races also became more frequent, many race-meet promoters giving a road contest as a side issue to the other.

After the Canadian championship meeting at Sarnia, on July 1 and 2, two of the most important events of the year were the second annual Queen City road race of 20 miles, held on the Kingston road, near Toronto, early in the summer; and the Athenæum Cycling Club's National road race, held over the same course, in the autumn. In the former, there were 173 entries and 139 starters; and in the latter, 204 entries and 166 starters. The record of 1 hour, 1 min., 43 secs., made by A. T. Crooks, of Buffalo, in the Queen City, was reduced to 1 hour, 20 secs., by W. M. Carman, of Toronto, in the National. Out of the last race arose a match race over the course between Carman and W. R. Hensel, who was only 20 seconds behind Carman's time in the National. Carman won on the track. The chief honors fell to Will Hyslop, of the Toronto Bicycle Club, who captured all five of the Canadian championships at the Sarnia meet, and was the principal winner at many of the other large meets of the season. His most dangerous competitors throughout the year were W. M. Carman and L. D. Robertson, Athenæum Cycling Club; C. C. Harbottle, his own club mate; W. Nicholls, Hamilton Bicycle Club; and, towards the close of the season, F. W. Young, Wanderers' Bicycle Club. All those mentioned were prominent winners on the circuit. Other track riders who made a name for themselves and gave promise of future brilliancy were H. D. McKellar, T. W. Carlyle, A. M, Lyon, S. Y. Baldwin, and J. E. Doane, of the Athenæum B.C.; W. G. Bender, J. F. Deeks, F. Bendelari, H. L. Daville, C. McQuillan, R. Jaffray, of the Wanderers' B.C.; M. R. Gooderham, F. B. Gullett, W. H. Lee, and J. Miln, of the Toronto B.C.; G. McIlroy, F. S. Gordon, G. McKay, and S. Aikens, of the Hamilton

B.C.; T. B. McCarthy, R. R. McFarlane, and W. N. Robertson, Stratford ; C. Manville, and J. F. and C. H. White, London ; R. O. Blayney, Simcoe ; J. Lang, Brantford ; W. Devine, St. Thomas ; H. Tolton, Galt ; W. R. Hensel, T. Proctor, S. H. Gibbons, and Wells, the Wanderers' cracker-jack, was away from Canada during most of the year, but, upon his returnin the autumn, he demonstrated that his championship form of 1892 had not deserted him. Two trials against time were made by Canadian riders at the close of

TORONTO B.C. RACING TEAM 1893.
C. C. HARBOTTLE, W. HYSLOP, J. MILN,
MR. GOODERHAM, (Trainer), F. B. GULLET.

G. Rolston, Royal Canadian B.C., Toronto ; L. Rowen and W. F. Mitchell, Guelph ; E. O. Sliter, Kingston ; G. E. Stellings and D. S. Louson, Montreal ; W. B. Parr, G. Harvey, and E. A. La Suer, Ottawa ; C. S. Schultz, Essex ; J. A. Reid, Aurora ; B. P. Corey, Petrolea ; A. E. Schmidt, Waterloo, E. J. P. Smith, Toronto and numerous others. G. M. the racing season. In the first, W. R. Hensel made new records from 6 to 11 miles, inclusive. In the second, W. M. Carman wiped out Hensel's figures, and continued the good work to 25 miles. Both trials were made on Rosedale track, Toronto, and in both the conditions were unfavorable and the pacing indifferent. The appointment of official time-keepers by the Racing Board of the Canadian Wheelmen's Association was of decided advantage to race-meets and time contests. The attendance at race-meets was usually gratifying to race promoters.

The principal records of the year were as follows:

World's records made in competition—

Distance.	Name.	Time.
¼ mile (flying start)	H. C. Tyler	.25 4-5
⅓ "	A. A. Zimmerman	.30 2-5
½ "	H. C. Tyler	1.00 2-5
¾ "	W. C. Sanger	1.35 3-5
1 "	"	2.08 1-5
2 "	"	4.31 2-5
3 "	J. S. Johnson	7.15 3-4
4 "	C. T. Knisely	10.12 1-5
5 "	A. E. Lumsden	12.36 3-5
6 "	J. W. Linneman	15.11 4-5
7 "	"	17.43 3-5
8 "	"	20.24 4-5
9 "	L. S. Meintjes	22.52 4-5
10 "	J. W. Linneman	25.32
15 "	L. S. Meintjes	38.05 4-5
20 "	"	51.18 2-5
25 "	"	1:04.39 3-5
30 "	"	1:17.56 1-5
35 "	"	1:31.02 2-5
40 "	"	1:44 11 4-5
45 "	"	1:57.33 2-5
50 "	"	2:11.06 4-5
55 "	"	2:24.59 2-5
60 "	"	2:39.47
62 "	"	2:45.53

World's records made against time (standing start)—

Distance.	Name.	Place.		Time
¼ mile	H. C. Tyler	Springfield,	Oct. 9, 1893	.29 1-5
½ "	"	"	Oct. 11, 1893	1.01
¾ "	"	"	" "	1.30 1-5
1 "	"	"	" "	2.00 2-5
2 "	"	"	Sept. 28, 1893	4.15 3 5
3 "	W. W. Windle	"	Oct. 17, 1893	6.43
4 "	L. S. Meintjes	"	Sept. 11, 1893	8.57 3-5
5 "	"	"	" "	11.09 3-5
6 "	"	"	Sept. 14, 1893	13.43 1-5
7 "	"	"	" "	16.05 4-5
8 "	"	"	" "	18.26 1-5
9 "	"	"	" "	20.46 3 5
10 "	"	"	" "	23.04 2 5
15 "	"	"	" "	34.37
20 "	"	"	" "	46.07
25 "	"	"	" "	57.40 3-5
26 "	"	"	" "	59.52 1-5

World's record made against time (flying start)—

Independence, Ia.—John S. Johnson, Nov. 10, 1893; 100 yards in 5 2-5 secs.
Independence, Ia.—John S. Johnson, Nov. 10, 1893; ⅛ mile in 12 1-5 secs.
Independence, Ia.—John S. Johnson, Oct. 31, 1893; ¼ mile in 24 2-5 secs.
Independence, Ia.—John S. Johnson, Nov. 10, 1893; ⅓ mile in 34 3-5 secs.
Independence, Ia.—John S. Johnson, Oct. 30, 1893; ½ mile in 55 secs.
Independence, Ia.—John S. Johnson, Nov. 9, 1893; ⅔ mile in 1 min. 16 secs.
Springfield, Mass.—W. W. Windle, Oct. 11, 1893; ¾ mile in 1 min. 26 3-5 secs.
Springfield, Mass.—W. W. Windle, Oct. 3, 1893; 1 mile in 1 min. 56 4-5 secs.

Records not accepted by the L.A.W.—

San Jose, Cal.—W. J. Edwards, Dec. 7, 1893; 100 yards (standing start) in 8 3-5 secs.
Nashville, Tenn.—M. F. Dirnberger, Nov. 15, 1893; 100 yards (flying start) in 5 secs.
Nashville, Tenn.—J. P. Bliss, Nov. 15, 1893; ⅛ mile (standing start) in 16 4-5 secs.
Nashville, Tenn.—J. P. Bliss, Nov. 15, 1893; ⅓ mile (standing start) in 38 1-5 secs.
Nashville, Tenn.—J. P. Bliss, Nov. 15, 1893; ½ mile (standing start) in 56 3-5 secs.
Nashville, Tenn.—M. F. Dirnberger, Nov. 15, 1893; ½ mile (flying start) in 54 secs.
Birmingham, Ala.—J. P. Bliss, Dec. 12, 1893; ⅔ mile (standing start) in 1 min. 17 secs.
Birmingham, Ala.—M. F. Dirnberger, Dec. 12, 1893; ⅔ mile (flying start) in 1 min. 12 2-5 secs.
Birmingham, Ala.—J. P. Bliss, Dec. 12, 1893; ¾ mile (standing start) in 1 min. 26 2-5 secs.
Birmingham, Ala.—M. F. Dirnberger, Dec. 12, 1893; ¾ mile (flying start) in 1 min. 21 3-4 secs.
Birmingham, Ala.—J. P. Bliss, Dec. 12, 1893; 1 mile (standing start) in 1 min. 58 2-5 secs.
Birmingham, Ala.—M. F. Dirnberger, Dec. 12, 1893; 1 mile (flying start) in 1 min. 51 secs.

American road records (competition)—10 miles, J. Willis, 27 mins. 26 secs.; 15 miles, W. B. Hurlburt, 43 mins. 18 secs.; 20 miles, W. B. Hurlburt, 57 mins. 46 secs.; 25 miles, F. Waller, 1 hr. 6 mins. 10 secs.; 50 miles, F. A. Foell, 2 hrs. 32 mins. 20 secs.; 100 miles, J. W. Linneman, 5 hrs. 48 mins. 45 secs.

American road records against time—

New York to Chicago—H. H. Wylie, June 17-26, 1893; 1,028 miles in 10 days 4 hrs. 39 mins.
Chicago to Milwaukee—E. Ulbricht, Nov. 4, 1893; 96 miles, 5 hrs. 46 mins. 3 secs.
Twenty-four hours—E. C. Yeatman, Nov. 15, 1893; 311 miles.
Chicago to New York (by seventy-six relays), May 18-23, 1892; 976 miles in 4 days 13 hrs. 8 mins.

English records against time—The following records against time were all made at Herne Hill, being from standing start, except the first, Harris' quarter:

Distance.	Name.	Date.		Time.
¼ mile	A. W. Harris	Sept. 22,	1893	.27 1-5
⅓ "	P. W. Brown	"	"	.32 4-5
½ "	F. G. Bradbury	June 15,	"	1.03 1-5
¾ "	E. Pope	Sept. 28,	"	1.33 2-5
1 "	"	"	"	2.07 2-5
2 "	G. E. Osmond	Aug. 19,	"	4.24 2-5
3 "	J. W. Stocks	Aug. 30,	"	6.55 3-5
4 "	"	"	"	9.14 2-5
5 "	"	"	"	11.36 4-5
10 "	"	"	"	23.20
20 "	"	"	"	47.17 3-5
25 "	"	"	"	59.06 4-5
50 "	"	"	"	2:05.45 4-5
100 kilo	"	"	"	2:43.02 2-5

English records (competition)—

Quarter-mile (flying start)—E. Pope, June 17, 1893; 29 1-5 secs.
Five miles—G. E. Osmond, July 8, 1893; 12 mins. 3 1-5 secs.
Ten miles—L. S. Meintjes, July 8, 1893; 24 mins. 14 2-5 secs.
One hundred miles—A. V. Linton, July 1, 1893; 4 hrs. 29 mins. 39 1-5 secs.
Twenty-four hours (bicycle)—F. Shorland, July 22, 1893; 426 miles, 440 yards
Twenty-four hours (tricycle)—F. T. Bidlake, July 22, 1893; 410 miles, 1,110 yards.

HALF-MOON BAY, THOUSAND ISLANDS.

SPORTS OF 1893—CYCLING, BOWLING.

CANADIAN RECORDS (COMPETITION).

DISTANCE.	NAME.	TIME.	PLACE.	DATE.
¼ mile	C. C. Harbottle .... (Flying)	.30 2-5	... Owen Sound...	Aug. 23rd, 1893
¼ "	J. S. Johnson	.33 1-5	.... Toronto	Sept. 23rd, 1893
½ "	" .....(Flying)	1.05 4-5	..... Sarnia......	July 1st, 1893
½ "	F. J. Osmond.............	1.07 2-5	.... Toronto	Aug. 30th, 1893
1 "	W. Hyslop	2.24 1-5	...Montreal.....	Aug. 26th, 1893
2 "	A. A. Zimmerman.........	5.03 2-5	....Sarnia......	Aug. 17th, 1892
3 "	W. M. Carman	7.38	....Stratford.....	Aug. 24th, 1893
4 "	G. M. Wells.....	11.15	....Kingston.....	July 1st, 1892
5 "	W. Hyslop	13.03 3-5	.... Toronto	Aug. 30th, 1893
6 "	G. M. Wells...............	17.55 4-5	....Hamilton.....	Aug. 12th, 1892
7 "	A. W. Palmer......	21.07	"	"
8 "	"	23.57 4-5	"	"
9 "	G. M. Wells...............	27.17 4-5	"	"
10 "	"	30.11 3-5	"	"

CANADIAN RECORDS (AGAINST TIME).

DISTANCE.	NAME.	TIME.	PLACE.	DATE.
¼ mile	G. M. Wells........(Flying)	.29 4-5	..... Toronto	Oct. 5th, 1893
1 "	J. S. Johnson...............	2.16 4-5	"	Sept. 23rd, 1893
2 "	W. A. Rhodes...............	4.50	"	Sept. 22nd, 1893
3 "	"	7.27	"	Sept. 22nd, 1893
4 "	W. Hyslop.................	10.05	"	Oct. 24th, 1893
5 "	W. A. Rhodes..............	12.33 1-5	"	Sept. 22nd, 1893
6 "	W. M. Carman	16.18 3-5	"	Nov. 4th, 1893
7 "	"	19.04 2-5	"	"
8 "	"	21.53 3-5	"	"
9 "	"	24.42 3-5	"	"
10 "	"	27.26	"	"
11 "	"	30.13	"	"
12 "	"	33.06	"	"
13 "	"	35.50	"	"
14 "	"	38.39	"	"
15 "	"	41.38	"	"
16 "	"	44.19	"	"
17 "	"	47.05	"	"
18 "	"	49.51 1-5	"	"
19 "	"	52.44	"	"
20 "	"	55.44	"	"
21 "	"	58.35 4-5	"	"
22 "	"	61.29	"	"
23 "	"	64.31 2-5	"	"
24 "	"	67.48 2-5	"	"
25 "	"	71.13	"	"

ONE-HOUR RECORD—W. M. Carman, 21 miles, 341½ yards.

Miscellaneous Records—

Springfield—One-hour record : L. S. Meintjes, Sept. 14, 1893; 26 miles, 107 yards.
Chicago—Two-hour record : L. S. Meintjes, Aug. 12, 1893; 45 miles, 1,530 yards.
Springfield—Fastest half mile ridden in competition in a scratch event : E. C. Bald, Sept. 14, 1893; 1 min. 3 2-5 secs.
Springfield—Fastest mile ridden in competition in a scratch event : W. C. Sanger, Sept. 13, 1893; 2 mins. 11 1-5 secs.
St. Petersburg to Paris—Charles Terront, Oct., 1893 ; 1,875 miles in 14 days 7 hrs.
Chicago—American twenty-four hour record : F. E. Spooner, July 8-9, 1892 ; 374 miles, 1,607 yards.
European mile record (standing start) against time— August Lehr, 2 mins. 6 2-5 secs.
One thousand miles on road—Lawrence Fletcher, 4 days 23 hrs. 30 mins.
Fastest lap race—H. A. Githens, of Chicago; two miles in 4 mins. 49 secs.

BOWLING.

In addition to the many local matches, there were two important bowling tournaments in 1893, in which Ontario clubs participated. The first, on July 12, was the contest for the Walker Trophy, held on the lawn of the Royal Canadian Yacht Club, at Toronto Island. The second was the Annual Tournament of the Ontario Bowling Association, held on the grounds of the Queen's Royal Hotel, Niagara.

A larger lawn than that of the Royal Canadian Yacht Club would offer more convenience for a tournament, but in no other respect could it be improved on. Away from the heat and dust of the city, almost surrounded by Lake Ontario and Toronto

JARVIS STREET, TORONTO, IN SUMMER.

Bay, it is always green and fresh, while the club-house offers every convenience to the players in the matter of dressing rooms and refreshments. The morning of July 12 was fine, and when play began rinks were present from the following clubs : Victoria, R.C.Y.C., Granite, and Prospect Park, of Toronto; Thistle and Victoria, of Hamilton ; and from the Kingston and Belleville clubs. Play continued over the next day, but was stopped by rain in the afternoon, and finished on the third day, the Walker Trophy being won by the Kingston club. McClain, of the Granites, won the consolation prize in the rink contests ; Dexter and McKay, of the Hamilton Victorias, won the doubles ; and P. Scott, of the Granites, won the singles.

On August 23, rinks from the same clubs met at the Queen's Royal Hotel, Niagara-on-the-Lake, for the annual tournament of the Ontario Bowling Association. A rink from Mitchell was also present. Play was on the commodious grounds of the hotel, and excellent weather favored the contestants. The Association Trophy was won by the Victoria club.

The annual meeting of the association was held, and the following officers elected for the current year : Patron, Lieutenant-Governor Kirkpatrick ; Honorary President, Col. Sir C. Gzowski ; President, John Harvey ; 1st Vice-President, J. Lugsdin ; 2nd Vice-President, R. McClain ; Secretary-Treasurer, L. D. McCulloch ; Executive, G. R. Hargraft, E. T. Lightbourne, C. Carlyle, F. O. Cayley, John Crerar, J. D. McKay, W. H. Biggar, J. W. Corcoran, R. L. Walkem, W. Elliott, Capt. Dickson.

BILLIARDS.

There were several notable contests during the year between the leading experts of Canada, the United States, and England. Jan. 20, George Sutton, of Toronto, defeated Joseph Capron, of Galt, for the 14-inch balk-line championship of Canada, and $500 a side, by 500 to 459 ; the game was played in Toronto. A week later these players met at the same place, in a straight rail game, for $500 a side, which Sutton won by 500 to 266. The winner's average was 25.9, and the loser's 9.8. March 28, a second game for the balk-line championship was played in Toronto, and was won by Capron from Sutton by 500 to 306. The stakes were $500 a side. A third game, on exactly the same lines as the previous balk-line contests, was played in Galt, April 20, when Sutton turned the tables on Capron, defeating him by 500 to 409.

The most notable event in English billiard circles was the visit of Frank Ives, the American champion, and his match with John Roberts, the English champion, which the former won. The game was one of 6,000 points, 1,000 points nightly, for six nights, and was played on an English table. The match began May 29, and was played in Henley's Circus, London. These experts played a return game, September 18-23, in Chicago, when Ives again won by 6,000 to 5,303. The English champion was, however, more fortunate when, on October 2 to 7, in New York City, he defeated Ives in an international match, for $10,000 and the gate receipts, by 10,000 to 8,738. The English champion then met Alfredo de Oro, October 16-21, in New York City, and was defeated in an international pyramid and American pool match, continuous, by 1,000 to 924.

November 21-25, Jacob Schaefer beat Frank Ives, in Chicago, 4,000 to 3,945, at the fourteen-inch balk-line game, for $5,000 and the gate receipts, 500 points per night.

CURLING.

The principal curling event of the winter in Ontario is the annual competition for the silver tankard of the Ontario Curling Association. In the winter of 1892-93, the primary competition in the various groups had the following winners : Group 1—1, Oshawa ; 2, Orillia ; 3, Bobcaygeon ; 4, Waubaushene; 5, Collingwood; 6, Hamilton Thistle ; 7, Hamilton Victoria ; 8, Toronto, Prospect Park ; 9, Toronto Caledonian ; 10, Woodstock ; 11, Galt Granite ; 12, Seaforth ; 13, Forest ; 14, Sarnia ; 15, Lucknow ; 16, Harriston. The final competition took place in Toronto in February, 1893. In the first round, Hamilton Thistle beat Orillia, 46-32 ; Prospect Park beat Sarnia, 38-33 ; Hamilton Victoria beat Collingwood, 39-31 ; Harriston beat Woodstock, 41-31 ; Waubaushene beat Galt Granite, 36-34. In the second round, Harriston beat Toronto Caledonian, 46-41 ; Oshawa beat Hamilton Victoria, 40-39 ; Prospect Park beat Hamilton Thistle, 40-39 ; Bobcaygeon beat Waubaushene, 42-21. In the third round, Oshawa beat Harriston, 40-37 ; Bobcaygeon beat Prospect Park, 42-41. In the final round, Bobcaygeon beat Oshawa, 48-37. The champion rinks were composed as follows: T. McCamus, W. T. C. Boyd, A. E. Bottum, W. J. Reid, skip ; George Bell, J. T. Robertson, T. Gage, W. Gidley, skip.

In Toronto the city trophy was won by the Granites, who took straight victories from Toronto and Prospect Park in the series.

ATHLETICS.

The principal athletic meeting of the year in America was the World's Fair tournament at Chicago on September 16, 1893. There four world's records were lowered and one equalled, and the honor list contained the names of two famous Canadian athletes. These were George R. Gray, who broke his best previous record by putting the 16-lb. shot a distance of 47 ft., and George W. Orton, of the Toronto Lacrosse and Athletic Association, who beat Tommy Conneff in the one mile run in 4 mins. 32 4-5 secs. J. S. Mitchell, of the N.Y.A.C., put the 56-lb. weight for height 15 ft. 4½ in.; E. B. Bloss, of Boston, made a hop, step, and jump record of 48 ft. 6 in.; and A. C. Green, of Chicago, in a pole vault for distance, covered 27 ft. 5 in.

In Canada, the great athletic event of the year is the annual meet of the C.A.A.A., which, in 1893, was held in Rosedale, Toronto. No records were broken, and the principal winners were: 100 yds. run, C. W. Stage, Cleveland A.C., 10 2-5 secs.; 220 yds., C. W. Stage, 23 secs.; ¼ mile, A. W. Gifford, Montreal, 51 2-5 secs.; ½ mile, A. W. Gifford, 2 mins. 5 secs.; one mile, G. W. Orton, Toronto L. and A.A., 4 mins. 39 secs.; two miles, G. W. Orton, 10 mins. 26 secs.; 120 yds. hurdle race, F. C. Puffer, N.J.A.C., 16 secs.; three-mile walk, W. H. Hazlitt, Toronto, 26 mins. 38 secs.; putting the 16-lb. shot (7 ft. run), Joseph Gray, Orillia, 39 ft. 8 3-4 in.; throwing 16 lb. hammer, W. Nichol, Toronto, 120 ft. 8 in.; throwing 56-lb. weight, W. Nichol, 29 ft. 6 1-2 in.; running long jump, F. Puffer, 21 ft. 7 3-4 in.; running high jump, A. Allison, Toronto, 4 ft. 10 5-8 in.; pole vaulting, J. Richardson, Toronto, 8 ft. 4 in.

The organization of, and erection of a palatial building for, the Toronto Athletic Club will undoubtedly greatly benefit Canadian athletics in the future. The building, which had been upwards of two years in course of construction, is now complete, and open to members. It is a magnificent pile, of modern Romanesque style of architecture, occupying a frontage of 90 feet on College Street West, by a depth of 110 feet. One of the best-appointed athletic institutions in the country, its chief interior features are its great gymnasium, 86 feet by 90, with the roof 30 feet above the floor, and its marble flanked swimming bath in the basement, 80 feet by 24. There are also Turkish, Russian, shower, and other baths in the basement, in close neighborhood to all of which are lounging rooms, and twenty dressing rooms, and bowling alleys. A barber shop and smoking room are also situated in the basement. On the principal floors of the building are a handsome billiard and pool hall, drawing rooms, card and chess rooms, fencing and boxing rooms, a large dining room, private dining rooms, committee rooms, and club offices. The building throughout is furnished in an elaborate and substantial manner. In rear of the building is a large open-air skating rink, which in summer may be used for tennis, cricket, and other games.

CASTLE REST, THOUSAND ISLANDS.

THE WORLD'S FAIR.

A SURVEY AND A REMEMBRANCE OF THE GREAT COLUMBIAN EXPOSITION.

HE event of the year 1893 (speaking broadly, the event of the century) was assuredly that wonder of a city that arose by a gray lake and sate with us—a message from the gods—all through one brief, sweet summer. 1893 was a crowned year, a very king. He gave to the tired old world a gift that rejuvenated, brightened, heartened her. He left with her a memory tender, keen, beautiful, like the ceasing of exquisite music that leaves an echo in the soul—like the refrain of a passion-laden song.

It is difficult to determine whence came the inspiration of the World's Fair. It is one of the things destined to be shrouded in mystery. Hosts of persons have claimed the honor of being called the father of the Columbian celebration; but, beyond reasonable doubt, it was a thought that dribbled into the public mind at the time of the Centennial of 1876, and took all the more root there from the fact that, although the Centennial was financially a failure, yet it attracted such world-wide attention to American industries that it made the public eager for another trial.

The opportunity for such a trial came with the 400th anniversary of the landing of Columbus. Here was the time, if ever, to hold a great international meeting; to invite the world to come and see what a comparatively new country could do and had done; to come and exploit their own arts and industries side by side with those of the mighty American continent. And the world came and wondered.

Once the great Columbian Fair project was mooted, came the question: Where will it be held? A vast murmur arose along the east. This huge exposition must be held in some eastern American city. The great west was entirely overlooked. People forgot, or were ignorant of the fact, that beyond the Alleghanies lay the great wealth, the natural wealth and power, of the vast continent. But the West—the hotbed of enterprise and commercial activity—put forth its voice, and there came a sounding note from Chicago, and immediately the world—old and new—burst into laughter. The eastern press became pregnant with gibes. New York newspapers pointed sarcasm after sarcasm at the audacity of this upstart city of the "wild and woolly West," and the comic papers sparkled with biting jests and absurd cartoons. What did she care for all this, the turbulent city by the Michigan Lake? Nothing. She entered into competition for the prize with her usual energy and force, subscribed her millions, sent her petition to Congress, and won by three votes!

Then, swiftly, an army of magicians gathered, and there arose on a wide stretch of marsh that edged Lake Michigan a wonder of white palaces, and domes, and

Hon. Lyman J. Gage,
President Chicago Exhibition.

stately buildings. Architects gathered—at first eager to exploit each one his particular idiosyncrasy; afterwards jointly, grandly, as one man, resolved to sink their individuality for the sake of one harmonious whole. With incredible swiftness the White City—so-called with instant poetry—flashed into light upon the wild park by the lake; and the world was invited to come within the gates, walk in the wide ways, and sail over the lagoons, see this wonderful congress of Science, Industry, Art, and Religion, and note the progress of the world from dim prehistoric ages to the present leaping, pulsing, hurrying moment.

The broad and generous invitation of the American people was responded to magnificently by the nations. A liberal allotment of space in square feet was made to the leading countries, many of which put up buildings of their own. It is not the purpose of this article to enter at length into arid lines of figures, giving the height and breadth of every building, its cost, and the number of the exhibits within (a task which would outrival the Herculean labors); but some statistics are necessary, and these we will lightly touch as we pass along.

The World's Columbian Exposition is said by some to have covered 750 acres of ground; by others, 984 acres. Whether the former or latter figures are correct is a matter of little moment; certain it is that a vast number of acres were covered by buildings, and a no less number were laid out in walks, and gardens, and beautiful little lawns. Buildings of different sizes and different architecture, but—with the exception of the Transportation Building, and the red roof of the Fisheries' Building—alike in pure whiteness, like to that of marble, sprang up all over the immensity of Jackson Park. Landscape gardeners gathered and planned the exquisite flower-beds that were a delight to the eye all through the short summer, and, presently, there lay upon the lagoons an island of roses—a wooded place where one wandered lost in a maze of enchantment and beauty on those soft, sultry nights, when the flowers flung their perfume on the night, and nodded time in shadowy places to the music that pulsed divinely through the air from the bands on the distant bridges.

To foreign countries alone 1,600,000 square feet were allotted, and the applications for space were many. Gigantic as was the scheme of the Exposition; gigantic as was the great Hall of Manufactures—a structure 1,687 feet long, with a gallery 50 feet wide—there were applications for four times the available space, and in several other buildings the deficiency was equally marked.

Rapidly the White City by the lake advanced towards its beautiful completion; and on the 1st of May, 1893, two years after the first ground was broken in Jackson Park, President Cleveland, amid unparalleled enthusiasm, pressed an electric button, and life came to the exquisite dream. The mighty machinery leaped to action; the flags of a world unfurled and swept to the breeze; the boats on the lagoons danced by to the sound of a mighty cheering; voices seemed to come from the clouds in answer to the plaudits below, as if the voices of the gods shouted mightily over the triumph of their White City; salvo after salvo throbbed the air, and there were tears upon the faces of the women; the orchestra of 500 pieces crashed out the glorious music of the Columbian March, and the air was filled with vibrant sound. Presently, looking eastward, those in the Court of Honor saw the shrouding flung from the divine figure of a woman, who stood—golden goddess! type of Liberty, Generosity, Nobility—on a pedestal that found footing in the waters that swept in through a white arch from the tossing gray lake beyond, and a cheer, mightier than the rest, broke from the people. The gods trembled. Such a wonder of rejoicing, such a triumph of all art, had never come before upon this earth. Men had looked into a corner of heaven, and were glad. The crown, that day, was set upon the loveliest city the world had ever known. The poem of the ages was complete!

Magnificent, indeed, was this realized dream. The white Court of Honor swept in lines of exquisite grace, serene, classic, exceedingly beautiful, along the sides of the great lagoon. Passing under the mighty dome of Administration, by the great statue of the discoverer of the country, one came upon this thing of beauty that will forever be a joy, in the memory of it, to the souls of men. Fling guide-book to the winds and look upon it! What matters the length or breadth of it! What matters anything but the beauty of it! What is this subtle pathos of it that makes your heart like to break!

Colossal, but full of grace and symmetry, the great Hall of Manufactures, Corinthian in architecture, with its four great entrances, its curved roof stairways, its long array of arches and columns, stretches—a shining wonder; on our left, headed by the wonderful Electricity Building, with its bobbing rooflights, and its wonderful whirling balls—golden, and blue, and red; the beautiful Palace of Agriculture, in itself a city of pavilions, pagodas, and kiosks; and Machinery Hall, with twelve of its great engines, representing a total of 3,000 horse power, stand on our right; and facing us, across the stretch of ruffled water, is the Peristyle—that corridor of the gods, with the great Quadriga as a crown upon it; with its slender pillars, white and chaste as the limbs of a Psyche, carved by Phidias; its archways, through which one could see, on rough days, the flashing of white-caps in the wild lake beyond, and, on still days, the glint of sunny waters, and the heroic figures—the gods themselves—standing along its summit, clear against the sky—stately sentinels

Bird's-Eye View of the World's Columbian Exposition, Looking West.

guarding the gateways of the world—the world that had gathered in the hollow of this city of light.

For the nations had gathered. Here were to be found the children of the earth. Every country was busy exploiting itself, and proud and light-stepping among them came and went everywhere the Dominion of Canada. Everywhere along the wide ways of this beautiful city one beheld the sign of this land, and everywhere the exhibits of her resources and manufactures were remarkable and amazing. The world wondered at the products of Canada. People had thought that there was but in this country those products which any rich and fertile land is capable of producing with judicious care and management. They expected a good exhibit of wheat and grain of all kinds, of timber from the vast woods of North America, and, possibly, of certain kinds of live stock; but they were not prepared for the magnificent and wonderfully copious display of manufactures, fruit, flowers, transportation, and the arts, made by the Dominion. Well might the Canadian flag wave proudly wherever it was placed! for, from the Palace of Mines to the beautiful Temple of Art that stretched in simple classic grandeur by the lagoons, Canada stood a wonder to the nations, and a keen contestant for the honors awarded to the successful countries of the world. A space of 70,000 square feet was allotted to Canada in the various buildings at the World's Fair, and she filled every foot of it with good things, besides erecting her own building. Close by the great tumbling gray lake, where the wide path by the shore made its splendid curve, stood the Canadian Pavilion, a pretty structure with walls and ceilings of native Canadian woods, and a wide balcony, commanding by far the best view of the lake. Canada's representative building was manned by representative men —men who exploited her artistic and commercial interests, and were untiring in their efforts to place her prominently before the eyes of the gathered nations. Competing with the world, as she was, it was highly necessary to Canada that her representative men should be men of tact, of foresight, of keen business acumen, and a better selection was never made.

The commissioners for Canada were Mr. G. R. R. Cockburn, the Hon. Joseph Tasse, and Mr. J. S. Larke, executive commissioner. The Quebec commissioner was the Hon. John McIntosh; and Ontario's commissioner was Mr. N. Awrey, M.P.P.; Mr. C. J. Law was commissioner for British Columbia; Senator Perley for the Northwest Territories. Great and capable work did these men for Canada, each acquitting himself of his duties with tact and geniality that won for him the plaudits and friendship of all who met him. But there were other workers who deserve honorable mention. These gentlemen were Mr. William Smith, press representative of the Canadian Government; Mr. F. Howard Annes, of Whitby, Ontario, who, with Mr. Charles W. Young, of Cornwall, represented the Ontario press.

MR. THOMAS B. BRYAN,
First Vice-President of the Directors of the Exhibition and Board of Administration.

The gratitude of the country is due to all these representative gentlemen—and no doubt others whose names are not mentioned here—who now, modestly, have gone back to their homes, content that they have done what they could towards spreading wide through the whole world the immense resources, mineral, agricultural, artistic, of this vast country; this colonial jewel of the British crown; this teeming and richly-dowered land.

Briefly, then, to speak of Canadian exhibits; for there is much to talk of, much to be said of the beauty of the White City, of the wonders of it, of its highways and waterways, its tragedies, sublimities, absurdities; much gentle gossiping of summer nights when a glory of light crowned the exquisite white places; of bright mornings, joyous with sunshine; of noons, fainting under a tropic heat. There is much to be said that this writing will not compass; so—let us drift.

Foremost among the provinces of the Dominion stood rich Ontario; rich in mines, in agriculture, in ales and liquors; rich beyond expression in her magnificent pomological display, her wonders of small and varied fruits, her giant vegetables, her gorgeous tropical plants; sweeping the prizes of a world in her live stock, and her cheese and dairy produce. Beautiful, hearty province! There was a ruddiness, a freshness, a hardiness about the exhibits of Ontario—of all Canada—that, somehow, bespoke of a healthy, hearty country, and a sturdy race. People spake of this many times. "Canadian folks are like their own apples—sweet and hardy." It was said by old farmer ladies from Ohio and Iowa, as they stood looking amazedly at the gigantic Goderich squashes—good little Goderich! —and those other wonders of vegetables from Canadian experimental farms. And with every fresh award, every fresh honor, the flag that floated from the roof of the Canadian Pavilion took a braver fling on the wind, and opposite, from Victoria House, stately England nodded approbation, while a ripple ran through the stout Union Jack.

Down in the stock barns, Ontario was written up many times in great letters, always with a string of colors and medals somewhere near. There, one might see old Yankee farmers talking with Canadians regarding the wonderful Ontario Southdowns, Cotswolds, Leicesters; those magnificent hackneys and Clydesdales; those shorthorn and Galloway bulls, that sent the fame of Canada, as one of the finest stockbreeding grounds of the world, abroad across the ways of the earth.

Nor is this a vain boasting. When, exclusive of the awards given for dairy produce, and for certain portions of the agricultural machinery exhibits, Canada captured—and this in competition with all the countries, old and new, of the world—no fewer than 1,914 awards (and some remain to be officially announced), the advantages which this country reaped from the World's Fair are ample and considerable. An immense outlay all this cost Canada; but when one considers the prominence the country gained by it, the insight she has given to the world of her magnificent resources, and the admirable manner in which those natural resources have been nourished and cultivated, the work done was good work. Never was money more wisely expended.

With what results? Patience for a moment, while figures—stolid facts!—speak. Canada won, to her grand credit: In live stock, 450 awards; in fish and fisheries, 24; in horticulture, 65; in mines and mining, 67; in manufactures, 191; in ethnology and natural history, 6; in fine arts, 5; in agriculture, 258. Nor do these figures give the sum total for the agricultural awards, for agricultural machinery and dairy produce are not set down here, owing to the fluctuations in these from month to month in field and dairy trials. So much, and yet more, for Canada. She, too, with the other nations, will have her share in the benefits that will accrue to all countries, to all peoples, from this Parliament of the World. What are these benefits? Knowledge of the vast movements all over the world—of science, agriculture, the arts; the comparison of her own powers as a producing country with those of all the nations; the liberality of thought such wide knowledge must bring; the loftiness of mind, the nobility, the courteousness that commingling of the peoples of the earth must necessarily teach; and—if the lesson be rightly read—the uprooting of all intolerance; the wider toleration of humanity, because we, too, are human; the great charity and love in which the nations should join, because, for every national interest for the progress of commerce, science, the arts, peace is necessary. All these are the lessons of the great Fair.

Every country set out to travel all over the world when it journeyed to this vast meeting of the nations. Each one came to exploit itself, to compare with others, to learn, *to travel*. It was like the setting out of a young man on the tour of the world. Each moment a fresh surprise overtakes him; each moment there is something to wonder at, to admire, to resolve, to emulate. He is always learning. He is finding out his own powers to enjoy, to study, to *do*. Canada went on the grand tour. She

MR. ANTHONY F. SEEBERGER,
Treasurer to the Directors, World's Fair.

learned the extent of her own mighty resources; she herself was astonished at the effect she had upon a world which had regarded her rather as a rural retreat than an active, progressive, cultured country. She learned, in this divine harmony of nations, this human poem of the White City, the present state of art and science in every field of development, and received a broad and comprehensive knowledge of every particular art and craft, while revealing to a world the wealth of her minerals and the magnificent yielding powers of her fruitful provinces. Results! benefits! one could go on naming them forever!

But let us pass from eulogies of country or countries, from facts and figures, and, treading to the sound of music, walk through the ways of the classic White City, remembering with tenderness its exquisite beauty, its gentle, happy crowds, its sublimity, its absurdities. The extraordinary success of the White City was absolutely due to self-abnegation. It was as if the gods came to the earth and asked of men to bury all of self and individual ambition, and the fame such might bring, and build a treasure-house for the world. And man, for once obeying the gods, the outcome was one exquisite harmony. All human passions, jealousies, feelings, were set aside; and the eleven architects (prominent men all of them, to whom fame was sweet), the five designers, the various sculptors, color artists, landscape gardeners, all labored, with a self-abnegation that was divine, to make an exquisite something that would astonish and fascinate a world. It may be—it must be—that this singleness of purpose, this superhuman generosity, this immense sacrifice of self and all other pettiness, became the soul of the White City, for she had one—she lived, she touched the soul of the meanest of us like a living art, like the throbbing of exquisite music; she, in a word, took hold of all men —cynics, philosophers, scientists, dullards, the blasé, the paltry, the great; and there is not one living who wandered through her wide ways, who knew the classic grace of her slender columns, the vast hollows of her painted domes, the flashing of wild waters through her curving arches, but was the better for it, the happier for it, the nobler for it, who did not feel his ideal of beauty realized, who to-day is not filled with gracious memories of it!

And, as if to show us we had not quite reached heaven, but were yet on the sorrowful earth, a tragedy sate upon the lips of this fair thing. In this, the White City was like to our grieving, common, worn world-cities. And not in many ways was she like to them. On July 11, the terrible disaster known as the Cold Storage Fire took place in the broad noonday, when the ways were crowded. Fifteen firemen and guards lost their lives, and the vast crowd swayed and groaned as it helplessly watched the brave men leap eighty feet of space, to meet death on the path below. Ever after, one might notice solemn groups standing on the cindered ways near the vast painted hollow of Administration—groups sobered from their joyousness for a moment, because, even here, in this city of love, and light, and all joy, pale Death, knocking importunately upon the gates, had found an entrance.

But, drifting always, we pass under the wide dome, and out to the Court of Honor. Ah, the wonder of it! Ah, but who and what were this people who could build a thing so fair that the world gaped at the beauty of it! The zeal of them! the patience and courage of this people of the West! Was ever before such fragility combined with such strength, such delicacy with such vigor! Look at it, this page torn from the Arabian Nights; this one reality that never fell short of the ideal! It is the autumn of the day. The sun, strong in his death-hour, smites in one glorious stroke the great dome, jewelling its crown; then, in one long line of quivering gold, he beats his way across the shivering waters, stopping to kiss the golden woman from brow to heel, and flings into one mighty shaft of light his dying strength, and the pallid gods on the wide roof of the Peristyle tremble into a glory of light. Diana, poised on the roof of Agriculture, leans in an ecstasy towards the stretching white palaces below, and, clear against the dusky blue of the sky, the flags of the world beat out on a dying breeze. There comes the wait of evening in the air; then dimly, redly, the sun falls into the enshrouding west, and the White City grows chill. The violet dusk gathers over the lagoons and gardens. Far across the sky a line of light pales swiftly till all the land lies dark. For a moment. Then the great hollow of Administration, holed with windows, sends its dull red eyes peering down at the pallid city, and now it hangs, the mighty dome, like a jewel from the concave of the sky—built in light. Up, up the curved roof creep the golden beads, till the crown is reached, and flings its painted summit far up, a glory of brightness against the darkening vault. And now the windows of the dome glow redly, each like a rose of fire. Below, the great electric fountains beat up in showers of gold, and red, and intensest green, and there is a murmur from the people. Out there, beyond the Peristyle, the lonely lake broods, peering with dark eyes between white archways at the glory within, like a lost soul grieving for a glimpse of heaven; out there it stretches desolate as an ocean, dark—vast, with the cry of the wind ever on it—a lonely voice. Then, within, along the mighty buildings that line

ILLUMINATION OF THE ART BUILDING, AS SEEN FROM THE LAGOON.

the Court, the lights burst in golden ropes, and lifting serene over the rim of the world comes a great moon, pale, surprised at this lighted wonder of a thing that lies crowned by the stretching lake, and the stars wheel, and the trees gossip, and the people, fascinated, awed, dazed at this vision of the gods, murmur always.

But what of it when, later, with a great booming, strange fires shoot up through the blackness, startling the peeping stars? What of it when Wooded Island shines a circle of colored lights, a jewel in a silver shield! What of the swinging lamps along the banks, the dancing of the electric boats over the lagoons, the slow, noiseless pushing of the gondolas! What of the medley of rising, falling, skimming lights; of the distant jargoning—exquisite soundings—of the bands; of the four great beams that crossed giant arms along the blackening sky, and silvered the limbs of the gods, and beat with fierce light upon the triumphant woman on the car of the great fountain; on the gracious bending forms of the Amazon rowers; on the wild sea horses that flung the spray in great gushes from their wide nostrils; on the dolphins, half leaping through the feathered mist; on the gold Diana, poised against a sky that leaned towards her broodingly! What of it but that it gave one a divine heartache; that it made men feel their souls! What of it but the foreshadowing of, somewhere, a resting-place for the tired ones! Very near were travellers in the White City to the land of God.

Away in the sober light of a gray morning to a vast building that lay in a quiet corner of the fair City. Away on the curving wonder of railway that ran among the domes and turrets of the place, and over the wide ways, twisting, serpent-like, along, and doubling in a great loop at one end, and so turning back and rushing again on its way over the heads of the people, down by the whirling windmills, past the old White Horse Inn, redolent of Pickwick, and extreme in its prices; past the strange brown mounds of the Cliff Dwellers, and opposite the rustic Forestry Building, fragrant with the breath of the woods, stood the curio-house of the White City, vast Hall of Anthropology. Here squatted the hideous mummies of the ancient Peruvians, forgotten of the world; here were the imprints of the giant footsteps of prehistoric animals from the permian age, when beasts that sprang from reptiles walked upon hind feet, to the tertiary or quaternary ages of mammals. Looking upon the footprints of prehistoric man, old fables leaped to the mind. "There were giants in those days," one said to oneself softly; and ranged along the wide gallery in Anthropology one came upon the mighty mammoth and the gigantic turtle, and a strange fossil reptile that stood upon hind legs like those of a horse, and had fin-like forepaws, and the flat head of a snake; and many mysterious wonders that made one a little silent and thoughtful for a time, recognizing one's ignorance. But, further on, one came upon a flashing of blue butterflies, on a glory of gaily-plumaged birds, on long rows of birds' eggs, on elk and moose, and black wolf, and otter, and the wild things of the woods, and these were a comfort to the heart— great tables weighted with the coins of the world, from old, old times, on which the great doorways of the past have forever closed, sent their stretching length across the wide galleries; and, further on, one made the acquaintance of the curious platypus of New South Wales, and of the bower-bird and lyre-bird, and other strange things.

On the ground floor of this vast building almost every nation of the earth contributed relics and curios. Here one learned for the first time of a race—not the Indians, but those who by many long and dim ages preceded them; and who had lived, and slept, and eaten on the very sites where Chicago's homes now are, and where the big humming business blocks of the great Western city thrust their roofs into the sky. The relics of this race are here. Hammerstones, rounded to fit into the hollow of the hand, their edges rugged from use, some of them pitted to receive the thumb and forefinger of the right hand, were here in plenty. So were models of the workshops of this strange people, as well as the various stone anvils they used for beating flint into shape. Also on this floor were cases of Indian curiosities, spear heads, arrows, ring stones, and pipes, of which Canada made a goodly showing. The weapons, dress, idols, and war-trappings of aboriginal peoples were hung in their various sections. Perhaps the most interesting of these was the collection of New South Wales, where the picture of "Mickey," the great chief of the Ulladullahs, the most expert boomerang-thrower in all Australia (a burly cannibal with a flat nose and a wrinkled forehead), hung in a conspicuous place, with his queer war weapons around him. When "Mickey" vanquished any of the chieftains who, with their tribes, came up from Solomon Islands or other places (for Mickey's fame had travelled far), he and his warriors set about eating the slain. Mickey, as a man of taste in these matters, always selected the heart as his particular portion, and, before he died, he had devoured eighty of these trophies of his skill in war. He was converted by the missionaries—not, however, until he had eaten a few Christian hearts, and found them not to his liking, and he died two years ago, in, no doubt, a certain "odor of sanctity." In this collection there was a vast bowl, so large that it left the visitor in doubt as to whether it was a bath-tub or a boat. It was curiously inlaid with clam shell and pearl; but the mighty interest attached to it, and which held those who looked at it silent with a dim horror, was that in it the victim of the cannibals was placed before he was served to the hungry savages. Near by stood a cannibal fork or spiker, with which warriors would pass choice morsels to their chief.

Great curio-house of the White City filled with the first beginnings of science, the first glimmerings of the intelligence of man, stored with the strange games of the world, with the fossils of the gigantic things that walked the mountains, and woods, and plains, and swam in deep waters when the earth was young; bright with the gewgaws of savage tribes, grim with the decaying mummies of a lost people, gay with butterflies, and birds, and strange beasts! What a world of curious knowledge it contained!

Not far off stood the convent of La Rabida, a quaint and mystic place, situated on a comparatively lonely spot, and, in its extreme dissimilarity to any other building at the World's Fair, attracting no small share of attention. Perhaps the most surprising thing about it was its thoroughly monastic appearance, and its look of age. It might have been built four hundred years ago, so misty with legend did it appear. A quaint place, stored with relics of Christopher Columbus, primitive charts, pictures, and curios of the court of Ferdinand and Isabella, and of the early history of La Rabida, in the time of America's discoverer.

Back over the winding Intramural to the Palace of Electricity, where the eye of Science looked out in leaping light upon the world. No longer will one be astonished after a visit to this wonder of a place, for one falls into a mental attitude which accepts all things as surprises. When one has seen real thunderbolts made and launched, facsimile drawings and figures transmitted, chickens hatched and roasted, shoes blacked, sewing machines run, surgical instruments worked, all by electricity, nothing wonderful can ever after surprise him. His surprise faculties become dulled, and, unless you administer to him an unexpected personal "shock," you will be unable to elicit from him any exclamation of astonishment. Seventeen thousand horse-power for electric lighting was provided at the World's Fair. That is three times the electric power in use in the city of Chicago, perhaps the best electric-lighted city in the world. It was ten times that provided for the Paris Exposition in 1889. Let us to figures for a moment. 9,000 horse-power was provided in the White City for incandescent lights, 5,000 for arc lights, and 3,000 for machinery power. This supplied 93,000 incandescent lights and 5,000 arc lights. No wonder that, viewed from the deck of the whaleback, on the wide lake of dark nights, the White City looked like a crown of light on the breast of the waters; like as though heaven had fallen for a moment, and was resting upon earth.

Who that watched the great Edison tower of light on the main floor of Electricity Building can ever forget it? There it stood, a tall shaft thrusting up almost into the roof, and ablaze with incandescent lights in red, and orange, and blue—lights always changing shape and color, and changing to the sound of exquisite waltz music. The beauty of it, the power and tenderness of it, combined with the wonder and the music, brought tears, often, to the faces of those who looked—so often are tears the visible manifestation in us of other things than grief.

There was exhibited in this building a great ring, known as the Teala Ring. Crowds always gathered here to watch things rotating slowly around this ring. It was made of soft iron wire, around which are wound four coils of insulated copper wire, so arranged in pairs that, each pair being connected with a distinct electrical circuit, carrying currents alternating in direction, and the "impulses" or changes of direction of the two currents alternating with each other in point of time," the action of the two currents on the ring and the space surrounding it produced what electricians call "a rotatory magnetic field." A copper egg, about the size of an ostrich egg, used to spin on its end if set in the centre of this ring. Bunches of keys and other metallic substances used also to rotate in the most mysterious manner, to the wonder of everybody. Marvellous building, this, of Electricity, with its whirling globes of blue, and crimson, and gold; its winking advertisements; its pillar of light, before which that which protected the Israelites would have paled; its scenic theatre of Pompeian red—the most exquisite thing imaginable; an Alpine village in faint evening light, which darkened as you looked, and the lights on

Front View of the Ontario Department at the Chicago Exhibition.

the stone bridge steal into a dim brightness. Then darkness; then the first pallid gray of the morning breaking in gold and rose into a broad noon. All gradations of light produced by automatic electric action.

Stepping across the wide white road, one comes upon Machinery Hall, with its annex and great power-house, with twenty-four thousand horse-power of steam; demoniac wheels revolve with awful rapidity; machines of all kinds jump up and down, and perform the most wonderful evolutions. Here it was that, in a wonder of a machine, a steel bar went in at one end and came out a broad network at the other, suggesting that terrible process at the Chicago stockyards, whereby a comfortable squealing porker, at one end of the line, turns out, at the other, in neat hams and strings of sausages. The noise of Machinery Hall was too much for us, and the odors too pungent. "Wheels," we said, looking in; then fled.

But who could describe huge Manufactures? Who, indeed, can fittingly describe any of the wonders of the White City? One could have spent a year wandering in the sumptuous courts, the gay pavilions, and yet not have seen all of it. A city under a roof it was, with its own wide and royal streets; its collection of the wonders of the world—the dreamings of the poets were, here, made into realities in delicate pottery, in shimmering silken fabrics, in twisted and beaten metals, in a flashing of diamonds and rubies, in a brilliancy of glass, in the working of wrought iron, and brasses, and bronzes. Great yellow eye of diamond, flashing wickedly on revolving cushion! Stately gates of iron, wrought in delicate device of leaf and scroll! Huge glimmering bath of porphyry, with the blush of beauty lingering in your polished depth! Dim rooms of ancient castles, in far-off countries, with your old carven chairs, and grim fire-dogs, and sombre richness! Wonderful kiosks, where fairy vases in shell, china, and curios in pottery, made a glory and a light! Stately pavilions, glimmering with the sheen of opal silk and golden embroidery! Wide courts of nations, with your riot of riches, your harmonies of color, your ivories, and fabrics, and sculptures! Imagination faints in the effort to depict you, and pen quavers over paper, and there comes a swimming of the brain.

So, resting for a moment in the wide corridor outside, watch the glory of the day. The golden sun, flashing upon this place of domes and palaces, beats upon the golden woman at the water gateway till the eye turns swiftly from a brightness that is too great to the flashing of cool waters through the arched chinks of the Peristyle. "Come and be cool," laughs the great tumbling lake; and the surf murmurs on the shore. One can hear it plainly, for the White City, for all its moving crowds, is, somehow, a silent city, which has never rung to the tramp of horses' feet, or the rolling of wheels, other than the water and mail carts. So silent is it that, as we sit—tired after the riot of color and fancy in the great roofed city we have just left—we catch, from the Casino, the swinging beat of music, and hear, now and then, the low cry of the gondolier, and hear the merry clinking of crockery from a restaurant near by. From the dome of Administration come little sparkles of light, as if fairies, diamond-shod, were dancing on its crown. It is the laughter of the sun as he peeps betwixt peaks and around turrets. With his gracious hand, he gilds every fleck of color, and flings a more intense whiteness over the stretching of fair palaces; and the White City lifts up her face for his caress, and the gods are glad, and send their breath along the lagoons, making the waters ripple. The band has stopped its braying of wind music, and the shivering of the violins comes across the ways, and the soul leaps to it. It is all so exquisite! All Nature—the winds that beat the air and the waters that forever heave and toss their turbulent bosoms; the trees that lean and whisper in the night-time; the roses that, generously, breathe their perfumed souls to us—all seemed to love this city of the gods, and all gave to her—that one sweet, dead summer—that the soul of her might be glad.

What strange creatures of the deep waters that were not to be found under the red roofings of the Fisheries' Building were few. In the vast tanks of sea water before which, each day, the people massed densely, in hollow sea grottoes, curious things crawled and swam. There were sea anemones that blossom miles below the surface of the ocean; great hooded crabs that carried their worlds, Atlas-like, upon their backs; queer sea spiders that tilted along sideways on slim, tall legs; quaint shell hermits that crawled about, tramp-like, investigating empty tenements, and immediately somersaulting into them; grasping lobsters, beating the waters craftily with cruel feelers in search of prey; and, strangest of all, a sea ostrich that buried his head deep in sandy places, leaving a sinuous, waving tail moving gently in the sea. Fishes, with the warty heads of toads, swam and dived in the wide tanks; and speckled beauties skimmed through the watery ways, while the plebeian catfish waved his ugly feelers and pressed his flaccid mouth against the thick glass. The teachings of the place were many and great.

The supply of sea water for the deep sea fishes was secured by evaporating the necessary quantity at the Woods Hall station of the U.S. Fish Commission to about one-fifth its bulk, thus reducing both quantity and weight for transportation about 80 per cent. The fresh water required to restore it to its proper density was supplied from Lake Michigan. Great was Canada in her fishery exhibit, her canned goods, her fishing boats!

Out again and across a bridge to Wooded Island, and over another and along by the Choral Building to where a great golden door glimmers in the sun. A favorite corner was this, by a lagoon, where the ducks and water-fowl gabbled and dived, and a little Venetian boat rocked lightly on the water's breast. A rest to the eye—dazed with the whiteness everywhere—was this great Hall of Transportation, with its soft terra-cotta harmonies, and great gate of gold and silver; with its wonders of portage inside. All the modes of carriage from Noah's Ark to the nineteenth century were exhibited in long lines in this vast place. Great locomotives stood—black giants—ready to pull their train of cars out at a few hours' notice; and foremost among these stood the business train of the world, the admired of all—the Canadian Pacific Railway Company's exhibit. The boat of the Sea of Galilee, with its weak little mast, was here; one said to be exactly like the one in which Christ rode on the Sea of Galilee. Here, too, was a representation of the ass, with all its trappings, like to that with which Mary and Joseph escaped from Nazareth with Christ. The chairs of India and China; the ox-cart of Mexico; my Lord Mayor of London's coach, and that of His Highness Dom Pedro; the canoe hewn from a tree of the Amazon River; Grace Darling's rotting boat; the prettiest baby carriage in the world; the grandest hearse! What a medley it was! What a wonder!

Not far from Transportation Building lay that devoted to Mines and Mining, a palace filled with the riches of the earth's deep heart. Here were dazzling displays of diamonds, opals, emeralds—all the jewels that make glad the heart of woman. One could see here how diamonds were washed and cut, and a great crowd was always attracted to the place where diamond-washing was going on. There were vast displays of iron and copper, ore, mica, asbestos, marbles of exquisite shadings, Mexican onyx, and all stones and minerals. Great gates of wrought iron—the work of Germany—swung in an arch at the south end of this building—work of many quaint devicings, vines, leaves, and roses were intertwined, and in the centre of each gate there sat a partridge, the feathers of which were most delicately wrought—they were a triumph of art in iron.

The great crystal dome, wide spreading, of

Mrs. Bertha H. Palmer,
President of the Board of Lady Managers.

Horticulture flashes in the sun's light, a beautiful hollow, lined with vines. The iron columns inside this building were painted a pallid green, and round them vigorous vines twisted their darker leaves, making a delicate harmony of color in two shades. Swinging gaily to right and left, catching a tendril here and there, the climbing green things met in the middle of the wide arches above, and, embracing, spread thickly, till all the place was roofed in green, making a pleasant, cool nook on sultry days for one tired of the garish sunlight and the white blaze outside. A pyramid of shrubbery flung to the roof from below; great palms waved their feathered arms; and myriads of flowers made the air fragrant. What would you see? Roof gardens? Climb to the top of the dome, and wander among the loveliest that were ever planned. Flower beds? Outside the great flower palace, beds of violet velvet pansies, in exquisite shadings, turned sweet faces up for a caress. Orchids? Step into the greenhouses and loiter among 18,000 of these delicate lady flowers—a ball-room of them. Or do you fancy strange things in the flower and shrub world? Then behold the night-blooming cereus; the dwarf cedar, 300 years old, shipped from Japan; the groups of giant cacti; the fern trees from Australia; the queer, warty, stunted shrubs, like little monsters, from some far country; the great cocoanut, leaning over, with her brown children close about her heart; the stately century plant—the pen might travel over miles of paper before the half of it would be set down.

Never, in all the world before, was there such a display of fruit gathered under one roof as in the Pomological section of the Horticultural Palace, nor such a gathering of the juices of the grape—from far Greece to Chicago itself. It made men young again to walk in the sweet-smelling place—the world's orchard! by the long rows of shining tables. Oh, Mother Earth, but thou art gracious, and sweet and wholesome and generous! Towers made of oranges, horsemen made of prunes, great heaping bunches of grapes, the biggest and rosiest apples in the world, stacks of lemons, bushels of cherries—sweet as lover's kisses, luscious berries, and great ripe pears, all were here. Wonderful gathering of the sweet fruits of the earth—who could enumerate you? The very memory of your freshness and perfume, and the rich ruddiness and pale delicacy of you, makes the mouth water!

Close by stood the Woman's Building, that museum of woman's work—of fair stuffs and broideries—in a lovely situation, by a lagoon, which here took the form of a small bay. Italian Renaissance was the style of architecture chosen, and the exquisite open colonnades which crowned the corner pavilions glowed every night with that dull Egyptian pink that is so exquisite in its tinting. Within was exhibited the work of the women of all countries, royal laces, paintings, ceramics, art-work, pottery—the most beautiful collection of woman's work that has ever been gathered. The library in the Woman's Building was one of the curio-places of the World's Fair. Here were the manuscripts of the famous women of the world. One could here compare the writing of gentle, unfortunate Lady Jane Grey with that of George Eliot, passionate Georges Sand, prim Jane Austen. A map of Italy, made by an Englishwoman in the time of Dante, and the "Boke of St. Albins," compiled by Dame Juliana Barnes in the 13th century, were among the most interesting curios. The faint, pale writings came to one like tender ghosts from the dim land. Those first two pages of "Adam Bede," "Evelina," and "Jane Eyre," filled, in volumes, the hearts that knew and understood.

Away, by the North Pond, serene and gracious, lovely in its exquisite and classic purity, stood the jewel of the great Fair of the World—the Art Palace; Victory, triumphant, winged, colossal, on the summit; caryatids, angels, and ideal figures of Art, Painting, Music, and Sculpture, stood without the walls; and great lions, couchant, guarded the portals. The art treasures of the world hung on the walls of the seventy-six galleries; and here, always, one found the people, crowding, wandering, and silent before the masterpieces of great artists. The pictures haunt one! Always, the dark eyes of La Cigale look into one's soul, and the shiver of winter trembles along the limbs of the poor grasshopper; and one sees the anguish of the wife in "The Poacher's Return," when they bring him back to her—her man—dead; and the anguish and beauty of many of the other pictures. In the wide courts where the marbles were, there were many exquisite groupings. Lovely Phrynes and Dianas stood poised for flight on lofty pedestals. Mercie's David, with one foot on the head of Goliath, stands, tall and beautiful, sheathing his sword. Fremiet's horrible "Man of the Stone Age" holds aloft the head of a boar; and Death, with her poppies in her hand, and a look of infinite pity and love on her beautiful face, and all a woman's yearning tenderness in her sad eyes, touches the young sculptor on the shoulder, and bids him come and rest on her deep bosom. All that there is of the beautiful in art lay in that vast palace by the lake through the beautiful summer that is gone; but will never be forgotten. Women walked through the gracious palaces with

MR. HARLOW N. HIGINBOTHAM,
President Chicago Exhibition Board of Administration.

tears upon their faces, for the souls of the people were stirred, and answered to the touching of the Beautiful. Vulgarities faded; hearts became open pages that one running might read; and, greatest lesson of the Fair! man was assured for the first time (having a realization of his dream of it) that there was a heaven, an immortality, an eternity wherein the soul of him would know its God: the White City was a foretaste of heaven, and the Art Palace was the heart of it!

And, now, whither away? To the beautiful State Buildings, filled with rare things; to the houses of foreign nations; to—for a resting moment—the wide walk by the beach, where the surf murmured ever its poem to the land, and coaxed back with each beating wave a little chattering string of pebbles that, like human hearts, went hopefully to the vast unknown. The buildings of foreign countries held no exhibits, and were merely headquarters for the entertainment of visitors of the several nationalities they represented; but in several there were curiosities of various kinds. Neither were the United States Buildings exhibit buildings, though many a rare curio was to be found in odd nooks among them. Strangely enough, the plainest of the State Buildings was that of Illinois, the dome of which—lean, shrunken, tall—was enough to ruin the grace of any structure. Beautiful was the building of Massachusetts, modelled after the old Hancock house, and breathing of the old-fashioned gentility of the good Puritans—simple, sober, gray. Filled was it with stately relics of stately men and their stately times, and many a woman's hand lingered for a moment on the cradle which had rocked four generations of Adamses. Great, old, reverend, was American history behind the gray walls of this beautiful building. Pennsylvania, sheltering her venerable Liberty bell, fairly quivered with echoes of stirring times; and Michigan—with her wide verandahs, her generous hearth (whereon in chill October great logs leaped and crackled), her fine collection of the children of her woods and creeks—was, to many, a comfortable home-place. Gay was New York, a fine lady among the buildings, with its imposing entrance, and heavy blue draperies, and great banqueting hall. Filled with curios of ancient Knickerbockers was she, hugging in one of her dim corners a grandame doll of a hundred years, watched over, in a little glass coffin, by the quaintest of gray-faced Dutch clocks. A Greek poem in Ionic columns was Utah, the Mormon State; while quaint Louisiana, in her old brown plantation house, was misty with legend and story. Priceless furniture of old Creole days was stored here; ancient pottery, cracked with the weight of years and adventures, glimmered on shelf and bracket, and, amid the gentle whirring of spinning wheel and loom, the Acadians of Longfellow sate at work—descendants of Evangeline—in high Norman caps and kirtle, while "the gossiping loom", murmured its love-poem to the wheel, which softly purred its answer.

California, with her flattened dome and lovely roof garden, breathed a subtle tropical fragrance of rich golden fruit; while Montana shone from the Mining Building, in the Rehan statue of pure silver, set upon a pedestal of solid gold. Indiana, with her red Gothic towers, her huge elephant chiselled out of one giant block of stone, and her curios, was a favorite among State buildings; and Iowa, stretched along the lake, with her beautiful Corn Palace, her seeds and grains of all kinds, and wonderful grasses, was a pleasant resting place. But most pleasant resting place of all was, in the gray of the day, a seat on one of the wooden benches on the wide curving walk by the lake—in the gray of the day, when dusk was falling, because then the crowds were moving joyously down the merry Midway, or to the fireworks, and this part of the White City—from the Iowa Building to the Victoria House—took to itself a loneliness, and there were strange soundings in the voice of the restless lake, and strange shapes rode atop the waves, and a divine sadness crept into the soul, and whispered there of wild, strange things. Slowly dies the day, while the solemn world of gray waters and graying sky wait. One by one the lamps along this wide way by the water glimmer, solitary lights! in their great white globes, like the eyes of giant owls. Behind, the White City is putting on her crown of light; but here by the lake, as the dusk gathers, it is dark and lonesome, a solemn place of stars. The passion and stir of life have gone from it all, gone to the pale waters with their rhythmic sw-is-sh, their low murmuring on the beach. Then, with a far booming, strange fires rush into the air, and drop in colored flame, flushing the sky, and the White City bursts into a glory of light—and the wild lake, gently lapping for the moment, whispers in its shroud of gray. Joy and sadness are blent together in the solemn transition of day into night, and the moon, frightened, peers in and out through scudding clouds. A wet glint comes across the sea, exquisite, evanescent; then, with a moan, the great north wind, sweeping the waters, cries shrilly, and the water-imps leap to meet him, and the mighty, desolate lake tosses wild, white arms into the black night, and the moon flees into the darkness, and the stars wheel, and the lonely soul, frightened, looks into the eyes of God!

* * * * * *

The White City had her business quarter, her Latin quarter. She herself, poised—an exquisite dream—between the sullen, dark city that was the mother of her, and that brooded

ILLUMINATION OF THE ADMINISTRATION BUILDING.

behind her, content to remain silent, forgotten for the moment in the white loveliness of her child, was a city of peace from traffic, leaving that to the more earthly places. She was a garden of all shining flowers, a poem in architecture—a fitting home-place for the treasures, and arts, and gatherings of the ages. The hurry of commerce she left the plodding world-cities; there, walking in her fair ways, men shook off much of their worldliness, and their souls found a freer scope. She was exalting, ennobling, elevating in her influence over men's minds—this place of the gods, this aristocrat among the shopkeeperish cities of the earth—who would have none of their noises, their street jarrings, their shriekings in great halls of trade, their smug, shop-walker's manners. A silent city in the common ways of men, she gave her voice forth in great beats of music, in the gossipings of her trees, the whisperings of her flowers, the murmurs and thunders of the waters that sate at her feet. Her white houses were open to all. One might wander free among her rich pavilions, her rare wrought brasses, her carvings in wood and ivory. One might enter her wide halls and stray among her wonders of Science—watch her giant wheels grind round, her strange lights revolve in vast globes, her glittering heaps of precious stones and minerals. One might amble from room to room in her great Art Palace, and weep out one's heart before the masterpieces of the world; or stand, awed, at the queer things of dead ages—the monster things that walked the earth, and the seas, and lived in deep caves; or stroll into the long rustic palace where great wood-giants lay felled, and scent the perfume of the forests. And it was free to all men. She stretched her white arms wide, that all might enter and know the beauty and the wonder of her. Mistress of all the cities of the world! crowned queen among them! The White City that flashed along the lake of Michigan alone gave of her beauty to the world without barter, without other coin than the silver price that gave admission to her gates.

But she had her business quarter. It was not white, as she was; therefore, it was not really a part of her, and she disdained it, in a way. But it lay within her walls, near to her, yet as far off as though an ocean lay between, noisy, laughter-loving Midway. Beyond a stretching viaduct (so far apart were they that you came to the Latin quarter through this dark and echoing way) there lay the greatest wonder—the greatest absurdity of a street the world ever saw. Midway Plaisance took to itself 80 acres of ground; and on these 80 acres were gathered representatives of nearly, if not all, the nations of the earth. The swarthy Turk, the wild-eyed Bedouin, the Algerian, Nubian, Persian, Dahomeyan, American Indian, Khabyle, here danced, and shouted, and shrieked their wares through the six months of heat and chill, and the people paid their grotesque pipers merrily. Quaint Midway, with your babblings in strange tongues, your grotesque leapings, your shrilling pipes and odors of charcoal and sandal-wood, your barbaric trappings, and your Hebraic eye to business! Great shop of the nations; wonderland of curiosities; stamping-ground for fakirs; Babel come again! How many merry memories the thought of you brings—of gay nights in old Vienna, where Zichrer wooed your soul from you with his exquisite jargoning of strings, and the waiter wrested your last coin from you with a bill whose dimensions were such as to invite indigestion, and many melancholy musings over the folly of acceding to stomachic requests for foreign viands when you do not understand the language of the country.

Merrily, merrily wag the pipes of the piper of Blarney, as you emerge from the dark ways of the viaduct and come out on the broad road, jangling with the cries, and laughter, and music of all the world. Bravely beats the forgotten green flag from the towers of Blarney Castle, and bravely does the piper blarney the coins from your pocket. In with you through the little turnstile that jerks you bodily (owing to the hurry of the fat Mullingar lady behind, and in a very undignified fashion) into the little square, where the colleens are in plenty, at the dairying, the lace-making, the "footing it," if you come in the evening, to the screech of the pipes. Up with you and kiss the blarney stone! as if you hadn't enough of it, be you lad or maid! and out, laughing always, to the wide street again, where a demoniac pipe calls you to the Beauty Show. "Bedad!" calls the Irish piper after you as you flee, "but the wurruld is full av fools, anyhow!" to which you sadly acquiesce when you leave the lovely congress and amble down the wide street, to be taken by a little ass, trapped in gay trappings, into the heart of Egypt.

Cairo! with its quaint carvings, its greasy, flat-nosed Egyptians, its not over-clean camels, its Temple of Luxor, pregnant with mummies; its cunning jugglers, and veiled flower-girls with the mystic eyes! Queer place of sandal-wood, bracelets, and live lizards was it, with its dim, cavernous shop-palaces hung with rugs, and spangled jackets, and bedizened pipes, and jangling bracelets! "Mustapha Ali, Shepherd's Hotel, Cairo." He pushes the dirty pasteboard into your hand, does Mustapha; and his great eyes gleam ; and the noise of the street dies, and a faint perfume of mingled roses and sandalwood flings across the street from the flowershops in the heart of the quaint place ; and again you are clamoring with mine host of Shepherd's, and wrangling with such another as Mustapha over your six bits of luggage, and there are strange cries in the streets, and you long for civilization and afternoon tea. But here comes the marriage procession, and Mustapha—how did he get there so quickly? —is atop genteel Ward McAllister, beating into that gentleman's aristocratic ears a tum-tum fit to break the drum of even the leathern ear of a camel.

Softly into Java, where the water-wheel sobs always. Graceful as all wild things, the delicate little people flit about the place, and the musicians, squatted in their corner, drop rhythmically their soft, sad music, that has a liquid sound in it. The great ape lounges in his cage, looking out upon life scowlingly, and hearing allusions as to his descent from the kings of Ireland with equanimity. In the theatre the archaic drama, old as the elder hills, goes to its end smoothly, amid no excitement of applause. The little actors don their masks and make their pretty, meaningless play, with outstretched fingers, spreading them, throwing drapery over them in artistic fashion to the sound of dropping music ; and you go out, when it is finished, and sip your Java coffee, and watch the small people flitting about their bamboo houses in the square, where they sell their tiny toy-like workings in basket and box, and you buy long slender cigarettes folded in palm leaves, and quaintly-devised handkerchiefs, and crying softly, "Salabad sorree," to the graceful little creature who serves you, you wander again into the wide street of grotesqueries, and stop a moment to talk to Simon of Smyrna, of the tribe of Zeïbek, an ideal representative of the Greek race ; but, not understanding Greek, which is the language of Simon, you admire, for a while, the extreme blue of the white of his eye—an Irishism is the only thing that will express it—and with mysterious words on both sides you separate.

The street of Constantinople gapes invitingly. Suave Turks, grown impudent with notice, call to you, as you pass, such coarse compliments as they have learned from coarse people, and shriek their wares in Americanese, and talk you over, with much jeering, in Turkish to their comrades. "Not for nothing," as the sharp boy said, did these sons of the Orient wear the hooked nose of the Hebrew. Syrians were these men of Chicago-Constantinople, with the bargain-loving, pushing, trading instincts of their race, but to the shrewdness of the Jew they added the courteousness of the East. Gay were the booths, red-lined, and hung with costly rugs and shimmering silks, and feather-light crêpes ! Gay were they with long, painted, stoppered perfume bottles, with stick-pins, and clinking coin-bracelets, and tiny idols in brass and pewter ! Bright were they with *souvenir* spoons, and pin trays, and tip-toed Turkish slippers ! Brave in tassels ; with beads from Jerusalem ; Turkish tops, made in Manchester ; swords of Damascene steel, fashioned in Sheffield ; wrought and beaten brasses from Algiers ; a thousand-and-one bits of genuine bric-a-brac—a million bits of Brummagem ! And the clatter of it, from the "bum-bum candy" personage in a shroud and turban to the wily Jew-Turk, who persuaded lonely ladies on investigatory and solitary promenadings into the dark little gallery, where they viewed Damascus and the Stations of the Cross through port-holes, so to speak, and came out done beautifully brown !

HON. THOS. W. PALMER,
President Exhibition Commission

Up and down, on the little blue Turkish theatre, bobs a little man, like a human wink. With much clapping of hands, and swishing of long garments, and hoarse shriekings, he invites people up to see the girls of the East squirm and shiver through their unholy dances ; and good old farmers from Iowa and Ohio toil up with their wives, and sit and watch the queer contortions that delight the Pashas of the East, and come away again, innocent of all evil, declaring their opinion, loudly, that three steps of a country dance. "was worth a hundred o' them foolish twistin's"; and lower down the mournful Arab women, brow-bound and grave, beat the drums with their naked hands, and chant, bleatingly, what sounds like the most grievous of tragedies; and the Bedouin chiefs sit cross-legged and grave, eyeing the pushing crowds with a grim disdain and a wondering; and the brown babies howl, like ordinary babies, and the sad mothers, in the pauses of song and dance, nurse them in the common way of all mothers. Shrill bleat the pipes along Midway, and loud brays the German band from the little beer-garden, where the waiters fly, carrying five "beers" in each hand — hollow "beers," with mighty heads of white bubbles and very little yellow bodies; and the people sit "unter der Linden," and listen to the music, and watch the shifting crowd and the little Egyptian ass, monkey-laden, who, with his half-human burden, parades to the shrilling of fierce pipes, and the shouting of turbaned Nubians, and drums in the crowd, to the street of Cairo, whence, presently, a mighty shout of laughter comes, trembling the walls of the Temple of Luxor, and proclaiming that some one has fallen overboard the Ship of the Desert.

And the night falls, and the sun is hidden, and out break the lights, and the fun waxes high, and the laughter of the people beats and throbs upon the air; and all the world, in this merry place, runs mad with glee. Then, bursting into a round glory of light, a giant wheel looms up against the darkness. The vast cobweb—with its multitude of fine lines, its huge rim, burdened with thirty-six cars, its low, churning sound, its circles and crossings of incandescent lights—beats its way, a brilliant circle seen afar from city, lake, and prairie, against the blackness of the night; and the units, looking smaller than ever, crowd into the little cages on its wings, which, in reality, are wide and capacious houses, and up beyond the cries and jarrings of Midway, beyond the pipings, and shrillings, and restlessness, they are lifted, till, looking abroad, all the glory of the White City flashes upon them, and you see this fairyland crowned in light, the black lake brooding beyond, the black city peering with red eyes out of the smoke behind, and again, and yet again, the wonder of it seizes you; and in the quiet and darkness of the little aërial house that throbs its way round, you thank God that you have lived so long.

There comes a night, in that summer of the White City, when the gods, being vexed, smote it with a mighty storm. Softly, all the day, it came creeping on it. The trees knew of it, and shivered, and the leaves fell with solemn rattlings, and little gusts of wind made a moan about the courts. Electricity bobbed merrily upon its roofs, and great Franklin, immovable upon his pedestal, held aloft his key to the elements, but cloud-compelling Zeus laughed, and bid Æolus unloose the winds; and great Jupiter, leaving his sea halls, descended upon Michigan, and the vast lake rose to meet him in a shrieking

Col. George R. Davis,
Director-General, Chicago Exhibition.

of laughter, and wound her white arms half way up to heaven in an ecstasy of turbulent joy, and the moon, frightened, stole behind a cloud.

Abroad, upon a bellowing wind, rode the storm king and his imps, and the sky, yawning, belched forth its fire, and, with one quavering wink, the bobbing lights on Electricity sank into the roof, and the face of Franklin paled yet whiter. A mighty god smote upon the great dome of the White City with a bar of iron, and shrank, afraid, at the beauty of her pallid face. Not even in Olympus had he—Hephaisto—seen so fair a thing; then, furious, he rode straight at a House of Art, that stood by the shivering lagoon. Mightily he smote, being angry, and she trembled, and gaped, and fell away, and Pluvius grieved, wept great tears upon her that mended not her sorrow, but, indeed, added thereto. Then the voices of the gods roared lustily, and Æolus, answering, tore across the world, ripping roofs, and hurling the small human things that stood in his way, beating them against walls and upon the ground, till he came upon a giant wheel, that, serene, churned its way up against the roof of heaven. Proof was it against the angry god, who smote it sharply upon its ears of glass, making them tingle. Then, calling Zeus, and Ares, and Hernes to his aid, he shouted to great Jupiter to send his sea horses leaping. And the three fell upon the giant wheel, and the voices of the gods broke in thunder from the sky, and the light of their anger smote the wheel, and Jupiter sent his white steeds flying ever and ever higher; but the great structure, made by little, human Man, went calmly on its way, wrapped in lightning sheets of blue, and silver, and pale violet, and the gods, amazed, shrank, crying, "Man is greater than are we!" And came their tears, drowning the sad earth, and the ways of the White City were turned to streams, and the bellowing winds died with a cry, and, sullenly, the great lake—deserted of Jupiter —spent her anger in mighty thunderings on the beach, and all through the night the skies wept; but when Aurora, ignorant of the warring of the darkness, thrust rosy feet over the blue of heaven upon the floor of the White City, and caressed her upon her soft-flushed bosom, while the great sun kissed the waters into laughter, and dried, with his fires, the tears of the gods, lo! the grief of the storm was forgotten, and once again the jewel of the world shone a white wonder by the waters of the flashing, glinting, restless lake.

And so, from the Babylon of Midway, from the dancing, and the piping, and the laughter; from serio-bright gossipings with the dignified Oriental scholar who drew finger-nail pictures for a living; from chats with "Far Away Moses," and Osman Mohammed, who is a policeman when he is at home; from the ostrich farm, where "Jim Blaine" looks at you as if he would give much to get you inside his prize-ring and batter the life from you; from the quaint feathered person of Brazil and the honey-voiced Hawaiians; from Hagenbeck's clever lions and low comedy bears; from all the merry jargon of it, back to the place that took the souls of us lovingly and caressed them—back to the White City, in the chilliness of an October evening, when, early, the twilight comes, and when the trees are fast shedding the pretty dun leaves, that made such a lovely shelter from the hot sun on sultry days.

The day is a gray one, and chill with a coming death; and the ways of the White City are clear of the crowds that a week ago jostled through them. Bravely beat the bands on the bridges, and the drums thrum down on Midway, and the boats shoot easily over the lagoons; and Wooded Island shrinks on the breast of the waters, mourning her dead roses. Men stand on roofs, muffled in great coats, close to the flag poles; and one feels they are the executioners. Swiftly flies the day. The lake, quiet, shivering a little in her gray shroud, gently tosses the three outlandish ships that have rested on her breast all summer; and the "Viking"—restless for change, for fight, wanting ever to break loose and ride over defiant waters on deeds of prey and rapine— restless, now that it knows the white gods on the Peristyle will leap to it presently, and, snatching the oars, beat (great giants!) their way to the unknown seas—rears at its moorings (a wild thing), its demon crest rising, a shimmering beast upon the waters. The White City, knowing her doom, waits for the death of the sun. Slowly a strange ship sails into sight, and the "Viking" strains and leaps against the wharf. It is the Death ship, and the pallid city shivers. One glorious burst of reddening light flings across the great dome, and quivers on the limbs of the white gods; then, quickly, the sun dies, falling suddenly into a cloud, to shut from him the death of his white love; and swiftly the men on the roof-tops do their work. Swiftly they tear the shrouding from the tall flag poles; and the naked, desolate, lost things lean into the graying sky. Great salvos crash from the strange ship, marking the passing of the White City. Paling, paling is the light of evening; and a gray ghost flies swiftly over the trembling waters in a shadow of mist, and the north wind, racing across the lake, has a keenness in its note. Softly falls the enshrouding night, and the lights leap out. But the gods have gone. Far out on the gray lake they are tossing in a wild Viking ship, and the soul of the White City has gone with them. The night thickens. A cold wind blows in from the trembling lake, and the last light has gone. Come away!   "KIT."

BUFFALO ROBES.

HOW HUMAN INGENUITY IS REPLACING THE VALUABLE ARTICLE—A CLEVER CANADIAN INVENTS SOMETHING SIMILAR, BUT BETTER THAN BUFFALO SKIN.

Among the thrilling tales that have stirred the blood, and fired the imagination of youth, few equal those stories of Wild West life written by Cooper, Ballantyne, and the equally vivid, but more truthful, narratives of Parkman, the historian. The most picturesque figures in these stories were the buffalo, those monarchs of the plain that roamed in countless herds over the virgin prairies. But, alas, for the romance and grandeur of the past! No more shall the plains rock with the tread of myriad feet rushing in a mad gallop that nothing could check. The plains where once they and

their relentless masters, the Indians, reigned supreme are now claimed by the peaceful occupations of the husbandman.

It is no longer possible for champion hunters like "Buffalo Bill" and Comstock to decide a wager of $1,000 as to who would kill the most buffaloes in an afternoon. A slaughter of this kind took place near Sheridan, Kansas, on a beautiful autumn afternoon in 1868, when "Buffalo Bill" came out the victor, having killed sixty-nine, while Comstock killed forty-six.

On the upper Missouri, for many years, at all the steamboat landings were to be seen bales of buffalo skins along the shore, piled up like cordwood, remaining for two or three years, waiting for purchasers. The last pile of robes, $10,000, were shipped from Fort Benton not more than five years ago, and they paid a handsome interest for storing and carrying them over. Two years ago the last buffalo robes were sold by the Hudson Bay Co., and they brought from $35 to $60 each. Many Canadians remember when from $5 to $12 would buy a good robe. Several attempts have been made in the West and Northwest to domesticate the buffalo, but without success. All that is left of this fine animal now are the bones that are bleaching on the prairie, and which are now being gathered up and shipped east to be manufactured into phosphates and animal charcoal for the refining of sugar. But nature always renews herself, and now thirty million of beef cattle graze on the plains that in 1859 furnished food for half that number of buffaloes. The only thing that remained unplaced was the handsome buffalo robe. A few years ago, however, it dawned upon an ingenious Scotchman, Mr. Newlands, of Galt, that if a substitute could be invented for the buffalo robe, a large demand must speedily spring up. To think, with Mr. Newlands, was to act, and thirty years' experience as a manufacturer and practical weaver and knitter, and understanding the manipulation of hair, wool, and fur, he set to work and spent nearly three years in perfecting a combined machine that wove and knit at the same time. Strength and elasticity were essential to give satisfactory results for a heavy fur cloth that was to give warmth and stand hard usage. With that dogged perseverance that is a characteristic of so many Scotchmen, Mr. Newlands at last succeeded, but not without many anxious days and nights, and produced a successful imitation of a buffalo skin that is made in one whole piece, without a seam, and is pronounced by experts to be equal in every respect to the original for all practical purposes.

This manufactured robe has been in use for years by the same classes that used the old buffalo skin, and one and all say that Mr. Newlands has solved the problem, and that the world has lost nothing, so far as the pelt and fur of the buffalo is concerned.

A large display of the Imitation Buffalo Robes, suitably lined and trimmed, were to be seen at the Canadian Pavilion in the Columbian Exhibition. They attracted thousands of Westerners, who would not believe but that they were the genuine robe, as they knew it a few years ago.

The first man in Chicago to secure a pair of these robes was "Buffalo Bill" himself. He has them in his Wild West show, and points them out to thousands who daily visit his wonderful delineations of Western life as the coming robe.

There are 45,000,000 of people living in Canada and the northern tier of States, that stretch from the Atlantic to the Pacific, and they must have a robe that will fill nearly all the conditions required for such a climate. It is claimed that the Saskatchewan Buffalo Robe has accomplished this. The American Buffalo Robe Co. was organized at Buffalo, N.Y., last year. They built commodious premises there, and are now manufacturing under Newlands' patent, which was secured in Canada and the United States.

GROUP OF BRITISH SOLDIERS AT TORONTO.

CANADIAN HAPPENINGS.

SOME OF THE PRINCIPAL EVENTS OF THE YEAR 1893.

January 8.

THE heavy snowstorm of the few days previous to this date gave the street railways in Canada a good deal to do; and in Toronto it may be said it was the first severe test of the electric system. The electric sweepers, each supplied with 100 horse-power, were brought into action. The severe weather did not prevent festivities and entertainments, among which may be mentioned the fancy fair in connection with St. Paul's Catholic Church, Toronto, which was opened by Hon. Wilfrid Laurier and Mr. Joseph Tait, M.P.P. When Mr. Laurier stepped to the front of the platform, he was accorded a pronounced ovation. He said that, notwithstanding the very great pleasure he had at being present on that occasion, he had not expected to be called upon to make a speech when Rev. Father Hand so kindly invited him to pay them a visit. As he was not an Irishman, they could neither expect wit nor eloquence from him. However, as a poor Frenchman, he was glad to be there, and gratified to know that the object which Father Hand had in view was a worthy one. "I am pleased to be here among my fellow-countrymen, co-religionists, and, I hope, friends," continued the speaker. "You are engaged in a noble work, and must surely succeed. The poet spoke truthfully when he said he who giveth to the poor lendeth to God." Mr. Laurier concluded by thanking them for having invited him there, and expressing his gladness at being able to do a little towards making the fair a success. Mr. Tait was then called upon, and the audience extended to him a warm reception. He had come down with Mr. Laurier in order that the latter might not get lost on the road. Mr. Tait was pleased to be there for many reasons. On his last visit he had drawn a pretty set of china, which he kept in memory of them. He then referred to Mr. Laurier's brilliant speech at the Board of Trade banquet, and expressed regret that there were not more men in Canada who were as much beloved as the Hon. Wilfrid Laurier. The speaker was glad to know that a good spirit permeated every class in that portion of the city. The work they were engaged in was charitable and Godlike. He admired the charitable sympathy which existed among all the various institutions of the city. They had had a Frenchman introduced by an Irishman, and he, a poor Scotchman, had nothing more to say.

A convention of farmers, under the auspices of the West York Farmers' Institute, was held at Woodbridge, Ont., at which papers on agricultural subjects were read by Mr. J. I. Hobson, Chairman of the Advisory Board of the Ontario Agricultural College, on "How to Keep the Farm Clear"; Mr. S. Hunter, of Rockville, on "Ensilage and the Silo"; and by Mr. J. C. Caston, whose subject was "The Orchard as Part of a System of Mixed Farming."

Jan. 10.—There was a conference at Toronto between the leaders of two great religious bodies, the Presbyterians and Congregationalists, with a view to overtures of union of their churches throughout Canada. The Congregational ministers who attended to lay their proposal before the Presbytery were Rev. Charles Duff, of Toronto; Rev. John Burton, of Toronto; and Rev. B. B. Williams, of Guelph. They had with them an address signed by ten ministers of the Congregational denomination, in which they expressed their belief in the possibility of a union between the two sects. This address was read by Rev. John Burton. The Presbytery cordially welcomed the Congregational ministers, and agreed to appoint the following members of the Presbytery to meet and confer with ministers of the Congregational churches on the subject of union between these churches, at such times and places as may be mutually agreed upon by both parties, and to report the result to the Presbytery: Rev. J. Cameron, Rev. Dr. Caven, Rev. Dr. Carmichael, Rev. D. J. Macdonnell, Rev. Dr. Gregg, Rev. G. M. Milligan, and Messrs. John A. Paterson and David Miller, elders—Dr. Caven to act as convener. Rev. Mr.

Burton expressed for himself and companions their sense of the courtesy of the Presbytery, and withdrew.

The opening ceremonies of a new homœopathic institution to be known as Grace Hospital took place.

Jan. 11.—The citizens of Toronto had an anxious time with regard to their water supply. Soon the reservoir emptied, the high level station failed to get a connection with the water sent through the mains by the pumps on the water front, and for the greater part of the day the whole district north of Bloor Street was entirely without water and at the mercy of fire, while, between College and Bloor Streets, the pressure was utterly insufficient to meet the demands upon it. In the central districts, elevators were kept moving, but very slowly. There was no burst in the mains, nor any valve open by which water could be lost. The conclusion was come to that the shortage was caused by citizens allowing their taps to run to prevent the water from freezing in the pipes. Towards night, when the elevators shut down and the factories ceased operations, the pressure gradually increased. Shortly before 9 o'clock, the high level station got into operation again, and all the north was supplied with water, though not at fire-pressure.

Jan. 12.—The twenty-fifth annual convention of the Western Ontario Dairy Association at London, Ont., closed, after a most successful meeting; indeed, many of the oldest members declared it to have been the most satisfactory ever held. The business was completed by 2 o'clock, although there were several subjects left on the programme which there was no time to discuss. The feature of the day was the visit of the Governor-General, who arrived from the west at 1.45 o'clock, and proceeded at once to the Victoria Hall, where he stayed for a few minutes, receiving and responding to an address of welcome from the assembled dairymen. His Excellency was not able to stay as long as he had expected, the heavy snow having detained his train, and made it a difficult matter to meet all his engagements. The morning session opened at 9.30 with an address by Prof. Fletcher, botanist of the Ottawa Experimental Farm.

Jan. 14.—A proposal having been made to remove the Toronto Observatory to Ottawa, a meeting of influential Toronto citizens was held to protest against such a change.

Jan. 16.—Great interest excited in Canada and New England by the announcement that Henry M. Whitney and a syndicate of Boston capitalists had obtained control of the coal mines of Cape Breton. From information gleaned in Boston, it seemed probable that the deal consummated was of even more gigantic dimensions than this, and embraced not only the coal mines, but a large area of undeveloped mineral properties and the railways connecting the mines with navigation. Many millions of Boston capital was to be invested in this enterprise, which was understood to include a great extension in the output of coal in that island; the construction of a railway from Sydney, where it would connect with the Intercolonial system to Louisburg, a port on the seaboard open all the year round; the opening up of iron, copper, and gypsum mines; and the establishment of smelting furnaces and other industries. All the coal mines were stated to have been consolidated under one lease, and the period of the lease, it was said, was fixed for sixty years.

Jan. 17.—Mr. Arthur Allan, youngest son of Sir Hugh Allan, and nephew of Mr. Andrew Allan, was suffocated by smoke in his lodgings in Montreal at an early hour. He left the St. James Club at midnight for his rooms, and an hour later was found dead, sitting in his easy chair. How the accident occurred, no one knows, beyond the fact that it was due to a fire which took place about 1 o'clock. It is supposed that, when Mr. Allan returned from the club, he lighted a cigar and flung himself upon the lounge in the sitting-room. Close to the lounge was a cuspidor. He may have aimed the end of his lighted cigar at the cuspidor. The cigar may have fallen on the floor and set fire to the carpet. Mr. Allan may, in the meantime, have fallen asleep. Awakened by the sensation of choking, he must have left the sitting-room and found his way along the hall to his bedroom, for it was in an easy chair of that room that he was found dead. There was no inquest.

A meeting in favor of the annexation of Canada to the United States was held at Stouffville; and a good audience assembled in Daley's Hall to hear Messrs. A. F. Jury, T. M. White, and S. R. Clark, all of Toronto, and all prominent members of the Continental Union Association, speak on this question, of which they are avowed apostles. It cannot be said that, while speaking, they received much encouragement in the way of applause, or that their auditors displayed any general sympathy with the views they expressed.

Jan. 18.— A most audacious robbery by daylight took place in Toronto, being perpetrated in a jeweler's store on Queen Street West by five partially masked men, armed with revolvers. Having overpowered the storekeeper, the five men went to the cash-drawer, extracted $20 therefrom, took $1 from the pockets of the proprietor, and then rifled the shop of its valuables. The loss sustained by the proprietor is placed at from $500 to $1,000. The property stolen consisted of sixty-three watches (a number of which are Waterburys), about 100 gold rings, and several chains. A portion of the goods was taken from the front window of the shop, and the whole affair occurred with the front door unlocked. The men left hurriedly by the front door with the stolen jewelry in their pockets.

The Royal Commission upon the Liquor Traffic resumed its session at Montreal. Mr. John A. Watkins, of the Inland Revenue Department, made some astonishing statements regarding the amount of illicit manufacturing and adulteration going on in Montreal. He said that bogus liquor labels were kept for sale by the leading lithographers of the city; that these bogus labels were for gin, whiskey, brandy, and other liquors, and sometimes bore the names of firms that did not exist; that they were kept in stock and sold to grocers, or anyone else who asked for them. He produced a bundle of these fictitious labels, and handed them to the commissioners, and added that he knew a man who made a good living by buying these labels and selling them again all over the country. Dr. J. W. Burgess, of the Protestant Hospital for the Insane at Verdun, was in favor of prohibition, but did not believe it could be enforced. Mr. James Patton, Secretary of the Committee of Management of the Montreal General Hospital, was also in favor of prohibition, and thought it could be enforced, but admitted that he knew no place where it is in force. Mr. Samuel Carsley, though not a total abstainer, was in favor of total prohibition on account of the misery induced by the liquor traffic. He thought brewers and distillers ought to be compensated in case of a prohibitory law, and was of opinion that such a law could be enforced, though he could not mention any country where it is now in force.

Jan. 20.—Professor Robertson, Dominion Dairy Commissioner, returned to Ottawa from England, after his trip to ascertain the possibilities of Canadian trade being extended in Great Britain. Mr. Robertson gave an interesting account of his tour and the hearty welcomes he had met, and dwelt on the requirements of the British markets. He said he had attended the great conference in London called to consider the agricultural depression, and added: "I did not quite see daylight through the mist of some of the speeches. Every reference to protection by the imposition of a tax upon all food products imported into Great Britain was received with vigorous applause. I do not think that the meeting represented the feeling of the British public, or the expectation of the mass of the farmers or farm laborers upon that question."

Jan. 25.—A coroner's jury sat at Chatham, Ont., on the body of Police Constable Rankin, who was alleged to have been foully murdered by having his skull fractured. A number of colored prisoners were held on suspicion. The deed took place at Raleigh. The spot is surrounded by a dense bush. It is said there are 500 acres of bush land between it and the lake. Bygrams' stave and saw mill is in the near vicinity. The place is seven miles from Charing Cross, five or six from South Buxton (the famous freedman's settlement).

The bishops of the Ecclesiastical Province of Canada met in the chapter-house of Christ Church Cathedral to elect a Metropolitan in place of the late Bishop Medley. The bishops present were : The Right Rev. J. Travers Lewis, D.D., Bishop of Ontario ; Right Rev. Arthur Sweatman, D.D., Bishop of Toronto ; Right Rev. William B. Bond, LL.D., Bishop of Montreal ; Right Rev. M. S. Baldwin, D.D., Bishop of Huron ; Right Rev. Charles Hamilton, D.D., Bishop of Niagara ; Right Rev. F. Courtney, D.D., Bishop of Nova Scotia ; Right Rev. R. T. Kingdon, D.D., Bishop of Fredericton ; Right Rev. A. Hunter Dunn, D.D., Bishop of Quebec ; and the Rev. James Baylis, Rector of Longueuil, the secretary. The only absentee was Bishop Sullivan, of Algoma, now in Europe. After a long deliberation, Bishop Lewis, of Ontario, was elected Metropolitan.

Feb. 2.—The masked daylight robbers who raided the jeweler's store on Queen Street West return part of the booty to its owner, accompanying it by an impudent letter signed "Dalton Imitators."

Rev. William Wilcox Perrin, Vicar of St. Luke's, Southampton, England, appointed Bishop of British Columbia.

Considerable apprehension prevailed in the various cities of Canada lest cholera should make its appearance from Europe, and precautionary measures were taken by the authorities.

Central Prison Grounds, Toronto

Photo by Harry English

Feb. 4.—The *Canadian Magazine*, a new serial, designed to answer the purpose partly of a national review and partly of a popular magazine, and edited by Mr. J. Gordon Mowat, appeared. The first board of directors comprised : Hon. J. C. Patterson, Minister of Militia; Hon. Thos. Ballantyne, Speaker of the Local Legislature ; Thomas Mulvey, T. H. Best, Dr. John Ferguson, Dr. L. Bentley, G. F. Frankland, J. Gordon Mowat (of Toronto), and Elihu Stewart (of Collingwood). The initial number contained political articles by D'Alton McCarthy and Principal Grant, besides an interesting list of non-political articles by other well-known men.

Feb. 5.—Mr. Thomas Edison gives his opinion that it would be more expensive to bring electrical power from Niagara Falls than to make the same in Toronto.

Feb. 6.—The masked robbers who adopted the name "Dalton Imitators" caught. Since the robbery at the jeweler's store in Queen Street West, they had made an attempt on the premises of a monetary institution in Church Street, Toronto, namely, the Home Savings and Loan Co.'s Bank. This attempt took place on Friday afternoon, January 27. The officials were engaged at 4.20 in balancing the books preparatory to closing, when three young men, apparently about twenty-three or twenty-four years of age, entered the building. One of the visitors took his stand in front of the teller's cage, and, putting the nozzles of two revolvers through the bars, ordered the teller, Mr. Wellington Wallace, to throw up his hands. Mr. Wallace did not comprehend what was meant. He thought the man was a friend of one of the clerks trying to perpetrate a silly joke, and with a jocular remark he went on with his work. The order was peremptorily repeated, and the official then realized that it was no joking matter. He did not, however, lose his head, but, seizing a chair, held it in front of him, and refused to comply. In the meantime, the second visitor went up to the adjoining counter, where James C. Mason, a nephew of the manager, was at work, and without a word jumped over the counter, and, rushing past Mr. Mason, made a dash for the rear door of the teller's cage. Fortunately, this was securely locked, and baffled any attempt to burst it in. Frustrated in this, the desperado turned as if to rush into the vault; but either fearing that he might get locked in, or realizing that the situation was getting perilous, he did not carry out his apparent intention. By this time, Mr. Mason and Mr. R. B. Street, the accountant (who was also at his desk), recovered from the surprise into which they had been thrown, and made an attempt to seize the intruder. A sharp tuzzle ensued, in which Mr. Mason was hit with some sharp instrument over the eye. The struggle was a brief one, for the would-be burglar, finding the odds against him, broke away, and, with his companion, succeeded in making good his escape, both men bolting out of the bank and rushing north and east along Adelaide Street. An alarm was quickly given, and one of the office boys in the bank followed the men, losing sight of them, however, before they had gone very far. They were, however, soon caught by the Toronto police.

Feb. 10.—An English lady wrote to the City Solicitor of Toronto, Mr. C. R. W. Biggar, claiming to own the land on which Toronto is built.

Feb. 14.—Hon. Mr. Gardner, President of the British Board of Agriculture, gave a sympathetic hearing in London to a large Scottish deputation, which urged the removal of the restriction on Canadian cattle. Lord Aberdeen, Lord Camperdown, Lord Breadalbane, and eighty representatives of Glasgow, Dundee, Aberdeen, and other Scottish bodies, urged the importance of the question to Scotland. President Gardner regretted that the deputation had not awaited the receipt of detailed official reports upon the present condition of Canadian herds, and upon the intentions of the Dominion Government regarding the Northwest quarantine against United States cattle. Seeing that his conviction was that the disease detected in Canadian cattle was contagious, the law compelled him to be assured that Canada was now absolutely free from disease before removing the schedule. The experience of the United States showed that, in a large territory, disease might exist without the knowledge of responsible authority. Mr. Gardner stated that, personally, he would be very glad to restore the privileges.

Feb. 18.—Hon. Edward Blake made his first speech in the British House of Commons. He spoke for an hour and a half, impromptu, in reply to Mr. Chamberlain, dealing forcibly with point after point raised by the latter, and holding the close attention of a full House. While he considered that the Home Rule Bill under discussion amply secured the supremacy of the Imperial Parliament, Mr. Blake said he objected to the suspension of the land question for three years. The Irish Parliament, he thought, ought to be empowered to deal at once with the land problem. Much enthusiasm was shown when the speech was finished, both Liberals and Irish members cheering loudly, the latter standing and waving their hats. Mr. Blake was warmly complimented by a distinguished member of the Cabinet, who is said to have declared the speech one of the best ever heard within the walls of Parliament.

March 6.—Hon. Hugh Nelson, ex-Governor of British Columbia, died in London.

March 14.—Lady Mowat, wife of Sir Oliver Mowat died in Toronto.

March 27.—The gang known as the "Dalton Imitators" sentenced to fifteen, ten, and three years respectively. George Bennett, the leader, was sentenced to five years in the Kingston Penitentiary on each of the three charges against him, making fifteen years in all. He pleaded for leniency for the sake of his young wife and child, who are left unprovided for; but Judge McDougall reminded him that they should have been a consideration to him before he entered on his evil life. William Archer received two terms of ten years in the penitentiary, the sentences to run concurrently. Archer also begged the clemency of the court, protesting that he had been led astray by Norris, who, he said, supplied him with money and liquor. The same plea was put forward by Edward Archer, the last of the trio, who said that on the day of the Roberts' robbery Norris (who, it will be remembered, turned Queen's evidence) had made him drunk and given him a revolver. His Honor remarked that he was persuaded that the prisoner had been equally guilty as his comrades in the Home Savings Company affair, despite the jury's acquittal. He sentenced the prisoner to three years in Kingston Penitentiary.

March 31.—Mrs. Alexander Mackenzie, widow of the late ex-Premier of Canada, died at Toronto.

April 5.—The new Parliament Buildings at Toronto were opened with great ceremony.

April 29.—The Sons of England lifeboat, the "Grace Darling," was put into commission in Toronto Harbor for the season in the presence of an interested and enthusiastic assemblage, numbering over 2,000 persons. The ceremonies were conducted by Mr. Richard Caddick, High Admiral, and other members of the Admiralty Board.

May 2.—The steamer "Chippewa," the biggest boat ever constructed in Ontario, launched at Hamilton. The "Chippewa" is 302 ft. long between perpendiculars, 307 ft. on the deck, and 311 ft. over all. Her moulded beam is 36 ft., and over the guards she is 67 ft., with depth of 13 ft. 6 in. The "Chippewa" is propelled by a walking beam engine of 3,100 horse power, with 57-in. cylinder and 11-ft. stroke. She has five boilers, each 21 ft. long, and 11 ft. 4 in. in diameter. She is a side-wheeler, of the feathering bucket type, and much after the style of the magnificent Hudson River steamers. In the matter of finishing and fitting, she is ahead of anything on Canadian waters.

May 3.—The steamer "City of Collingwood" launched at Owen Sound. The "City of Collingwood" was constructed by Owen Sound's veteran shipbuilder, Captain John Simpson. She is 214 ft. long over all, with 34 ft. beam; depth of hold, 13 ft. Her hull is painted black and her bottom red. She is fitted with triple expansion engines, and is calculated to run about 20 knots an hour. Her cylinders are 18, 30, and 48, with 30-in. stroke. The boilers are steel Scotch tight, 9 ft. in diameter, 11 ft. in length, tested to 162 lbs. The propeller wheel is 10 ft. 8 in. in diameter. The engines and boilers were manufactured by Messrs. Inglis & Sons, Toronto; while the steam-steering gear and capstans are from the Scotch firm of Messrs. Fisher & Co., Paisley. The propeller and hoisting gear, together with the rudder fittings, were supplied by the local firm of Messrs. Kennedy & Sons. All of these contrivances are of the most modern design. The vessel is roomy, there being a large deck space for freight and live stock. Aft of the engine-room are the purser's and steward's offices and quarters, smoking-room, baths, baggage and engineers' rooms, all on the main deck. The saloon is 180 ft. long, and the dining saloon will comfortably seat 100 passengers. The furnishings are handsome, being oak throughout, and are supplied by Messrs. Allan & Co., Toronto. There are fifty-one state-rooms, which will accommodate 150 passengers.

May 10.—The magnificent structure erected by the Confederation Life Association on Richmond, Yonge, and Victoria Streets, Toronto, was formally opened, the auspicious occasion being celebrated by an elaborate banquet tendered by the president and directors to a large number of prominent and representative citizens.

June 3.—A dreadful murder was committed at St. George de Clarenceville, in the County of Missisquoi, Que., whereby Omri Edy, an old farmer of seventy-one years, and his wife and daughter, lost their lives. The deed was discovered by John Gilbert, a French-Canadian, who worked the Omri farm and shared in the profits. His house was about half a mile south of the scene of the tragedy. Between the two intervened extensive barns, stables, and outbuildings, which, with the shade trees, shut out the view from one to the other. According to custom, Gilbert rose about 4 o'clock, and proceeded to the barn to feed the stock. He was there probably twenty minutes; and when he came out at the north side, as near as he could judge, about 4.45, he saw the Omri house was on fire. To use his own expression, smoke "big as a barrel" was rising from the summer kitchen in the rear. He ran across the garden, a space about 100 yards, and, rushing up to the west door, facing the road, broke it in with his foot and shouted "Fire! fire!" An outburst of smoke drove him away. He was well acquainted with the plan of the house, and knew that the old couple were in the habit of sleeping in a bedroom on the ground floor in the northeast corner, and that the daughter generally occupied the room above them. He therefore ran around the house in order to arouse the sleepers. Looking through a window, which was near the bed of Mr. and Mrs. Edy, he observed that it had never been occupied. Breaking a pane, he thrust his hand in, and pulled off the counterpane to satisfy himself that no one was really there. He then ran back to the door which he had first broken in, and, as the outburst of smoke had cleared away, he observed a woman lying on her back on the floor at the left of the threshold, and about four feet from it. Thinking that she had been suffocated, he picked her up and carried her out to the lawn. He there recognized her as Miss Edy, although her

"NINA," 16-FOOT SKIFF, ON TORONTO BAY.

eyes were blackened and her face covered with blood. The perpetrators of the crime were not discovered.

June 12.—In the Police Court, George Pyke, the defaulting accountant of the Imperial Bank, who had been brought back from Kansas City, pleaded guilty to the charges of embezzlement preferred against him, the amounts named in the four specified charges totalling about $3,700. Magistrate Baxter occupied the Bench. The prisoner asked the Crown Attorney if he might go immediately before the County Judge for sentence, and, that official agreeing, Mr.

Baxter committed him for trial accordingly. Pyke was thereupon taken across to the chambers of County Judge Morgan, and repeated before him his plea of guilty. Judge Morgan, in passing sentence, alluded to the prisoner's excellent character previous to the offence of which he now stood convicted, and to the fact that the bank officials had asked for clemency on his behalf. He sentenced him to three months' hard labor in the Central Prison.

June 28.—Facsimiles of the fleet in which Columbus sailed on his voyage of discovery in 1494 visited Toronto. The vessels were the "Santa Maria," the "Pinta," and the "Nina"; and they were in charge of Spanish crews, under the command of Captain Victor ma Concas y Palan, Capitan de Fragata. They were visited during the day of their stay by thousands of the citizens.

June 30.—The following bulletin recording the weather of the past month was issued at Toronto Observatory:

Atmospheric pressure.—The mean atmospheric pressure reduced to sea level was 29.974, being 0.023 above the average. The greatest pressure—30.241—occurred at 8 a.m. of the 8th, and the least—29.526—at 2 p.m. of the 22nd, giving a monthly range of 0.715 in.

Temperature.—The mean temperature was 66.47, being 4.40 higher than the average of fifty-three years, and 1.43 higher than June, 1892. The highest temperature—90.7—occurred on the 19th, and the lowest—48.5—on the 7th. The warmest day was the 19th, mean temperature 77.20; and the coldest the 1st, mean temperature 59.62. On each of twenty-four days the mean temperature was above the average of that particular day, and below on six days.

Dew Point—The mean temperature of the dew point was 58.2.

Humidity—The mean humidity was 75, being 2 per cent. above the average.

Cloudiness—The mean amount of cloud was 48, being 5 per cent. below the average.

Sunshine—The number of hours of direct sunshine was 252.1; number of hours possible, 465.7; ratio, 0.54.

Precipitation—Rain fell on fifteen days to a depth of 1.830 in., being 1.089 in. below the average. Heaviest day's fall, 0.560 in., on the 10th.

Wind—Average velocity without regard to direction, 6.70 miles per hour. Most windy day, 11th; mean velocity, 15.5 miles; greatest velocity in one hour, 28.0 miles, from 3 to 4 p.m. of the 22nd.

Aurora on 18th. Fog on 3rd, 5th, 14th, 21st, and 22nd. Solar halos on 6th and 14th. Thunder or lightning on 2nd, 4th, 10th, 15th, 17th, 21st, 24th, and 25th.

July 1.—Great celebration of Dominion Day at the Chicago Exposition. The Maple Leaf and Beaver (of Canada), the Union Jack and Lion (of England), the Stars and Stripes and Eagle (of the United States), and the Tricolor (of France), mingled at the Exposition during the celebration of Dominion Day, the twenty-sixth anniversary of the Provincial Federation. The Canadian-American League, the French-Canadian Society in Chicago, visiting and resident Canadians and Englishmen, officials from both the mother country and colony, and the whole brigade of British artillery, cavalry, infantry, and bandsmen who make up the tournament here, participated enthusiastically in the demonstration. Chicago's Mayor aroused a succession of hisses in Festival Hall, in the afternoon, by carrying his annexation talk a little too far to suit many of the Canadians who heard him. One of them, a young man, was so carried away by his desire to show himself a loyal subject of the Queen that he tried to tear down one of the British flags resting against the Stars and Stripes over the platform above him. He was unable, however, to pull it down to wave it before the audience, as he had intended to; so he contented himself by interjecting remarks in the Mayor's speech and joining in the hisses. The Mayor's annexation sentiments at first were taken as a joke more than seriously; but when he went on to speak of the Union Jack being wrapped out of sight in the folds of the Stars and Stripes, the Britons in the audience showed their disapproval by vigorous hissing, and the same unpleasant sounds came from the distinguished persons on the platform. The celebration began with the British military officers and men, headed by their band, marching into the park through the 57th Street Gate. An immense throng of people followed the waiting veterans, and kept step with the music. The route was past the State Building, and by the Lake Shore drive to the Canadian Pavilion. A mass of people filled the interior of the building and the avenues leading to it. The flags of England and the Dominion floated from every flag-staff on the pavilion and across the roadway on Victoria House. The band played a little on the pavilion, and then the military procession went to the Transportation Building, where stands the draped model of the sunken battleship "Victoria." There was no standing-room to spare in the main aisle of the building as the band played the "Dead March in Saul," and the crowd stood with uncovered heads. The procession was late in reaching Festival Hall. Nearly 30,000 persons were present. The hall was prettily decorated with the Canadian flag and Union Jack. On the platform sat more than 200 prominent Canadian men and women (some in private life, but many occupying public places). Among them were: The Lieutenant-Governor of Ontario, Mr. George A. Kirkpatrick; Mr. George R. R. Cockburn, M.P. for Centre Toronto, Honorary Commissioner to the Fair and Chairman of the Exercises; Senator Tasse, of Montreal, Honorary Commissioner to the Fair; Mr. John Pearson, President of the Canadian-American League of Chicago; Mr. E. R. Goudie, President of the World's Fair Scottish games; Mr. E. R. Baker, President of the Scottish Assembly of Chicago; and Canon Bruchesi, of the Montreal Cathedral. Others on the platform were: Mayor Harrison; Col. J. Hayes Sailer, British Consul; Sir Henry Truman Wood, of the British Commission; Mr. Walker Fearn, Chief of the Foreign Affairs Department; Mr. Frederick Douglass, and many French-Canadian business men of Chicago.

July 6.—The great International Christian Endeavor Convention was opened at Montreal under the most auspicious circumstances. The visitors were treated to beautiful weather, and the arrangements made by the local committee were so perfect that everything was conducted without the slightest hitch. Early morning prayer meetings were held in St. James' Methodist Church, St. Matthew's Presbyterian Church, Erskine Presbyterian Church, Douglas Methodist Church, and the American Presbyterian Church. Notwithstanding the early hour— 6.30 in the morning—the services were all well attended. When President Clark took the chair at the Drill Hall at 10 o'clock, and called the convention to order, the immense hall contained between five and six thousand delegates. The fair sex predominated, and, in fact, one of the most noticeable features of the convention is the prominent part taken by the women in the proceedings. While the actual attendance of delegates is not up to the first estimates, there must be nearly ten thousand visitors in the city, and both the Drill Hall and tent were thronged with great crowds during the day.

A distinguished excursion party passed over the new Electric Line along the Niagara River. The road is the best equipped electric line on the continent, and nothing was left undone in its construction that could in any way add to its safety or convenience. The ballast is of broken stone; the ties are large; the rails are heavy, and of the very best steel; the bridges are of steel, resting on abutments and pedestals of the finest masonry; and all curves are thoroughly protected with guard rails and rail braces. Specially designed observation cars are used, with three tiers of seats running longitudinally, from which passengers can view the scenery without rising from their seats. The whole road is of the most solid description, and reflects great credit on Mr. W. T. Jennings, under whose direction it was built. The electrical apparatus was furnished by the Canadian General and Electric Company, and is giving every satisfaction. On the arrival of the "Cibola" at Queenston, special open cars were in waiting for the excursion party, and no time was lost in making a start. The road first goes along the edge of the river a short distance until opposite the company's Queenston power-house, after which the cars begin to go along the grade up the mountain, through the village of Queenston, passing within a few feet of where General Brock was killed in the war of 1812. At the Whirlpool, where the river takes an abrupt turn, the cars give the tourists a splendid opportunity of seeing the river and densely-wooded banks. From the viaduct, which is 500 ft. long and 135 ft. high, over the Whirlpool ravine, the Whirlpool Rapids, Suspension and Cantilever bridges, and the town of Niagara Falls, are seen in the distance. On the return journey, a visit was paid to the power-house near the Falls, which is a solid stone structure, fitted up with the latest improvements in electric apparatus. The water from which the power is obtained is taken from the rapids just above the Falls by a flume, 200 ft. long, to the gates, where it plunges a depth of 62 ft. on to the turbines below, and is then carried away by a tunnel 600 ft. long, discharging underneath the Falls. The power is conveyed by the proper shafting and belting to the dynamos in such a manner that any required number of these machines may be used as necessity demands.

July 11.—First day of the National Rifle Association at Bisley Camp, England. The Canadian team arrived, being composed of the following: Col.-Sergt. M. B. Henderson, 63rd Battalion, St. John, N.B.; Lieutenant A. D. Cartwright, 47th Battalion, Toronto; Lieutenant T. Mitchell, 12th Battalion, Toronto; Lieutenant M. Pope, 3rd Victoria

INTERIOR, CHURCH OF THE GESU, MONTREAL.

Rifles, Montreal; Staff-Sergt. J. Crowe, 1st Battalion, Peterborough; Staff-Sergt. J. H. Simpson, 12th Battalion, Toronto; Staff-Sergt. J. Rolston, 20th Battalion, Hagersville; Private W. Langstroth, 62nd Battalion, Hampton, N.B.; Private H. G. Heaven, 20th Battalion, Boyne, Ont.; Staff-Sergt. A. J. Green, 21st Battalion, Essex, Ont.; Sergt. J. Drysdale, M.G.A., Montreal; Private R. Tink, G.G.F.G., Ottawa; Sergt. M. C. Mumford, 63rd Battalion, Halifax; Sergt. B. R. Bent, 93rd Battalion, Amherst, N.S.; Lieutenant J. Limpert, 29th Battalion, Preston, Ont.; Lieutenant T. C. Boville, 43rd Battalion, Ottawa; Lieutenant R. J. Spearing, 53rd Battalion, Sherbrooke, Que.; Battery Sergt.-Major Case, H.G.A., Halifax; Lieutenant J. Dover, 78th Battalion, Truro, N.S. The team were all in the best of health, the commandant being Lieut.-Col. F. C. Denison, of Toronto.

At the Montreal Presbytery, the heresy case of Rev. Prof. John Campbell was taken up. The Moderator, Rev. W. R. Cruikshanks, presided; and among the more prominent delegates present were: Revs. A. J. Mowatt, James Paterson, James Fleck, J. Nichols, Dr. Robertson, Prof. Ross, T. Bennett, S. J. Taylor, Prof. Beadreau, J. MacGillivray, Prof. Scrimger, J. M. Crombie, W. D. Morrison, Dr. McDonald, Dr. Warden, J. L. Morin, Principal MacVicar, Dr. Robert Campbell, J. E. Duclos, C. B. Ross, Prof. Coussirat, F. M. Dewey, G. C. Heine, W. Forlong, R. T. Duclos, Dr. Mackay, W. D. Reid, and Messrs. D. Morrice, J. A. Stewart, W. D. McLaren, John Murray, Stephen Thompson, and William Drysdale. Dr. Robert Campbell moved that the following report of the committee be received and considered: "The committee appointed to confer with Prof. Campbell beg to report that they met with him on the 7th day of this month, all the members being present. Prof. Campbell having acknowledged the substantial correctness of his lecture, a lengthened conference was held with him. Prof. Campbell acknowledged that he had spoken somewhat strongly in the lecture, but declared that he still adhered to the main position taken therein, as previously communicated to the Presbytery in his letter of June 6, 1893, namely, his disbelief in the entire inerrancy of the inspired revelation of the Old Testament. All of which is respectfully submitted. D. H. MacVicar, W. R. Cruikshanks, Robert H. Warden, Robert Campbell, James Paterson.

July 12.—Immense gatherings of the Orange Order in all parts of Ontario.

July 13.—The Governor General and Lady Derby paid their farewell to Montreal, where they have had many pleasant times during their five years' sojourn in Canada. The day was a busy one for the distinguished visitors. During the early part of the morning, they received a number of callers at the Windsor Hotel, including Chief Justice Sir Alexander Lacoste, Administrator of the Province in the absence of Lieutenant-Governor Chapleau, and Lady Lacoste. At 11 o'clock they left the hotel in an open carriage, and, escorted by a troop of the Duke of Connaught Hussars, drove to the new Board of Trade Building. Here the party, which consisted of the Earl and Countess of Derby, Lady Isabella Stanley, Mrs. Lyster, and Major Walsh, A.D.C., were received by Mr. W. W. Ogilvie, the President of the Board, and members of the council. The visit was a purely informal one, there being no address or speeches. There was a large number of members on 'Change at the time, and, as the distinguished visitors passed through the Exchange Hall, the members sang "God Save the Queen." After being shown through the new building, the visitors re-entered their carriage and were driven to the City Hall, where the civic reception took place. The party was received by Mayor Desjardins, City Clerk David, and the members of the Civic Reception Committee. A guard of honor, composed of one hundred men from the 6th Fusiliers, was in attendance. As the visitors passed into the City Hall, the guard of honor saluted and the band played the National Anthem. Lord and Lady Derby and the members of the party were escorted to the Council Chamber, which had been beautifully decorated with natural flowers. There was a large attendance of the aldermen and their friends, and the public was fairly well represented.

Mayor Desjardins read the following address, first in English and then in French:

"To the Right Honorable Frederick Arthur, Earl of Derby, G.C.B., G.C.M.G., etc., etc.

"My Lord: We, the Mayor and Council of the city of Montreal, would assure your Excellency on this, the eve of your departure for England, of our sincere regret at the interruption of the happy relations that have existed between you and the people of Canada. Of the long line of able and illustrious administrators who have occupied the seat of viceregal power in this Dominion, no representative of Her Majesty came to us with loftier claims to respect, both for hereditary honors and personal character and services. Associated for years with our affairs as head of the Colonial Office, your Excellency, in coming to Canada, came not as a stranger among strangers, but as a veteran Minister and an expert in matters colonial among those who knew you by reputation. From the day of your Excellency's arrival, the heart of the Canadian people was wholly yours. The confidence which we had previously based on your repute was deepened by personal knowledge into profound trust and strong attachment. We learned to prize your high sense of justice, your strict impartiality, your generous disregard of the clamors of prejudice. Every year of your Excellency's administration tended to strengthen in Canadian breasts the sentiment of loyalty to the throne and of good will to your Lordship's person. With heartfelt sympathy, the people of Canada shared in the distressful suspense that awaited, not without dread, the fate of a beloved son. With joy we hailed the news of that son's recovery. Again, when the hand of Fate touched the chief of your noble race, we condoled with the sorrowing household, knowing what virtues had vanished from the earth. But we felt the solace of the poet's words, '*Non omnis moriar*,' as doubly true, and that a noble example is a grand heritage. It is the lustre of such examples that gives significance to your Lordship's motto, '*Sans changer*,' and makes true nobility a deathless heirloom.

"My Lord, our functions authorize us to speak for one city only. We have gone beyond our mandate, and have spoken for the whole Dominion; but we speak in an especial manner for Montreal, which is our country's business metropolis. We speak for both sections of our twofold population, for all creeds and classes; and, in bidding your Excellency adieu, we would respectfully include in our homage your gracious consort, the Countess of Derby. In a sense peculiarly true, Her Excellency has been the first lady of the land, and the mothers and daughters of Canada are sorry to part with her.

"Be assured, my Lord, that, whatever Destiny may have in store for you, the good wishes of the people of Montreal will accompany the Countess and yourself, and all the members of your family."

July 26.—First trip of the new steamer "Chippewa" to Niagara.

Aug. 1.—The sixty-fourth session of the Grand Orange Lodge of British America commenced at Sault Ste. Marie, Mr. N. Clarke Wallace, M.P., Grand Master, in the chair, and the following delegates also being present: Hon. Mackenzie Bowell, P.G.M.; E. F. Clarke, M.P.P., D.G.M.; Rev. J. Helliwell, Grand Chaplain; R. Birmingham, Grand Secretary; W. J. Parkhill, Grand Treasurer; James Kelly, Grand Lecturer; E. Floody, G.D. Cor.; Rural Dean Cooper, D.G. Chaplain; James Thompson, D.G. Lecturer; John Sheppard, D.G. Lecturer; Major S. Hughes, M.P., Grand Auditor; W. H. Stewart, Grand Auditor; Thomas Keyes, P.G., Secretary. Members — E. Cochrane, M.P., Dundonald; Senator Clemow, Ottawa; W. A. McCulla, ex-M.P., Brampton; Lieut.-Col. R. Tyrwhitt, M.P., Bradford; W. T. Hodgins, M.P., Hazeldean. Ontario West—James L. Hughes, Grand Master; D. M Jermgan, J.D.G.M.; Rev. W. Walsh, Grand Chaplain; William Lee, Grand Secretary; E. F. Clarke, Grand Treasurer; Charles H. Bailey, G. Lee, Major W. H. Cooper, G.A.O.W., P.G.M.; Major James Bennett, Major H. A. White, His Honor Judge Fitzgerald, William Nicholson. Ontario East—J. H. Delamere, Grand Master; Major T. A. Kidd, D.G.M.; John J. Moore, Past Grand Treasurer. New Brunswick—Major A. J. Armstrong, P.G.M.; James Kelly, D.G.M. Nova Scotia—John C. Glass, G.M. Quebec—William Galbraith, G.M. Manitoba—W. J. Marshall, G.M.; Major Stewart Mulvey, P.G.M.; James Morrow, P.G.M.; Frank D. Stewart, Grand Treasurer. N.W.T.—A. G. Hamilton, G.M. County Masters—Major Thomas H. Elliott, Algoma; Major W. J. Glenn, South Perth; John Bennett, Halton; James Elliott, South Grey; Major John Hughes, West Durham; John Bell, ex-M.P., Lennox and Addington; A. Bradley, Carleton; E. A. Loney, Prescott; A. Sweet, Dundas; W. Griffith, Wentworth; Joseph Harrison, Peterborough; John Mooney, North Huron; Lieut.-Col. J. H. Scott, West Bruce; John J. French, Kent; Captain A. M. Todd, South Huron; W. J. Green, West Peterborough; Lieut.-Col. John Hogg, West Simcoe; Henry Burnett, J.P., Peel; Thomas Telford, East Bruce; A. John Elliott, North Grey; C. W. Cosens, North Perth; Lieut.-Col. W. W. White, West Wellington; James Little, Nipissing; John Blizzard, Northumberland; Jas. Brownlee, Lincoln, P.C.M., three years; E. A. Lanark, P.C.M. County Proxies—Thos. Woods, East Lambton; Rev. Phillip Jones, East Simcoe; James A. Keyes, Lincoln. District Masters—William Bleeks, Richmond; J. Stewart, East Toronto; Thomas Henry, St. Vincent; E. W. Powers, Centre Toronto; James A. Orr, West Nipissing; David Lynn, Macdonald; D. J. Bailey,

Manitoulin; J. J. Hodgins, Bell's Corners; John A. Sissons, Howard and Harrich; Johnston Hoople, Caledonia; Joseph White, East Nipissing; D. C. Masters, William Johnston, West York; Samuel Hagan, Thessalon. District Masters—J. M. Beers, North Ridge; Elijah Miller, Kincardine. District Proxies—John Cox, Montreal; Wm. Little, Nottawasaga; A. F. Campbell, M.PP., Derry West; Dr. R. B. Orr, Northwest Toronto; Robert Hoath, Owen Sound; C. W. Sawers, West Peterborough; Robert Weir, G.M.R., Black Inst. Primrose; D. Goldie, Ayr; Fred Rollins, Madoc; Jacob Steinmiller; Alex. Dobson, Beaverton; J. H. Harvey, Coboconk; A. Wolverton, Wolverton; R. B. Cooper, Belleville; J. G. Bechtel, Burford; J. R. Dafoe, Napanee; A. Hilburn, Neustadt; H. L. Rice, St. Marys; H. A. Mulhern, W. Walker, J. S. Robertson, Toronto; P. R. Hoover, Green River; John Campbell, St. Thomas; Charles Smith, Campbellford; A. H. Stevens, Chatham; J. Rutherford, Blenheim; Joseph Kidd, Tilbury Centre; T. O. Kemp, Seaforth; Angus Plewes, Markdale;

THE IMPERIAL INSTITUTE—BRITISH AMERICAN CONFERENCE ROOM.

Aug. 9.—A large number of anglers gathered at Niagara-on-the-Lake to celebrate the anniversary of Izaak Walton.

The second annual meeting of the Dominion Millers' Association was held in Committee-room A of the Board of Trade Building, Toronto. The President, Mr. M. McLaughlin, presided; and there were present the following members: Vice-President A. H. Baird, Paris; James Hamilton, Glen Huron; James Stark, Paisley; James Hodd, Stratford; M. McLaughlin, Toronto; E. S. Edmondson, Oshawa; James Wills, Plattsburg; Fred Heimbecker, Hanover; Adam E. Ratz, Tavistock; William Pearson, Singhampton; J. E. Pearen, Brampton; J. H. Dracass, Streetsville; Geo. Shepherd, D. C. Thomson, Orillia; William Galbraith, Toronto; John Galbraith, Allandale; F. L. Green, Greenwood; N. Wenger, Ayton; Joshua Howard, Hagersville; James Old, Caledonia; Jas. Huxtable, Horning's Mills; Robert H. Vick, Orillia; S. R. Stuart, Mitchell; W. J. Howson, Teeswater; A. McFall, Bolton; T. F. Brown, Welland; John Brown, Toronto; J. D. Saunby, Toronto; G. S. Baldwin, Aurora; James Fair, Clinton; John Hull, Lakefield; T. T. Dexter, Sebringville; Thomas Soulds, Oakville; Robert Noble, Norval; John Mackay, Bowmanville; George H. Harper, Dundas; W. H. Meldrum, Peterborough; John W. Megers, Listowel; John D. Flavelle, Lindsay; Thomas Sadler, Lindsay; William

Snider, Waterloo; W. D. Mace, Tamworth; G. S. Middaugh, Dunnville; H. B. Schmidt, Newtonbrook; and N. B. Rolston, Hamilton. Baseball Grounds during six days.

Aug. 21.—Grand military parade in Toronto of a company of British soldiers. Exhibitions of military tactics given at the Royal Canadian Dragoons arrived in Toronto from Quebec per special C.P.R. train. They disembarked at the Queen's Wharf, where they were met by Lieut.-Col. Otter and the band of the Royal Canadian Infantry, who escorted them to their new quarters in the fort, where they received a rousing welcome from those who will now be their comrades. The corps numbers fifty-two men, in two detachments; one mounted, the other on foot. The commanding officer is Lieut.-Col. P. G. Turnbull, who served through the Northwest with distinction. Under him are Captain F. T. Lessard, adjutant, and Lieutenant William Forrester, the latter an athlete of some reputation. Many of the men have seen active service and wear honorable decorations. Twelve of the men are English born, four Irish, two Scotch, and the rest Canadian. The uniform is scarlet tunics and trousers of dark blue with yellow facings. The corps was organized ten years ago by Lieut.-Col. Turnbull in Quebec, where it speedily became very popular. They were originally called Hussars, and a few weeks ago were converted into dragoons, when their uniform was changed from dark blue to red. The corps has the reputation of having been always smart and soldier-like in the city where it was born, trained, and fitted for duty; and "their conduct during the ten years of its existence," says *The Quebec Chronicle*, "has been circumspect to the highest degree."

Aug. 26.—Considerable agitation having taken place on the Sunday Street Car question in Toronto, the vote was taken on the subject, and resulted as follows:

Ward.	For.	Against.	Majority For.	Majority Against.
1	1,412	1,386	26	..
2	2,347	2,769	..	422
3	3,177	3,319	..	142
4	2,749	2,876	..	127
5	2,079	2,282	..	203
6	1,390	1,525	..	135
Totals..	13,154	14,157	1,029	
		13,154		26

Total majority against Sunday cars. 1,003
Total votes cast................ 27,311

The following shows the official figures by wards of the vote upon the Sunday Car question recorded at the municipal elections of January, 1892:

Ward.	Yea.	Nay.
1	1,047	1,408
2	1,763	2,643
3	2,669	3,506
4	2,193	2,777
5	1,585	2,352
6	1,094	2,601
	10,351	14,287

Total vote cast.............. 24,638
Majority against 3,936

Sept. 5.—Mr. Wilfrid Laurier, the Dominion Liberal leader, inaugurated his Ontario campaign of political meetings at Newmarket, and was enthusiastically welcomed by an audience numbering from six to seven thousand people. Speeches were delivered by several of the Reform leaders, and all agreed that the demonstration was the most successful they had ever attended. Mr. Laurier spoke for over an hour and a quarter, dealing with the arbitration in Paris on the sealing question, the Canadian tariff, and the Manitoba school question. He inveighed against the policy of protection at considerable length, and pleaded for a tariff for revenue only, stating that protection took more from the people than it put into the treasury. In support of this, he said, among other things, that while the Canadian tariff on sugar puts $80,000 in the treasury, it puts $600,000 in the pockets of the refiners. Mr. A. S. Hardy, M.P.P., Commissioner of Crown Lands, announced that, before long, the people would have an opportunity of expressing their opinion of Sir Oliver Mowat and his government. While Mr. Laurier was speaking, the crowd on the platform became so great that the whole structure went to the ground with a crash. It broke down evenly, and, fortunately, no one was injured. There was danger of a stampede towards the ruins; but Mr. James Sutherland, M.P.P., calmed the rising terror by commanding all to remain quiet. None remained calmer than Mr. and Madame Laurier. Mr. Laurier stood erect where he had dropped, turned his head slightly around, saw that his wife was seated calmly on the bench upon which she went down, and slowly said to those about him who showed signs of excitement: "Oh, I see she is all right; I always said she would make a good soldier." In a few minutes Mr. Laurier was standing on the reporters' table, and from that eminence concluded his address.

Sept. 7.—Mr. C. H. Tupper, Minister of Marine and Fisheries, received notification that Her Majesty, in recognition of the value of his services as British agent in the Behring

Sea arbitration, had conferred upon him the title of Knight Commander of the Order of St. Michael and St. George. As his father, the High Commissioner, is a baronet, his title will, of course, descend to his eldest son, Mr. Stewart Tupper, of Winnipeg. The Minister of Marine and Fisheries received the notification in the form of a message from General Montgomery Moore, administrator pending the arrival of Lord Aberdeen.

Sept. 13.—A gathering of the first importance to the Church of England in Canada took place in Toronto, and was continued several days. In pursuance of a call issued by the Metropolitan of the Province of Canada, suggested by resolution of the Provincial Synods of Canada and Rupert's Land, delegates from seventeen dioceses met in Trinity College for the purpose of forming a General Synod for the Dominion of Canada. There are twenty dioceses in British America, of which three were not represented—Newfoundland, Selkirk, and Caledonia. Of the seventeen other dioceses sending delegates, the bishops of fourteen were present. The episcopal heads of Montreal, Moosonee, and Mackenzie River were those absent. Besides their Lordships, there were seventy-two duly accredited delegates present, of whom thirty-four are laymen. In the early part of the day a solemn service was held in St. Alban's Cathedral, and at 3 o'clock the delegates assembled in the Convocation Hall of Trinity College to get down to business. Some surprise was created by the action of the bishops, who, after the Metropolitan of Canada had named a temporary chairman, marched in a body out of the meeting, leaving the clergy and laity to shift for themselves. Their Lordships proceeded to the library, and in private conclave proceeded to the House of Bishops, while the delegates discussed for a couple of hours the best method of getting them back again. It appears that the bishops assumed that the General Synod was in session when the meeting was opened; whereas the delegates, or the majority of them, considered the proceedings as merely preliminary to the formation of the General Synod. If the assumption of their Lordships were acknowledged as correct, the question of an Upper and a Lower House would be tacitly settled; but the clerical and lay delegates desired evidently that that question, along with all others affecting the constitution, should be freely discussed and voted upon.

The following report of a joint committee was ultimately agreed upon: "That having considered the actions of the Provincial Synods of Canada and Rupert's Land, and of the several dioceses, your committee are of the opinion that the position of this body now is that it is prepared to declare itself a General Synod on the following basis, subject to any amendments which may be made and assented to at this session: We, the bishops of the Holy Catholic Church, in full communion with the Church of England, together with the delegates from the clergy and laity now assembled in the first General Synod of the Church in the Dominion of Canada, hereby make the following solemn declaration: We desire the Church, in the Dominion of Canada, to continue an integral portion of the great Anglican communion composed of the churches which—united under one divine Head in the fellowship of one Catholic and Apostolic Church, holding one faith, revealed in Holy Writ, and defined in the creeds as maintained by the undivided Primitive Church in the four Ecumenical Councils, receiving the same canonical scriptures of the Old and New Testaments, as containing all things necessary to salvation —teach the same Word of God, partake of the same divinely ordained sacraments, through the ministry of the same apostolic orders, and worship one God and Father through the same Lord Jesus Christ, by the same holy and divine Spirit, which is given to those that believe to guide them into all truth; and we are determined, by the help of God, to hold and maintain the doctrines and sacraments of Christ, together with the order and government of the Church as the Lord hath commanded in His Holy Word, and as the Church of England hath received and set forth the same in the Book of Common Prayer, and administration of the sacraments, and other rights and ceremonies of the Church according to the use of the Church of England, together with the Psalter or Psalms of David, appointed as they are to be sung or said in churches, and the form or manner of making, ordaining, and consecrating all bishops, priests, and deacons, and in the Thirty-nine Articles of Religion, and to transmit the same, unimpaired, to our posterity."

The following constitution was also agreed upon:

"1. There shall be a General Synod, consisting of the bishops of the Church of England in the Dominion of Canada, and of delegates chosen from the clergy and the laity. The delegates shall be chosen by the several Diocesan Synods according to such rules as they may adopt, or, in a diocese which has no synodical organization, may be appointed by the bishop. The representation

Mount Pleasant, North Toronto.

Photo. by Harry English.

shall be as follows: Dioceses having fewer than twenty-five licensed clergymen, one delegate from each order; dioceses having twenty-five and fewer than fifty licensed clergymen, two of each order; dioceses having fifty and fewer than one hundred, three of each order; dioceses having one hundred licensed clergymen and upwards, four of each order.

"2. The Synod shall consist of two Houses—the bishops constituting the Upper, and the clergy and laity together the Lower House. The clergy and laity shall vote by orders, if required.

"3. The president of the General Synod, who shall be styled the Primate, shall be elected by the House of Bishops from among the metropolitans or bishops not in any ecclesiastical province. The Primate shall hold office for life, or so long as he is bishop of any diocese of the General Synod; nevertheless, he may resign at any time.

"4. The General Synod shall have the power to deal with all matters affecting in any way the general interests and well-being of the Church within its jurisdiction; provided that no canons or resolutions of a coercive character, or involving penalties or disabilities, shall be operative in any ecclesiastical province, or in any diocese not included in an ecclesiastical province, until accepted by the synod of such province or diocese, and that the jurisdiction of the General Synod shall not withdraw from the Provincial Synod the right of passing upon any object falling within its jurisdiction at the time of the formation of the General Synod.

"5. The following, or such like objects, may be suggested as properly coming within the jurisdiction of the General Synod:

"(a) Matters of doctrine, worship, and discipline.

"(b) All agencies employed in the carrying on of the general work of the Church.

"(c) The general missionary and educational work of the Church.

"(d) The adjustment, with consent of the dioceses, of the relations between dioceses in respect to Clergy, Widows' and Orphans', and Superannuation Funds.

"(e) Regulations affecting the transfer of clergy from one diocese to another.

"(f) Education and training of candidates for holy orders.

"(g) Constitution and powers of an appellate tribunal.

"(h) The erection, division, or rearrangement of provinces, with the consent of any existing provinces interested. But the erection, division, and rearrangement of dioceses, and the appointment and consecration of bishops, within a province, shall be dealt with by the synod of that province.

"(j) That nothing in the foregoing scheme or in the constitution to be framed thereunder shall affect any canons or enactments of the provincial or diocesan synods in force at the time of the ratification of said constitution by this Synod.

"7. For the expenses of the Synod, including the necessary travelling expenses of the members, there shall be an annual assessment of the dioceses, proportioned to their representation, exempting those which are entitled to send only one representative of each order.

"8. The words, 'ecclesiastical province,' heretofore used, shall mean any group of dioceses under the jurisdiction of a Provincial Synod.

"9. We declare that the General Synod, when formed, does not intend to, and shall not, take away from or interfere with any rights, powers, or jurisdiction of any diocesan synod within its own territorial limits, as now held or exercised by such diocesan synod.

"10. We declare that the constitution of a General Synod involves no change in the existing system of Provincial Synods, but the retention or abolition of Provincial Synods is left to be dealt with according to the requirements of the various provinces as to such provinces and the dioceses therein may seem proper."

On *Sept. 18*, in St. James' Cathedral, Toronto, a solemn and impressive service was held in celebration of the organization and establishment of the General Synod of Canada. The sermon was preached by the Bishop of New Westminster, the cathedral being crowded to the doors.

At the meeting of the General Synod, on the following day, the announcement was made that the most Rev. R. Machray, Metropolitan of Rupert's Land, had been elected by the bishops Primate of all Canada. By this action he becomes Archbishop of Rupert's Land; and by virtue of a resolution passed by the General Synod, the Metropolitan of the Province of Canada, Bishop Lewis, becomes the Archbishop of Ontario. Shortly after the House of Delegates opened, the House of Bishops sought an audience. When they reached the platform, Bishop Machray ascended the throne. This was the first intimation of his election, and it was received with loud applause.

Oct. 7.—John R. Hooper, who is charged with the alleged murder of his wife, is arrested at Port Hope.

A great demonstration held at Glencoe, Ont., in favor of Sir John Thompson's

Government. On the platform were the following members of the Cabinet: Sir John Thompson, Sir Adolphe Caron, Mr. John Haggart, Mr. T. Mayne Daly, and Mr. N. Clarke Wallace, who joined the party here, and the following gentlemen: Dr. Roome, M.P.; Messrs. A. D. Ingram, M.P.; J. A. Leitch, Reeve of Glencoe; A. H. Backhouse,

THE MOST REV. ARCHBISHOP MACHRAY,
Primate of Canada.

President of the East Elgin L.C.A.; George Richardson, Secretary of the West Middlesex L.C.A.; George M. Harrison, Town Clerk; Chiefs Joseph Fisher, of the Chippewa Band, and Scobie Logan, of the Muncey Band; Messrs. Mark Master, John Oldrieve, J. F. Simpson, R. F. Munson, J. H. Brownlee, and A. J. Campbell, Glencoe; R. W. Barker, A. G. Chisholm, London; H. F. Fell, G. W. Huston, W. J. French, M. J. Simpson, George Young, O. N. Sexsmith, Dr. McIntyre, Angus Campbell, Rev. W. Lowe, W. Swaisland, J. G. Roome, J. M. Corneil, R. Clanahan, S. J. Walker, David Cowan, E. L. Mott, and George Parrott, Glencoe.

Oct. 10.—The sound of war was heard all day in Halifax, Nova Scotia. Five thousand men under arms manœuvred in and about the eight forts at the entrance to the harbor and on the warships of the British fleet. The regular forces were augmented by all the militia at this point. The object of the operations was to test the ability of the land forces and fortifications to resist a possible attack, either by land or sea. Early in the morning the "Blake" and "Tartar" went to sea, and military were stationed in all the forts. The first movement was the landing by a torpedo boat of a party of sailors at Herring Cove. They stole along the road two miles to York redoubt, and surprised the garrison there. An alarm was given and hostilities began. In the engagement a sailor had one arm blown off, and the other hand split to the wrist. In the hurry of firing, the field gun was improperly sponged out, and the new charge exploded prematurely. Following the attack on York redoubt by the land forces was a bombardment by the "Blake" and "Tartar." Then the cannonade became general from all the forts and ships. Meantime, another landing party of 250 sailors was making its way along the road towards the northwest arm to reach the city. They were met by the 66th, and another engagement took place. Another casualty occurred here, a private of the 66th having his ear blown off by a comrade's rifle. The progress of the invaders was stopped, and the interest was again centred in the firing between ships and forts. The official announcement of the result of the tactics and manœuvres has not yet been made. To-day's engagement is understood to be more favorable to the defending forces than at former operations. York redoubt was more effective than before. A prominent officer in the Royal Artillery said that the ships were well within range of the guns at the redoubt and McNabb's Island, and that they could never have stood the fire from the forts; that at times the other forts would have been very destructive.

Oct. 23.—Royal Prohibition Commission opened their investigations in Toronto. There were on the commission: Sir Joseph Hickson (chairman), Judge McDonald, Messrs. E. F. Clarke and G. A. Gigault. Mr. L. P. Kribs, acting for the antis, was also present.

Oct. 25.—Lord and Lady Aberdeen warmly received by Toronto.

Oct. 31.—The trial of Luckey, for the murder of his sister, began at Brockville.
Sir John Abbott, ex-Premier of Canada, died at Montreal.

Nov. 1.—The memorial statue to the late Sir John A. Macdonald was unveiled in Hamilton. Canada's Premier was present to pay hearty tribute to his predecessor and friend, and representative statesmen from the various parts of the Dominion congregated to do honor to a Canadian patriot. The men who came together to do honor to the occasion were Canadians before everything else. And the gathering, the addresses that were delivered, and the noble spirit of nationalism and loyalty that breathed through it all, were not only a fitting tribute to the first of Canada's Premiers, but were an honor and credit to the country as a whole.

Nov. 9.—The Quebec Legislature was opened by the Lieutenant-Governor.

Nov. 20.—Three foolish youths made an attempt to blow down the Nelson Monument at Montreal.

Nov. 22.—Thomas McGreevy and Nicholas K. Connolly, who have been on trial seven days on the charge of conspiracy against the public treasure chest, were found guilty at Ottawa, and were sentenced by Judge Rose to one year's imprisonment in the county jail there, without hard labor. This was the end of the great conspiracy trial.

Dec. 7.—Funeral of the late ex-Governor Boyd at St. John, N.B., the largest ever seen in that city.

THE LATE MR. W. H. HOWLAND,
Ex-Mayor of Toronto.

Dec. 12.—Death of Mr. W. H. Howland, ex-Mayor of Toronto, and a well-known philanthropist.

Dec. 15.—Execution of Charles Luckey at Brockville for the murder of his parents.

Dec. 17.—Mr. and Mrs. James Williams, a highly-respected old couple living on the public road about a mile and a half north of Port Credit, were found murdered in their house. The murder is supposed to have been committed on the 15th inst. The bodies were discovered by the neighbors, whose suspicions had been excited by the absence of any signs of life about the Williams' place. The old man was found sitting in a chair, with a coat thrown over his head, which had been crushed in by repeated blows. Mrs. Williams had been struck down at the door and her body dragged into the house. It would seem that she had been attempting to escape when overtaken by the murderer. The house had been ransacked, but nothing can be said as to what booty was secured. From the marks in the snow, it would appear that the murderer or murderers drove towards Toronto.

Dec. 18.—Great storm on this Friday night and Saturday morning, which was particularly disastrous in Toronto and neighborhood, where traffic was, for a time, stopped, and electric wires and poles were blown down in all directions. The first indication that the Observatory had of the storm was on Wednesday morning, when a general decrease in the pressure was observed over Wyoming, U.S. The storm moved in a southeasterly direction, and on Thursday evening it was central over Colorado. At the rate of 800 miles a day it advanced, and on Friday morning it was central over Iowa. It then developed considerable energy, and on Friday night was central over Grand Haven, Michigan. From there, it moved northeastward to the Gulf of St. Lawrence and dispersed. While the storm was passing over Toronto, its centre was slightly to the north of the city. Farther to the north there was a heavy snowstorm, and farther to the south a heavy rainstorm. Along the dividing line of these two currents of cold and warm air melted snow and rain fell, and froze on all objects. This line of demarcation extended as far eastward as Kingston, where it went into American territory, and did not again come into Canada till it reached the Bay of Fundy, giving a heavy fall of rain to the south, and a heavy fall of snow throughout the Provinces of Quebec and New Brunswick. The storm was followed by higher pressure, and colder air drawn in from the north and northwest. An important cyclone set in over the Northwest, which gave decidedly milder weather, and caused a gale throughout Alberta and Manitoba.

St. Catherine Street, Montreal, in Winter.

THE WORLD'S RECORD FOR 1893.

EVENTS IN GREAT BRITAIN AND IN THE PRINCIPAL COUNTRIES OF THE GLOBE.

HE year 1893, in Great Britain and the world at large, was not marked by any very great events. It saw the marriages of two of the Queen's grandchildren. In the British Parliament, it saw the Home Rule Bill forced through the House of Commons by a narrow majority, and rejected by the Lords. The greatest disturbances were those which took place in the labor world, there being three disastrous strikes — the cotton strike, the Hull dock strike, and the great coal strike. A terrible disaster came to the Navy in the loss of H.M.S. "Victoria." There was a great demonstration of French and Russian vessels at Toulon. There was a threatened dispute between France and Britain in connection with the Siam matter, and a war between the forces of Cape Colony and King Lobengula, the chief of the Matabele.

THE ROYAL FAMILY.

On March 25, the Queen left Windsor for Florence, travelling *via* Cherbourg and Mont Cenis, but, before leaving, witnessed a performance at Windsor of Lord Tennyson's "Becket," by Mr. Henry Irving and the Lyceum Company. Her Majesty was accompanied abroad by Prince and Princess Henry of Battenberg, and was received at Florence by the British Ambassador to Rome and the Duke of Aosta. Her Majesty took part in the festivities at Florence in honor of the silver wedding of the King and Queen of Italy, and saw the illuminations of the city in the evening. The Queen left Florence on April 26, after bestowing several gifts of jewelry and leaving money for the poor with the authorities, and, travelling *via* Strasburg and Flushing, reached Port Victoria in the "Victoria and Albert" on the 28th. The Court remained at Windsor for some time, where the Queen received many visitors, and formally announced, on May 3, the engagement of the Duke of York to Princess Victoria May of Teck. Wednesday, May 10, saw the first of the great ceremonies of the year, when Her Majesty opened the Imperial Institute, South Kensington. The weather was perfect, and the pageant a most splendid one, additional brightness being lent to it by the presence of the Maharajah of Bhownagar, the Rajah of Kapurthala, and the Thakore Sahib of Gondal, with their suites, and by the contingents of troops from the colonies, which included officers and men from Canada, New South Wales, and the Indian Army. The Queen arrived in a carriage drawn by six cream-colored ponies, and was received at the entrance to the Institute by the Prince of Wales, as president, the rest of the Royal Family, and the officials and suite. The opening ceremony was performed in the Great Hall, which had been arranged for the occasion; and when the building was declared open, the Prince, by turning a key in the model of the Institute, set the peal of new bells in the tower ringing. After the ceremony, Her Majesty was conducted over the building. As this was the first appearance in public of the Duke of York and Princess May since their betrothal, the event caused a good deal of interest, and the Prince and Princess were received with much enthusiasm. During the third week in May Her Majesty left Windsor for Balmoral, where the Princess of Wales paid her a visit, and again returned south on June 20, to superintend the preparations which were taking place for the marriage of the Duke of York. At the beginning of July, the Queen received a succession of guests at the Castle, and the Comédie Française went down to Windsor to play "La Joie Fait Peur" and "L'Eté de Saint Martin" in the Waterloo Chamber. Her Majesty also came to town on Coronation Day to unveil the statue of herself by Princess Louise in Kensington Gardens. On July 5, the Court came to Buckingham Palace for the Duke of York's wedding, and returned to Windsor on the Friday, where Her Majesty entertained most of the Royal guests who came to England for the ceremony. On the 15th, "Cavalleria Rusticana" and "L'Amico Fritz" were performed at the Castle; and

The Loss of the British Battleship "Victoria."

after receiving many deputations of congratulations on her grandson's marriage, and addressing a letter of thanks to the nation, Her Majesty went to Osborne on July 20, where she was attended by the Duchess of Connaught and Princess Beatrice. On the 29th, the German Emperor arrived at Cowes to visit the Queen and to take part in the Cowes Regatta, for which purpose he had brought over his yacht "Meteor," formerly known as the "Thistle." Towards the end of the month, the Queen heard, with great grief, of the death of her cousin and brother-in-law, the Duke of Saxe-Coburg-Gotha, the only brother of the Prince Consort; and on the 28th the Court left Osborne for Balmoral, which was reached on the evening of the following day. There the Queen led a quiet and retired life, among those visiting at the Castle being Prince and Princess Henry of Battenberg and their children, the Duchess of Connaught and her daughters, the Duke and Duchess of York, Prince Arthur of Connaught and his father, and the Duke and Duchess of Fife. Early in September, Her Majesty laid the foundation stone of a new church at Crathie, which is to be built in the early Scottish style. Towards the end of October, private theatricals were held at the Castle, the Princess Beatrice appearing in the "Scrap of Paper," and afterwards Mr. John Hare's Company gave a representation of "Diplomacy," while, on November 13, the Carl Rosa Opera Company gave a performance of "Fra Diavolo." Her Majesty returned to Windsor on the 18th, after a rough and boisterous journey, and the various members of the Royal Family paid her short visits in turn.

The Prince and Princess of Wales began the year very quietly at Sandringham, as no return to public life was made until after the anniversary of Prince Albert Victor's death, the only incident of note being that the Duke of York was promoted to be a captain in the Royal Navy on January 1. But in February the Princes began to resume their places in the life of the nation, the Duke of York making his first appearance in public as president of the banquet of the National Society for the Prevention of Cruelty to Children, and the Prince holding his first levee on February 20. Both the Prince and the Duke were extremely busy all through the spring, the Prince, among other things, opening the Tate Free Library at Brixton on March 4. Early in the month, the Princess and her daughters came to Marlborough House, but did not appear in public, only accompanying the Prince to Windsor when the body of the late Prince Albert Victor was placed in a sarcophagus in the Albert Memorial Chapel. Shortly afterwards the Princess and her daughters went yachting in the Mediterranean in the "Osborne," visiting many places on the coast of Italy, calling upon the King and Queen of Italy at Rome, and having an audience of the Pope. The Princess also stopped at Naples and Syracuse, and towards the end of April was met by her brother, the King of Greece, at Corfu, whence the whole party went on to Athens. After staying about six weeks abroad, the Princess returned to England, and having paid a visit to the Queen at Balmoral returned to London, and appeared several times in public with the Prince. Meanwhile, the Prince of Wales and the Duke of York were very busy with public meetings and functions of all sorts, and later on were joined in London by the Empress Frederick. In April a second daughter was born to the Duke and Duchess of Fife, and shortly afterwards the Prince paid a busy five days' visit to the Duke of Edinburgh at Devonport. Two more levees were held on April 24 and April 29, and, among other public events, the Prince commenced another year of office as Grand Master of the English Freemasons, dined with the Benchers at the Middle Temple, and visited the Wilts Yeomanry at Devizes. The Duke of York represented Her Majesty at Naples and Rome on the occasion of the silver wedding of the King and Queen of Italy, and on May 3 his betrothal to the Princess Victoria May of Teck was made public. He also opened the "Forestries" Exhibition at Earls Court on May 13. The Prince was present at the opening of the Imperial Institute; and on June 6 laid the memorial stone of the new buildings of the Royal United Service Institution, which cover the site of the old Dover House stables, and will contain the library, reading-room, and a lecture hall, and was present at the bazaar held after the ceremony, having the day before attended the dedication of the north transept of St. Bartholomew's, Smithfield. On June 10, the Duke of York opened the new municipal buildings at Richmond. June 24 was a busy day for the Prince of Wales. First, he went to Clerkenwell with the Duke of York to unveil the memorial to the late Duke of Clarence at St. John's Gate, erected by the Order of St. John in honor of their late Sub-Prior. Then he accompanied the Princess and the young Princesses to open the new wing of the Great Ormond Street Hospital for Sick Children, where the Princess received purses on behalf of the institution, and in the evening he dined at the Trinity House

THE DUKE OF YORK, MARRIED JULY 6, 1893.

banquet. Meanwhile, preparations were busily going on for the Royal wedding; but this did not prevent the Prince and his whole family from being present at the opening of the National Workmen's Exhibition at Islington, nor from opening a bazaar in the Westminster Town Hall in aid of the Alexandra Hospital for Children with Hip Disease. The Royal party at Marlborough House for the Duke of York's wedding included the King and Queen of Denmark and the Czarevitch—the Princess of Wales' nearest foreign relatives. On the Saturday following the Royal wedding, the King and Queen of Denmark visited the city with the Czarevitch and the Prince and Princess. The Royal guests were received in the Guildhall, and the Queen of Denmark was presented by the Lady Mayoress with a lovely bouquet, while Miss Brookman offered another to the Princess of Wales. The Common Serjeant read an address to their Majesties from a large roll of vellum, mounted in crimson silk and bordered with gold; and after this ceremony the Royal party were present at the banquet given in their honor. The Prince of Wales, with the young Princesses, the King of Denmark, and Prince Waldemar, were present at the State ball; and after the State concert, which closed the Court festivities of the season on July 14, went down to Sandringham for a short rest with the King and Queen of Denmark and Prince Waldemar, the Czarevitch having returned to Russia. But, before leaving London, the Prince and Princess accompanied the King and Queen about London, visiting many charitable institutions, picture galleries, studios, and theatres. The Prince also ran down to Dover to lay the memorial stone of the new harbor works, and then went to Winchester for the quincentenary celebration of the college foundation, when he attended a thanksgiving service in the cathedral, lunched with the Mayor, went over the college, and distributed medals, going on afterwards to Goodwood to stay with the Duke of Richmond for the races. By this time the Sandringham party had dispersed, the King and Queen of Denmark having gone home, while the Princess and her daughters, and, shortly afterwards, the Duke and Duchess of York, returned to London. On July 29, the Prince welcomed the German Emperor at Cowes, having entered his new yacht, the "Britannia," for the races during the Cowes week. The Prince's yacht arrived at Cowes with sixteen winning flags, and at once won the chief match at the Royal London Yacht Club Regatta, when the Prince and the Emperor were on board and took part in the working of the yacht. The following day the "Britannia" was beaten on time allowance by the "Meteor" for the Queen's Cup; but the "Britannia" was, as a rule, very successful, and beat the American yacht "Navahoe" on several occasions. The Princess and her daughters generally viewed the racing from the "Osborne," and only went ashore to visit the Queen. The Prince and Princess left Cowes on August 14, and shortly afterwards the Prince went to Homburg for the waters, and the Princess and her daughters embarked in the Royal yacht "Osborne" for a cruise along the coast of Norway. They arrived at Stavanger on the 18th, and went on as far as Gudvagen before returning, arriving at Fredensborg on September 2. There was a large party at the Castle, including the Czar and Czarina and the King and Queen of Greece; but the death of King Christian's brother put a stop to the festivities. The Prince of Wales left Homburg on September 10, and went to Scotland, where he remained shooting and fishing until the family reassembled at Sandringham. Meanwhile, the Duke and Duchess of York, after spending some time in the Highlands, had great receptions in Edinburgh and York, and, on their arrival in town, laid the foundation stone of the Mission to Seaman's Institute at Poplar—their first public appearance in London since their wedding day. The Prince of Wales joined them in London; and after taking part in several public ceremonies, such as opening the South London Fine Art Gallery at Camberwell, went to Newmarket for the autumn meeting. In the third week in October, the Prince and his family were once more united, the Prince having returned from Essex, the Princess and her daughters from Denmark, the Duke of York from Sandringham, and the Duchess from visiting her parents at the White Lodge, Richmond Park. After spending a short time in London, and paying a few visits, the whole party reassembled at Sandringham early in November, and entertained a large number of guests to celebrate the Prince's birthday. The Prince opened a new recreation and reading room at Wolferton, and gave his annual dinner to the men employed on his estate. Among the house party were the Comte and Comtesse de Paris and Lords Cadogan, Rosebery, and Houghton. Soon afterwards the party broke up, and the Prince came to London to dine with the Benchers at Lincoln's Inn, to open the St. Bride's Printers' Institute, and to attend the first winter lecture at the Imperial Institute.

Since the marriage of the Prince and

The Princess May of Teck, Married July 6, 1893.

Princess of Wales, no Royal wedding has excited anything like such general and widespread interest as that of the Duke of York and Princess Victoria May of Teck. For more than a week before the ceremony, an army of carpenters was engaged in putting up the decorations in the streets; but what was most unusual was the crowd that thronged all parts of London to watch the preparations being made. On July 4 the Princess, accompanied by the Duke and Duchess of Teck, left White Lodge for Buckingham Palace; and on the same evening a gala performance was held at the Opera, the work chosen being Gounod's "Romeo et Juliette," with Madame Melba and the De Reszkes. A few days before the wedding, the distinguished guests began to arrive from abroad, among them being the King and Queen of Denmark and Prince Waldemar, the Czarevitch, the Grand Duke of Hesse, the Crown Prince of Belgium, and Prince and Princess Henry of Prussia. On July 4 the Prince of Wales gave a garden party at Marlborough House, at which Her Majesty, the Royal guests, several Indian princes, and all the most celebrated personages of the day, were present. From an early hour of the morning of Thursday, July 7, an enormous crowd thronged the streets, and all traffic was stopped on the line of route, some 7,000 troops being called into requisition to line the roads. About .11 o'clock the invited guests began to arrive at the Chapel Royal, St. James', and were shown to the seats reserved for them. Shortly before 12, the Archbishop of Canterbury and the officiating clergy assembled, and then those members of the Royal Family who took no part in the procession entered. The first procession, starting from Buckingham Palace, comprised all the Royal guests, the Royal Family, and the bridesmaids, who were ten in number, namely, the Princesses Victoria and Maud of Wales, the Princesses Victoria, Alexandra, and Beatrice of Edinburgh, Princess Victoria of Schleswig-Holstein, the Princesses Margaret and Patricia of Connaught, Princess Victoria Eugenie of Battenberg, and Princess Victoria Alice of Battenberg. The bridegroom was accompanied by the Prince of Wales and the Duke of Edinburgh, and the bride by the Duke of Teck and Prince Adolphus of Teck. Shortly before midday the Queen's procession of four carriages, attended by a field officer's escort of Life Guards and a detachment of native Indian troops, arrived at the Ambassador's Court, where Her Majesty was received by the Great Officers of the Household and conducted to her seat in the *haut pas* of the chapel. Her Majesty wore a dress of black watered silk, richly draped with Honiton lace, the Blue Ribbon of the Garter, and a magnificent necklace and coronet of diamonds. The Queen moved alone, supporting herself by her stick, and was followed by the Princess of Wales, leaning on the arm of her father, the King of Denmark. A quarter of an hour later, the bridegroom's procession

LORD ROBERTS.

came up the chapel, the Prince of Wales, the Duke of Edinburgh, and the Duke of York, being all three in naval uniform. Soon afterwards came the bride's procession, the Princess May being escorted by her father, the Duke of Teck, and having her brother, Prince Adolphus, in Lancer's uniform, on her right, the bridesmaids following to bear the train of her bridal robe. The bride's dress of white satin was specially woven in the Spitalfields looms, and was ornamented with orange blossoms and fine old Honiton point lace; the bodice was made of white and silver brocade, and the veil fell from a diamond tiara, which was surrounded with wreaths of orange blossoms. The ceremony was performed by the Archbishop of Canterbury; and when he pronounced them to be man and wife, the distant booming of a Royal salute of 101 guns was heard, announcing to the crowds outside that the Prince and Princess were married. After the ceremony, the Duke and Duchess advanced and kissed the Queen, the Queen of Denmark, and the Princess of Wales; and then the bride and bridegroom's procession was re-formed, and left the chapel. The Queen shortly afterwards followed, leaning on the arm of the Grand Duke of Hesse, while the trumpets sounded a fanfare and the band

THE DUCHESS OF EDINBURGH.

THE DUKE OF EDINBURGH.

played "God Save the Queen." At Buckingham Palace, the Queen and the bride and bridegroom appeared on the balcony; and then, when the marriage register had been signed, the wedding breakfast was held in the large State dining-room and the ballroom at a number of separate tables. Shortly before 5 the bride and bridegroom left for Liverpool Street, *en route* for Sandringham, their drive to the station, along the Strand and through the city, being one continued ovation. In the evening London was brilliantly illuminated, and the streets were thronged with huge crowds till far into the following morning. In the following week, Her Majesty knighted the Sheriffs of London at Windsor, the Lord Mayor attending with them in State.

THE BRITISH PARLIAMENT.

Parliament reassembled on January 23; and the most remarkable thing about the Queen's speech was the small space allotted to Ireland, only two paragraphs being given to it. Her Majesty's advisers declared that the peace of Europe was assured, and that matters in Uganda and Egypt were satisfactory. The agricultural distress was touched upon; the state of Ireland noticed; and an announcement made that a bill would be submitted to Parliament which had been "prepared with the desire to afford contentment to the Irish people, important relief to Parliament, and additional securities for the strength and union of the Empire." Other

LORD ROSEBERY.

subjects introduced were: Improvement of Registration, Bills on Labor Questions, Parish Councils, Enlargement of the Powers of County Councils, Bills relating to the Church in Scotland and Wales, and the Direct Veto of the Liquor Traffic. The mover and seconder of the Address in the House of Lords were Lords Thring and Brassey, and in the House of Commons Mr. George Lambert and Mr. Mark Beaufoy. The debate on the Address continued till February 11, and on the 13th Mr. Gladstone introduced his Home Rule Bill in a House crowded to the utmost. He spoke for nearly two hours; and, after some debate, the bill was read a first time on the 17th.

LORD HOUGHTON,
Lord-Lieutenant of Ireland.

Then Mr. Fowler introduced the Registration Bill, and Mr. Asquith the Employers' Liability Bill. Several other bills were also read a first time, and on the 23rd the Church Suspensory Bill for Wales was read a first time, the majority being 54. This was a bill in one clause, enacting that in all appointments coming within the scope of the bill, which were made after its passing, all emoluments should be held by the new incumbents subject to the pleasure of Parliament. The result would be that they would have no claims to compensation should a Disestablishment Bill ever be passed. Lord R. Churchill summed the matter up by saying that plunder was the local motive for the bill, and a desire to obtain votes at any price the political motive of the Government. On February 27 the first reading of the Liquor Traffic (Local Control) Bill took place, and its provisions may be summarized thus: One-tenth of the electors in any area may requisition for a poll on the question whether, in houses for the retail sale of intoxicating liquor, total closing shall be adopted within the area, a majority of two-thirds of the persons voting shall decide, and no further appeal shall be permitted for three years; the poll is to be taken by the local authorities; the area is the parish—in small boroughs the whole borough, in larger boroughs the wards; the voting is to be by ballot; all expenses, except the bare expense of taking the poll, are to be illegal; hotels, refreshment rooms at railway stations, and eating-houses, are exempted; the authority of the present licensing body will not be interfered with for three years, though the question of Sunday closing is to be determined in each area by a bare majority, and may be brought into operation at once. On the 24th there was an animated debate

LORD SALISBURY SPEAKING.

on the Army (Annual) Bill, and the House endured an all-night sitting. This bill was read a third time on the 27th; and on the same evening Mr. Balfour moved a vote of censure on the Government, which was defeated by 319 to 272. On the 24th, Sir William Harcourt introduced his Budget, and made his annual statement, which was almost universally pronounced to be the feeblest effort at finance for many years past. The Chancellor of the Exchequer estimated the expenditure for 1893-94 at £91,464,000, and the revenue at £89,890,000, thus showing a deficit of £1,574,000. Customs were estimated at £19,650,000; Excise at £25,140,000; stamps at £13,600,000; land tax, etc., at £2,460,000; and the income tax at £13,400,000. The taxable revenue thus showed a falling off of £590,000. Of the other sources of income, the Post Office was put down at £10,600; Telegraphs at £2,480,000; Crown Lands at £430,000; Suez Canal interest at £220,000; and miscellaneous receipts at £1,950,000. Thus there was a total deficit of £1,574,000; but by placing another penny on the income tax, Sir William estimated that he would obtain a surplus of £176,000. He also proposed to do away with the adhesive stamp in foreign and colonial share certificates, and other securities payable to bearer, and to increase the duty on contract notes from sixpence to one shilling. The Indian Budget statement was taken on September 21, and the third reading of the Appropriation Bill on the following day; and, that done, the two Houses adjourned, the Lords till November 9 and the Commons till November 2. On resuming after the recess, Mr. Gladstone read a carefully-worded minute, in which the Government declared that they felt it their duty to confine, as far as they could, the business of the sittings to the Local Government (England and Wales) Bill and the Employers' Liability Bill, and to the final disposal of those Government bills which were passed through the House of Commons earlier in the session. No new bills were to be introduced unless demanded by financial or administrative necessities, and, to facilitate this, Mr. Gladstone demanded the whole time of the House. The progress of the Employers' Liability Bill was smooth, except in one particular, and that was on the clause prohibiting the workman from contracting himself out of the operation of the Act, as many workmen, especially railway men, were desirous of doing.

THE HOME RULE BILL IN PARLIAMENT.

The debate on the Address having been concluded, Mr. Gladstone introduced his second Home Rule Bill into the House of Commons on February 13. The professed

MR. GLADSTONE,
As he appeared when speaking on the Home Rule Bill.

object of the bill was to establish a legislative body in Dublin for the control of Irish legislative and administrative business consistently with the integrity of Imperial unity.

Eighty-one Irish members were to sit at Westminster, but to vote only on matters of Imperial interest. (This was one of the most contentious points of the whole bill.) The Viceroy was to be appointed for six years, and freed from religious disabilities; his Cabinet was to be an executive committee of the Irish Privy Council, and he himself was to have a veto. Two Chambers were

LORD ROSEBERY,
Speaking in the House of Lords.

to be appointed, a Legislative Council and Legislative Assembly, the former elected on a £20 franchise and 48 in number, and the latter 103 in number and popularly elected for a maximum of five years. The Upper House was to have a suspensory veto for two years, after which the fate of a bill was to be decided by the joint assembly of the two Houses. The powers of this Irish Parliament were defined to make laws for the peace, good government, and order of Ireland in exclusively Irish matters; but certain powers were reserved to the Imperial Parliament, and certain disabilities imposed on the Irish Parliament. Among the powers reserved were: The Crown, Regency, and Viceroyalty, peace, war, and defence, treaties, foreign affairs, dignities and titles, external trade and coinage; while under the incapacities imposed came securities for religious freedom and personal freedom. If the Irish Legislature acted *ultra vires*, appeal was to lie to the Judicial Committee of the Privy Council; but if the Irish Parliament passed any law which was contrary, in any respect, to an Act of Parliament, the law was to be good except so far as it was contrary. The judges were to be irremovable, but the Constabulary to be gradually abolished and replaced by a force owing its existence to the Irish authority. On the question of Finance, all legislation for Customs, Excise, Post Office, and Telegraphs, was to be Imperial; but as far as possible the fund to be appropriated as

Ireland's contribution to the Imperial expenditure was to be the Customs duties, the net sum contributed being estimated at £2,370,000 a year. Finally, land legislation was to be left in the hands of Imperial Parliament for a period of three years. This was the outcome of the seven years of incubation. Great anxiety was shown by members to hear Mr. Gladstone's speech, and at 9.30 the first arrivals came up to the door of the House. At 10.30 about forty members were present, sitting on chairs and even on a waste-paper basket; and when the doors were opened at noon a most unseemly rush took place, members tumbling over one another in their haste to secure seats. Mr. Gladstone rose at 3.30, and spoke for two hours and a quarter. The debate lasted till the 17th, and among those who spoke were Mr. Balfour, Lord R. Churchill, Mr. Labouchere, Mr. Chamberlain, Mr. Courtney, Mr. Goschen, and Mr. John Morley. The points against which criticism was chiefly directed were the retention of the Irish members, which was disapproved of by members on both sides of the House, and the schedules dealing with the redistribution of seats in Ireland. Those relating to the Irish repre-

COL. SAUNDERSON,
The Irish Unionist, making a point in the House of Commons.

sentation at Westminster were considered the worst, owing to their gerrymandering tendencies, as five boroughs which could only muster some fourteen thousand electors between them were to have a member apiece, while the County of Antrim, which contained thirty-three thousand voters, was put off with three members. Then came a long pause, and Parliament was occupied with other matters until April 6, when Mr. Gladstone opened the debate on the second reading, which was opposed by Sir Michael Hicks-Beach. The opening days of the great debate were comparatively orderly; and the speakers who addressed the House as the debate went on, day after day, included Mr. Barton, Mr. Chamberlain, Mr. Justin McCarthy, Mr. Plunket, Sir G. Trevelyan, Mr. Davitt, Mr. Chaplain, Mr. Courtney, Mr. Asquith, Mr. Blake, Mr. Goschen, Lord R. Churchill, Mr. J. Morley, Mr. Sexton, Colonel Saunderson, Sir Henry James, Mr. Balfour, and Mr. Gladstone. The bill was read a second time on the 21st of the month, being carried by 347 to 304 votes. Prolixity was the chief characteristic of the debate, for, though everyone agreed that the speeches would have no effect upon the voting, yet every one was anxious to put on record his opinion of the bill. On May 8 the House went into Committee on the bill, with Mr. Mellor in the chair, and, as an experienced observer remarked, very soon became a bear-garden. Mr. Gladstone, Mr. Balfour, Mr. Chamberlain, and Lord R. Churchill were in constant attendance, and party passion soon blazed up, mocking the authority of the Chairman. Mr. Chamberlain at once brought forward a motion for the postponement of Clause 1, which was negatived by 270 to 213; and on the same evening Mr. Darling's amendment against the restriction of the Imperial Parliamentary power in all matters was rejected by 285 to 233, and Lord R. Churchill's motion to report progress by 307 to 265. Amendments by Mr. Bartley, Mr. W. Redmond, and Mr. T. W. Russell were also negatived, and, on the 12th, Clause 1 was passed by 309 to 267. On the 15th, Clause 2 was debated, Mr. Cavendish's amendment to the effect that the bill should enumerate the specific subjects to be delegated to the Irish Legislature, and several other amendments, being negatived; and the Clause passed two days later by 287 to 225. Clause 3 was under discussion from May 30 to June 13, when Clause 4 was entered upon and continued till the 23rd. By this time the Ministerialists were in despair at the slow progress of the measure, and the Government were being urged to adopt some measures to get the bill through Committee. The Government yielded to these representations; but, before putting on the gag, Mr. Gladstone issued the text of his new financial proposals in connection with the bill. These provided that the public revenue of Ireland should be divided into general revenue and special revenue, the former consisting of (a) the gross revenue; (b) the portion due to Ireland of hereditary revenues of the Crown; and (c) an annual sum for the Customs and Excise duties (if any) collected in Great Britain on articles consumed in Ireland. One-third part of the general revenue of Ireland, and also any Imperial revenue to which Ireland may claim to be entitled, was to be the contribution of Ireland to Imperial charges, the residue forming part of the special revenue of Ireland. After six years, the contribution of Ireland to Imperial charges was to be revised. As to the special revenue, the Irish Parliament might impose taxes which were to form a Consolidated Fund for the public service of Ireland, and various regulations were laid down for the imposition and collection of local taxation, and the Irish Post Office revenue and expenditure. Then, on June 29 and 30, Mr. Gladstone's proposals for applying the closure on the Home Rule Bill were debated, and finally carried by 299 to 267. Under these drastic regulations, most of the clauses were passed without debate; and on July 27, the day appointed, the bill was through Committee, a final battle between Mr. Gladstone and Mr. Chamberlain marking the close of the discussion. But if all members had equally observed the bounds of Parliamentary decorum, the House would have been spared the disgraceful scene which took place that day, and ended in a free fight. Mr. Chamberlain was closing his incisive speech on the bill when one of the Irish members raised the cry of "Judas!." Mr. Gibbs attempted to call the Chairman's attention to it, but the division was allowed to progress. Mr. Logan, a Gladstonian member, crossed the floor of the House close to the Front Opposition Bench, and a rude exchange of words followed, mingled with shouts to Mr. Logan that he was out of order. He then committed a breach of Parliamentary etiquette by sitting down on the Front Opposition Bench. A general fight ensued, and at once fifty or sixty members were engaged in it, and blows were interchanged. Strangers in the gallery hissed loudly. Mr. Mellor took down the word "Judas," and order was restored by the return of the Speaker. The next day apologies were made at the Speaker's instigation, and the incident closed as far as Parliament was concerned. The results of the gag were these: The printed bill extended to 1,495 lines; of these 1,164 were gagged, and only 331 debated. The report stage of the bill began in August, and continued through the month, the third reading being moved by Mr. Gladstone on the 30th, the closure having again been called in to put an end to

Poets' Corner, Westminster Abbey.

the debate. Early on Saturday morning, September 2, the bill was read a third time in the Commons, and was at once hurried across to the Lords, where it was read a first time, thus ensuring its being printed and circulated in time for the second reading on the Tuesday. Earl Spencer moved the reading to the House, crowded in every part, with peeresses in the galleries, the Strangers' Gallery crowded, and members of the House of Commons packed close at the Bar. The Duke of Devonshire moved its rejection, and, during the three days' debate which followed, the Duke of Argyll, Lord Ashbourne, Lord Ripon, Lord Selborne, Lord Rosebery, Lord Dunraven, Lord Herschell, Lord Halsbury, the Bishop of Ripon, and others, spoke. Lord Salisbury wound up the debate in a masterly speech, and, on September 8, the second Home Rule Bill was rejected.

THE BRITISH COAL STRIKE.

In July appeared the first symptoms of the great coal strike, which lasted until November. In Derbyshire the miners voted against the proposed reduction of 25 per cent., and the Lancashire and Cheshire men decided to accept no reduction in wages. Towards the end of the month, some members of the Coalowners' Association gave notice of their intention to reduce wages by 25 per cent., and a special conference of the Miners' Federation opposed any reduction, and made arrangements for a strike. Both sides gave their reasons for their action, and on Friday, July 28, the men struck over the greater part of Central England and North Wales, and the South Wales' miners determined to support the strikers. When notices expired, about two hundred and seventy thousand men were standing idle, and smelting works, potteries, and other manufactories, had to cease work. Early in August the Scotch miners also struck, but in Northumberland the men stuck to their work. In South Wales the men on sliding scale were indignant at the conduct of the strikers, who mobbed Mr. Abraham, M.P., when he advised them to submit to arbitration, and the situation became so threatening that the authorities applied for protection. By the middle of the month two hundred men of the Devonshire Regiment were sent to Ebbw Vale, as some thousands of colliers, armed with clubs, insisted upon the work of the collieries being stopped, and men were being violently assaulted. A number of strikers from Blaenavon and other places marched across the hills to Ebbw Vale, but were stopped by the military and police; so they held a meeting, at which were many Ebbw Vale men armed with sticks. When the strikers began to retire, it was rumored that they meant to return in force, so the Ebbw Vale men attacked them and put them to flight. Soon afterwards another large body of strikers, armed with clubs and spiked sticks, invaded the vale, but were stopped by the military. So threatening was the aspect of affairs that urgent telegrams were sent to Plymouth for additional troops, and upwards of a thousand more men were drafted into the district. This display of force, and the fact that the iron, steel, and tin workers thrown out of employment supported the non-strikers, prevented any more rioting, and the march of the men of the Rhondda Valley to Ebbw Vale ended in a complete fiasco. In South Wales, men were returning to work at the beginning of September, but in many places the strike still went on. In the Midlands an outrage took place at a colliery near Loughton, and both the coalowners and miners held conferences, but without any effect upon the situation, as the masters declared that the attitude of the men afforded no basis for a settlement. In September the interest began to shift from South Wales to the Midlands, where several riots took place, and much damage was done to property. The prolonged strike produced a great deal of distress in the country, and, but for the local residents and tradesmen, the miners' wives and families would have been without food. In Yorkshire, attacks were made upon the collieries at Barrow, Wath, and Pontefract, and coal, timber, and houses were set fire to. At Pontefract, especially, much damage was done before the authorities acted, and when, after much delay, the Riot Act was read, the mob stoned the troops, who then fired. In this unfortunate disturbance lives were lost, and the affair became the subject of an inquiry appointed by the Government. By the beginning of November some way of settling the dispute was ardently desired on all sides, and on Friday, the 3rd, a joint conference of coalowners and miners met in London. Great things were hoped from it, but the members were unable to agree. The deadlock seemed more hopeless than ever, in spite of the desire of all parties to end the struggle; so the suggestion of Mr. Gladstone that another conference should be held, with Lord Rosebery, a man in whose tact and judgment both sides had confidence, in the chair as moderator and adviser, was eagerly welcomed. Friday, November 17, at 11 a.m., at the Foreign Office, was the date fixed for the meeting, and late in the afternoon a compromise was effected in these terms: A Board of Conciliation was to be appointed

His Holiness Pope Leo XIII.

FESTIVITIES AND CELEBRATIONS.

Of festivities the tale is brief, and even the family affairs of the Sovereign houses of Europe have given less occasion than usual for public holidays. The chief function of this kind was the celebration, in April, of the silver wedding of the King and Queen of Italy. On this occasion, the German Emperor and Empress, and a brave gathering of princes, princesses, and envoys extraordinary, visited Rome. For the better part of a week, the whole of Italy gave itself up to imposing rejoicings, and touching evidences were afforded of the genuine affection in which the Royal couple are held by their subjects. A golden jubilee of a different kind was signalized at Dresden in October, when the veteran King Albert of Saxony received congratulations on the completion of fifty years of his military career. The tireless Emperor of Germany offered his felicitations to the King in person, accompanying them with a splendidly jeweled marshal's baton. Some months previously, the Pope had celebrated his Episcopal jubilee. Rome was filled on the occasion with some 30,000 pilgrims, contributed from nearly every quarter of the globe, and laden with rich gifts for the venerable Pontiff. The most important popular festival of the year was, however, contributed by the great Republic of the New World in the shape of the Chicago Exhibition, which is fully treated of in other pages of this book. In magnitude and magnificence, this review of the forces and products of the world's industry transcended all previous efforts in the same direction. Three days before the opening ceremony, an official welcome to the nations was organized at New York, when President Cleveland reviewed the foreign warships which had been despatched with greetings to the United States. The vessels were anchored in two lines, each stretching over a length of three miles. The two following days were filled with ceremonial functions, and on May 1 President Cleveland formally opened the Fair in the presence of an enormous cosmopolitan crowd. During the six months the Exhibition remained open, it was visited by 21,458,910 persons, besides the holders of free tickets.

THE WAR CLOUD.

Considerable impetus has been given to the movements of the Peace Party everywhere on the Continent by the further increases which have taken place in the armaments of the great Powers. The burden is becoming unbearable, especially in Germany, Austria, and Italy; and it is probably only due to the unmistakable demonstrations which have been afforded of the reality of the rival Franco-Russian Alliance that the protests against the inflated military budgets have not taken a more definite shape. As it is, the new German Army Bills were only passed after a struggle in the constituencies which has revealed a great extension and intensification of popular discontent. The relations of France and Italy were not improved during the year. Riots at Aigues Mortes and elsewhere in France against immigrant Italian workmen tended to embitter the anti-French feeling on the other side of the Alps. In the middle of August, the lamentable proceedings at Aigues Mortes gave rise to turbulent popular demonstrations in Rome, in the course of which an attempt was made to attack the French Embassy. Both Governments, however, acted with promptitude, and in each case the leading rioters were punished.

THE TOULON FESTIVITIES.

The armaments of the Triple Alliance were not permitted to go unanswered by the rival Powers in the east and west of Europe—Russia and France. No special military measures have been necessary in these countries, inasmuch as their respective military and naval plans are on a level with their requirements. In the early stages of the German Army Bill, the necessity for some counter-demonstration in France was much spoken of in the newspapers, and a rumor obtained currency that it was the intention of the Russian Government to despatch a squadron to Toulon in return for the visit of the French Admiral Gervais to Cronstadt in 1891. The project did not assume any definite shape until September, when the Italian Crown Prince attended the German and Austrian army manœuvres, and the Emperor William made a triumphal tour of Alsace and Lorraine. The result was one of the most remarkable outbursts of popular enthusiasm ever witnessed. For nearly a fortnight the whole of France was *en fête.* The Russian Squadron, under Admiral Avellan, reached Toulon on October 13, and received an imposing reception from the French fleet and the military and civil authorities. On the 17th, the Russian Admiral and a detachment of his officers proceeded to Paris. Here a superb welcome awaited them. The city was magnificently decorated, and an uninterrupted series of banquets and other functions were organized in their honor. They were publicly received by the President. The demonstrations in the streets reached such a pitch of enthusiasm that even kisses were showered by patriotic Frenchwomen on the Muscovite guests, and several of the latter

THE LATE MARSHAL MACMAHON.

lost their voices through too hearty an acknowledgment of the compliments offered them. The festivities derived their unique *éclat* from the fact that, for the first time in many years, all factions and classes in France were united in a public ceremonial. Even the Socialists gave a tentative approval to the national rejoicing. The death of Marshal MacMahon on the opening day of the Paris *fêtes* was not allowed to interfere with the programme. Indeed, it added to the solemnity of the celebration, inasmuch as the Russian officers, at the particular command of the Czar, prolonged their stay, so that they might testify their sympathy for France in her loss by attending the funeral of the distinguished soldier at the Invalides. On their way back to Toulon, the progress of Admiral Avellan and his colleagues was punctuated with splendid ovations and entertainments. At Toulon itself, President Carnot bade farewell to his visitors at a review of the combined squadrons; and the visit ended with an exchange of telegrams between the President and the Czar, in which both testified to the close and cordial relations which linked the two nations.

GREAT BRITAIN IN THE MEDITERRANEAN.

The Franco-Russian festivities had an unexpected result. In Germany, Austria, and Italy, they failed altogether to disturb the national equanimity. It was soon appreciated on the Continent that, so far as they revealed a new danger, it was not the Triple Alliance which was affected, but Great Britain. The first note was struck by a series of articles signed "Nauticus," and published in *The Independance Belge*, in which it was argued that the creation of a Russian Mediterranean Squadron destroyed the naval supremacy of Great Britain in that sea. The cue was taken up very widely by the Continental press; and it was shown that, in the Mediterranean, France and Russia had no identity of interests which affected any European Power except Great Britain. Some idea of this kind seems to have dawned on the Cabinet at home, for, concurrently with the anchorage of Admiral Avellan at Toulon, the British Mediterranean Squadron paid ceremonial visits to the Italian ports of Taranto and Spezia, where they were received with splendid hospitality. Unhappily, a very decided emphasis was given to the new view of the Franco-Russian *entente* by the difficulties which had arisen in Egypt and on the northwestern and eastern frontiers of India. It became manifest that Great Britain would one day have to reckon in the East, not with Russia alone, but with Russia and France together. Curiously enough, too, the whole year in France had been marked by outbursts of Anglophobia, more or less serious, which showed that the normal tendency of the French people with regard to England was the reverse of benevolent.

EGYPTIAN AFFAIRS.

French hostility to Great Britain assumed its most threatening forms in regard to Egypt and Siam. Except for a rather severe brush with Osman Digna's dervishes at Ambigal early in January, when a British officer was killed, the outlook in the Nile Valley wore a serene aspect at the beginning of 1893. On January 16, however, a profound sensation was caused over all Europe by the announcement that the young Khedive had abruptly dismissed his Premier and his Ministers of Finance and Justice without previously consulting his English advisers, and had appointed in their stead men of notoriously reactionary and anti-British predilections. It was not difficult to recognize the hand of France in this startling revolt. Lord Rosebery dealt with it, however,

The New British Battleship, H.M.S. "Revenge."

with exemplary promptitude and firmness. The rights of the Khedive in the matter of the appointment of Ministers had been distinctly limited by a despatch of Lord Granville in 1884, and on this limitation the British Cabinet vigorously insisted. A stormy interpellation took place in the French Chamber on the 18th, in the course of which M. Develle, the Minister for Foreign Affairs, announced that France would be "calm," but that adequate representations for the protection of the Khedive's "rights" would be made to the Cabinet of St. James. Meanwhile, however, Lord Cromer, by an action at once vigorous and conciliatory, had brought the Khedive to a sense of the peril of his position, and after a little hesitation His Highness capitulated. At the same time a strongly-worded despatch was sent to Cairo by Lord Rosebery, and it was resolved to strengthen the British position by reinforcing the army of occupation. The failure of the intrigue and of the efforts of French diplomacy led to an animated debate in the French Chamber, in the course of which M. Develle pledged himself to an active insistence on the rights of France. The counterpart to this debate was supplied in May by a speech by Mr. Gladstone in the House of Commons, in which the Premier not only expressed approval of the action of Lord Rosebery, but declared that "France had no special title to interfere on this subject." Still hankering after an assertion of his supposed rights, the Khedive visited Constantinople in July, but apparently failed to obtain any support from his suzerain. Since then it is believed that he has accommodated himself to his position, and he has announced his intention of journeying to

LORD CROMER,
British Minister in Egypt.

England at an early date in order to visit Queen Victoria.

THE SIAM AFFAIR.

There can be little doubt that the irritation created in France by the British triumph in Egypt led more or less indirectly to the predatory campaign in Siam. Since the arrival of M. Lanessan at Saigon as Governor-General of French Indo-China, a "forward" policy had been strongly advocated by that gentleman. On the ground of certain shadowy historic traditions of the Annamites, claims had been formulated for the advance of the French frontier to the left bank of the Mekong. These pretensions, which involved one-third of the entire kingdom of Siam, including some of its richest provinces, only excited merriment among the easy-going Siamese; and the so-called "negotiations" at Bangkok dragged on lazily and ineffectually. The claims of the French had, however, roused the apprehensions of English travellers, notably Lord Lamington, the Hon. G. N. Curzon, and Mr. Archer; and, at the height of the Anglo-French conflict on the Egyptian question, it seems to have dawned upon one of those nameless persons who frequently make history that an opportunity for retrieving the shattered prestige of France existed in the far East. However that may be, serious collisions began to take place in the disputed

ABBAS PASHA,
Khedive of Egypt.

provinces between Siamese and Annamite troops, in the course of which the latter incurred certain losses. These were soon magnified into outrages; the patriotic emotions of the French were stirred, and the diplomatic situation on the Menam assumed the forts; and Lord Dufferin, who had been hurriedly despatched to Paris, found it impossible to persuade M. Develle to abate one jot of his extravagant demands. The King of Siam, finding himself without support, accepted the ultimatum; and in October a treaty was signed at Bangkok surrendering to France the whole region she had claimed.

The situation thus created for Great Britain was of undoubted gravity. Apart from the loss of prestige in Siam, the loss of trade in the annexed provinces, and the possible diminution of commercial intercourse with the peninsula generally, the effect of having France for a neighbor on the Burmese frontier, while Russia was pressing forward on the Pamirs, was to place

ADMIRAL HUMANN,
French Commander at Siam.

a threatening aspect. The French preferred a request for immediate redress, which the King promised should be forthcoming as soon as the facts were ascertained. The reply to this was an ultimatum demanding the evacuation of the left bank of the Mekong and a money indemnity. On the expiry of the ultimatum, the French Minister left Bangkok, and a squadron was ordered to the Gulf of Siam. These events caused no little perturbation in England, on account of the important commercial interests of that country in Siam, and the strategical value of the country as a buffer to our Burmese frontier. Lord Rosebery gave pledges in the House of Lords that Great Britain would watch over the integrity of Siam, and, further, announced that the French had promised that no belligerent action should be taken without the English Cabinet being advised. For some reason or other, these assurances proved illusory. French warships forced the Menam, after a gallant resistance by

THE KING OF SIAM.

our Indian Empire between two fires. The seriousness of the position was intensified by the alliance of the two advancing Powers, and by their anti-British demonstrations in the Mediterranean. Recognizing the peril, Lord Rosebery made a somewhat lame effort to avert it. A convention has been concluded with France for the creation of a buffer State in Northern Siam, which will prevent the French and English frontiers from becoming actually coterminous. Towards the creation of this State, which can never be an effectual protection, Great Britain contributes a slice of her Burmese possessions, while France generously yields a small corner of the vast region of which she has despoiled Siam. The net effect of the whole dispute is, then, that France acquires a splendid empire in Indo-China at the expense of Siam, and, at the same time, England is shorn of a small portion of her Eastern dominions. The revenge for Egypt have been subdued with a firm hand; and Lord Lansdowne, on visiting Burma in the fall of the year, was able to testify to the consolidation of the British position in that country. The course of events on the

M. PAVIE,
French Minister at Siam.

THE QUEEN OF SIAM.

northwestern frontier has been more satisfactory. With Russia no further difficulties have arisen, and, pending negotiations with regard to the Pamirs, our neighbors have abstained from any further military expeditions to that inhospitable region. The troubles with the Ameer of Afghanistan, which filled so large a portion of the history of 1892, have been overcome. In October a British Mission, under Sir Mortimer Durand, proceeded to Cabul, and was received with a hospitality which recalled the splendors of the "Arabian Nights." In public durbar, the Ameer assured the British envoy of his unalterable fidelity to Great Britain. All points in dispute between the Indian and Afghan Governments were satisfactorily settled. The relative spheres of influence of the two States were defined, and the Ameer's subsidy was increased from twelve to eighteen lakhs annually. On November 17, the British Mission left Cabul.

was complete. The necessity for keeping France at arm's length on our Burmese frontier has been illustrated during the year by the turbulence of the Kachins and other tribes, who would afford combustible material for the intrigues of an unscrupulous and predatory neighbor. These rebel movements

FORTIFIED ISLAND NEAR BANGKOK, SIAM.

THE WAR IN SOUTH AFRICA.

In July a conflict broke out between the British South Africa Company and Lobengula, King of Matabeleland. The latter claimed the right of raiding and enslaving the natives of Mashonaland, and sent a powerful impi to Fort Victoria to enforce his claims. The British settlements were at once placed in a state of defence, and it was urged on the Home Government that the security of the Zambesian colonies depended upon a decisive blow being struck at the military organization of the Matabele. Mr. Labouchere and his friends raised a loud cry against the policy of the Chartered Company, and for a time Lord Ripon refused

KING LOBENGULA,
From an authentic early photograph.

his consent to a forward movement. Early in October, however, a detachment of Matabele attacked an Imperial force near Tati. Mr. Rhodes, the Premier of Cape Colony and Chairman of the South Africa Company,

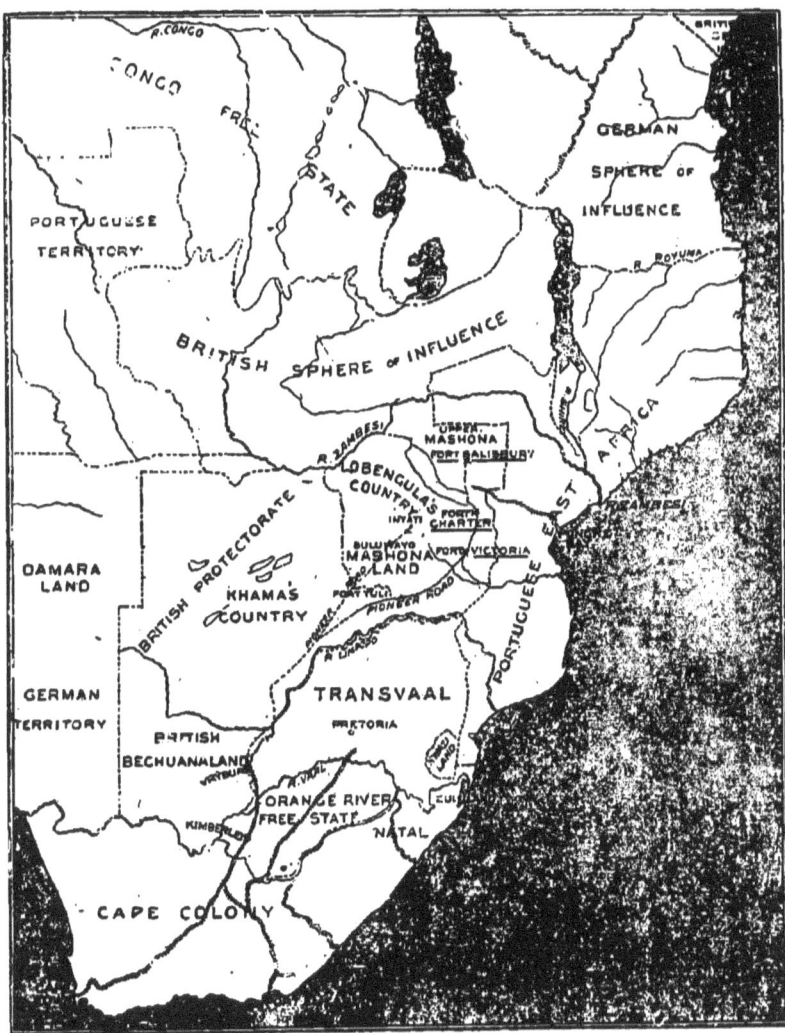

SOUTH AFRICA—Showing Position of Matabeleland.

proceeded north, and two well-equipped columns, composed of colonists, under Dr. Jameson, were despatched against the Matabele. At the same time a force of Bechuanaland police, under Major Goold-Adams, advanced from the south. By a rapid and brilliant series of operations, the forces of the Chartered Company completely defeated the armies of Lobengula, and in November occupied Buluwayo, his capital. Negotiations for the future administration of Matabeleland are now pending between the company and the High Commissioner, Sir H. B. Loch; but meanwhile an administration has been established at Buluwayo, and considerable progress has been made in the pacification of the country. The prospects of the Chartered Company were further improved by the opening of the Beira Railway in October.

THE ANARCHISTS.

Anarchy reared its head with unmistakable vigor and treachery in Europe in 1893. In the early part of the year, anarchist outrages were reported from Rome and Vienna, and infernal machines were sent (happily without evil results) to the German Emperor and Count Caprivi. The most destructive outrages took place, later, in the Spanish province of Barcelona, where an anarchist named Pallos attempted the life of Marshal Campos with a bomb, and a band of hitherto undiscovered miscreants threw two bombs from the gallery of a crowded theatre into the stalls, killing thirty persons. The whole province was, in consequence, placed under martial law. An attempt to imitate this outrage, with more dramatic circumstances, was made in Paris, where an anarchist named Vaillant threw a bomb from one of the galleries of the Chamber of Deputies, fortunately without killing anyone. This daring crime produced a deep impression throughout Europe, and almost every Legislative Assembly sent messages of sympathy to the French Parliament. Severe repressive measures against the anarchists were immediately passed in France, and proposals were made for an international and uniform campaign against them.

FRANCE AND GERMANY.

The Panama scandals seemed at one moment to have involved the whole French Republic. The gloom of the outlook was intensified by the death of M. Jules Ferry—the one strong and uncompromising statesman left to France—which occurred a few days after his sensational election to the Presidency of the Senate. All its good luck seemed to have deserted the Republic. The populace, however, remained calm; and it received its reward at the General Elections, when, for the first time in the history of the Third Republic, a fairly compact majority of Moderates was returned. When the new Parliament met, the impotence of the Radicals and the majority enjoyed by the Opportunists rendered this Cabinet no longer a fair representation of its constituents. Ac-

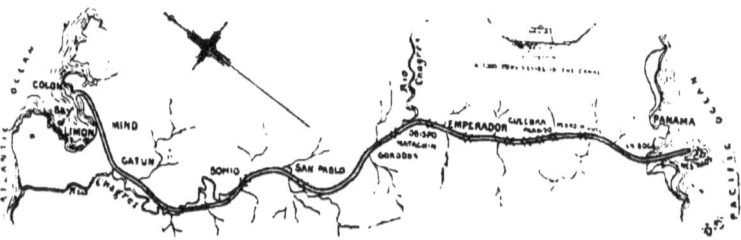

PLAN OF THE PANAMA CANAL'

cordingly, in the beginning of December, it was succeeded by a fresh Ministry under M. Casimir Perier. The only serious breach of the peace in Paris took place in July when the Quartier Latin, after a difference with the police, broke out in open riot. The manifestations assumed serious proportions, and led to the resignation of the Prefect, M. Lozé. Although Germany has also been the scene of both general and local elections, the working of the national pulse does not seem to have been abnormal. The great successes of the Socialists at the polls indicate, as we have already pointed out, an increase in popular discontent. How far this is counterbalanced by the Conservative successes is not clear, since not a few of Count Caprivi's nominal supporters were returned by anti-Semitic and agrarian votes representing forms of discontent almost as aggressive as those which have found their mouthpieces among the Socialists. The tranquillity in Germany was also largely due to the circumstance that, since the passage of the Army Bills, no great controversial measure has reached a critical stage. Evidence is, however, not wanting that the commercial treaty with Russia and the proposed new taxes on wine and tobacco will be strenuously resisted by the Reichstag, and it is not at all improbable that they may lead to a Chancellor crisis. One of the most striking acts of the Reichstag was to pass a resolution advocating the repeal of the anti-Jesuit law. The resolution has, however, yet to be sanctioned by the Federal Council.

OTHER COUNTRIES.

Outside the Suffrage agitation, very little of special interest has occurred in Austria. In Bohemia, the agitation of the Young Czechs has reached so threatening a point that the Government has found itself compelled to resort to a partial suspension of

KING ALEXANDER OF SERVIA.

the constitution. The one event of conspicuous importance in Hungary has been the introduction into Parliament of the Civil Marriages Bill, with the Emperor-King's consent. In Italy the chief events, beyond those already dealt with, have been the continuance of financial difficulties and the consequent fall of two Cabinets. In Russia, the year has been still less eventful. There has been no great calamity like the visitations of famine and cholera in 1892, nor was there any hardening of the Russifying policy which, in previous years, has inflicted such dire hardships on dissenters, like the Jews and Stundists, or on non-Russian nationalities, like the Fins and Poles. In Southeastern Europe, the course of events

was rather more exciting. Difficulties with the Armenians cropped up again in Turkey, and the trial and execution of several who had been implicated in riotous proceedings at Angora were much criticized in England. In Greece, the aggravation of the financial

EX-KING MILAN OF SERVIA.

situation led to a change of Ministry in May, and the return to power of M. Tricoupis in November. The first duty of the new Cabinet was to announce the inability of the country to meet its financial obligations. The most pleasing feature in

EX-QUEEN NATALIE OF SERVIA.

Greek history during 1893 was the completion and inauguration of the Corinth Canal. Servia was the scene of a series of sensational events. Early in January it was announced that the ex-King and Queen had become reconciled, and their divorce was quashed.

THE GREAT MOSQUE AT WAZAN, MOROCCO.

DEPARTURE OF DR. NANSEN, THE SWEDISH EXPLORER, IN THE "FRAM."

In April, the young King effected a *coup d'état* by assuming the reins of power while yet lacking a year to his legal majority. The Regents who showed a disposition to resist were arrested ; but, as the King had secured the adhesion of the Army, no disturbance of the peace ensued. A new Cabinet was formed under Dr. Dokies ; but it resigned in December, owing to a quarrel with the Austrian Government. In Bulgaria (the powder magazine of European politics), events pursued an orderly and serene course. The *status quo* was strengthened by the marriage of Prince Ferdinand, and the national spirit experienced a striking re-awakening over the bier of Prince Alexander of Battenberg, the first ruler of the Principality, whose remains were interred at Sofia amid the most impressive manifestations of national mourning. Financial embarrassments were the main features in Spanish and Portuguese history during the year, and Spain plunged rather more deeply into her difficulties by embarking on a war in Morocco. Beginning with a series of small engagements with the Riff Kabyles at Melilla, successive defeats of the Spaniards led to operations on a large scale. In July, Senor Castelar announced his retirement from public life. In Scandinavia, the contest between Sweden and the Norwegian Home Rulers continued with undiminished bitterness, and as yet no prospect of a solution has been disclosed.

NANSEN.

A pleasanter aspect of life, which also combines the brave and adventurous, is to

DR. NANSEN,
The Swedish Explorer.

be found in the departure of Dr. and Mrs.

Nansen, the Norwegian explorers of the Arctic regions, in their specially built ship, the "Fram," which sailed from Christiana in June.

In honor of Dr. Fridtjof Nansen and his crew, a public banquet, or "kold seksa," was given in the Freemasons' Hall of that city on June 17. Between three and four hundred ladies and gentlemen were present, and the occasion was remarkable for the warm-hearted enthusiasm expressed by the company, which was thoroughly representative in character. The function was conducted in true Norwegian style. At the conclusion of the feast, Professor Mohn, of Christiana University, delivered a short and effective speech, in the course of which he paid a high tribute to Dr. Nansen, both as a man, and as a brother professor and scientist. He alluded to Dr. Nansen's feats in Greenland, and concluded by saying: "Dr. Nansen and his crew will all share the one cabin on the 'Fram'; they will all share the same dangers and the hardships of the voyage; and when they all return, as I firmly believe they will, they will all share equally the honors and congratulations which their success will warrant."

The company then pressed forward to clink glasses with Dr. and Mrs. Nansen, amid lusty shouts of "Skàäl! Skàäl!"

THE AMERICAN CONTINENT.

Ex-Secretary of State James G. Blaine died at Washington on Jan. 27. The President, Mr. Cleveland, issued the following announcement: "It is my painful duty to announce to the people of the United States the death of James Gillespie Blaine, which occurred in this city to-day at 11 o'clock. For a full generation this eminent citizen has occupied a conspicuous and influential position in the nation. His first public service was in the Legislature of his native State. Afterwards, for fourteen years he was a member of the National House of Representatives, and was three times chosen as Speaker. In 1876 he was elected to the Senate. He resigned his seat in that body in 1881 to accept the position of Secretary of State in the Cabinet of President Garfield. After the tragic death of his chief, he resigned from the Cabinet, and, devoting himself to literary work, gave to the public in his 'Twenty Years in Congress' a most valuable and enduring contribution to our political literature. In March, 1889, he again became Secretary of State, and continued to exercise this office until June, 1892. His devotion to the public interests, his marked ability, and his exalted patriotism, have won for him the gratitude and affection of his countrymen,

CATHEDRAL OF ST. JOHN THE EVANGELIST, NEW YORK.

CLEVELAND AND HIS CABINET.

J. S. MORTON,
Secretary of Agriculture.

RICHARD OLNEY,
Attorney-General.

W. S. BISSELL,
Postmaster-General.

PRESIDENT CLEVELAND.

HOKE SMITH,
Secretary of the Interior.

J. G. CARLISLE,
Secretary of the Treasury.

WALTER Q. GRESHAM,
Secretary of State.

DANIEL S. LAMONT,
Secretary of War.

and the admiration of the world. In the varied pursuits of legislation, diplomacy, and literature, his genius has added new lustre to American citizenship. As a suitable expression of the national appreciation of his great public service, and of the general sorrow caused by his death, I direct that on the day of his funeral all the departments of the executive branch of the government at Washington be closed, and that in all public buildings throughout the United States the national flag shall be displayed at half-mast, and that for a period of thirty days the Department of State be draped in mourning."

On December 27 there was laid the corner stone of what promises to be one of the most notable structures in the western hemisphere;

Albany; Littlejohn, of Long Island; Scarboro, of New Jersey; Whittaker, of Pennsylvania; Starkey, of Newark; Talbot, of Wyoming; Brewer, of Montana; and Wells, from far-distant Washington. They were

PRESIDENT PRIXOTO, OF BRAZIL.

supported by an imposing array of clergy, archdeacons, seminary professors, and students, many of whom had come from distant points also.

Political labors in the United States were practically monopolized by President Cleveland's efforts to overturn the economic system of his predecessors. Towards the end of February the President's Cabinet was completed, and early in March his Presidency was solemnly inaugurated. To the struggle which then ensued over the Silver Repeal Bill, and to the preparations which had been made for the abolition of the McKinley tariff, reference has already been made. The local elections held in November seemed to indicate a revulsion of political feeling, but the Democrats contend that the striking successes of the Republicans on that occasion were due to purely personal and local causes.

RT. REV. H. C. POTTER,
Protestant Episcopal Bishop of New York.

for it is confidently expected that the great Cathedral of St. John the Divine, which is to rise on the heights of Morningside Park, in the northern part of Manhattan Island, will be the most impressive religious structure in the new world.

The ceremonies attending the inauguration of so memorable an event were in every way worthy of the occasion. In the huge white tent that had been erected to shelter the company from the blasts that swept up from the Hudson were gathered many of the foremost men of the Episcopal Church in the United States.

Nine bishops were present to add authority to the occasion. They were the presiding bishop, Potter, of New York; Doane, of

ADMIRAL MELLO,
Brazilian Insurgent Leader.

Early in the year a revolution which received the countenance of the retiring President, Mr. Harrison, broke out at Hawaii, and the Queen was dethroned. It having been discovered that the change of government was effected by a minority of the inhabitants, assisted by a force of United States bluejackets, President Cleveland has announced his intention of reinstating the deposed Queen. In the South there have been the usual insurrections and pronunciameintos. The sputter of rebel movements which have marked the history of Brazil since the proclamation of the Republic culminated, in September, in a formidable naval revolt in the Bay of Rio Janeiro. The whole squadron, under Admiral de Mello, turned against the Government and bombarded the capitol. The struggle is still in progress,

QUEEN LILIUOKALANI.

neither side having achieved any decisive success. The rebels established a provisional government in the Province of Santa Catherina, while the Government have been chiefly occupied in purchasing new vessels abroad and organizing a fresh fleet. The Argentine passed through another stormy year of insurrections and Cabinet changes. A revolution has been accomplished in Nicaragua, and the Presidents of Guatemala and Honduras have dispensed with the constitutional machinery of government and proclaimed themselves dictators. Peru and Chili have both experienced Ministerial crises, and the former has lately become involved in a quarrel with Ecuador.

MISCELLANEOUS.

In Australia, the financial crisis has thrown everything else in the shade. The Colonies have, however, not escaped from the epidemic of Cabinet instability which has compassed the whole globe. New Ministries have been formed in Victoria, Queensland, South Australia, and New South Wales. Queensland has been much occupied with the Separation Question, but as yet no satisfactory settlement has been arrived at. In February, the colony was visited by very destructive floods. New Zealand has adopted Woman Franchise, and, in the general election which ensued, the experiment was found to tend in a Conservative direction. Western Australia has passed Manhood Suffrage. In India, the early part of the year was occupied in bidding farewell to Lord Roberts, who had retired from the commandership-in-chief. Considerable difficulty was experienced by the Home Government in finding a successor to Lord Lansdowne in the Viceroyalty. The appointment was offered to Sir Henry Norman, who at first accepted and then declined the offer. Eventually, the Earl of Elgin was nominated, notwithstanding spirited protests and criticisms from the Indian press. A wave of the *odium theologicum* passed over our Eastern dependencies, culminating in serious riots between the Hindoos and Mohammedans at Bombay and Rangoon. Africa has been the scene of many interesting events. The chief of these—the Matabele and Melilla wars, and the Uganda evacuation question—are dealt with in another section of this survey. Mr. Cecil Rhodes, the Cape Premier, found it necessary to reconstruct his Cabinet early in the year. The New Constitution has been proclaimed in Natal, and a responsible Ministry, under Sir John Robinson, has been formed. The Swaziland question has been settled on the basis of a conditional cession of the country to the Boers. The suppression of the slave trade has involved several small campaigns in Nyassaland and the Congo Free State, and the work of delimiting frontiers between Great Britain and France and Germany in the lesser known regions of the Dark Continent has made substantial progress. No addition to the British Empire was made during the year, except that the Solomon Islands in the Western Pacific have been annexed to the Crown.

DISASTERS.

The world's struggles during 1893 have not been prosecuted without the usual tale of calamities and sorrows. In this respect

The Entrance to Rio de Janeiro.

however, the year compares favorably with its predecessor. We have not had any serious visitation of famine, cholera, and influenza; but, on the other hand, we have still a by no means light catalogue of "natural shocks" to look back upon. Zante has been twice shaken by earthquake, and the visitations were accompanied by enormous destruction of property. Blizzards and cyclones on a terrific scale have again ravaged several of the American States, and a storm on the Gulf of Mexico is reported to have ghastly accident of this kind occurred in November, when a vessel loaded with dynamite exploded in the Spanish port of Santander, laying nearly the whole town in ruins. Of accidents by sea, the chief have been the wreck of the Anchor line "Trinacria," off Cape Villano, when thirty lives were lost; the loss of the French despatch vessel, "La Bourdonnais," and twenty-five lives; and the foundering of the English battle-ship, the "Victoria," with Admiral Tryon on board. The latter occurred in smooth

RIVAL RELIGIONS—A MELEE IN BOMBAY.

been attended by the loss of 2,000 lives. Hungary and Roumania have suffered from floods, and a similar calamity swept away many lives and homesteads in the Indian State of Manipur. In May, a landslip occurred in Norway, when 120 persons were killed. Among the miscellaneous disasters in America, which have included the usual catalogue of railway accidents, must be mentioned the burning of a lunatic asylum in New Hampshire and the collapse of Ford's Opera House at Washington. Both disasters involved the loss of many lives. The most water off the coast of Syria, during the evolutions of the Mediterranean Squadron. A miscalculation on the part of the Admiral led to a collision between the "Camperdown" and the flagship, when the latter was rammed and sank within a few minutes. Admiral Tryon and 400 of his crew perished. The disaster plunged the whole country into mourning, and was the occasion for many sympathetic messages from foreign States. In July, a court-martial was held at Malta, extending over ten days. The result was a verdict in accordance with the above facts.

BIOGRAPHICAL MISCELLANEA.

NOTICES AND MEMORIALS RELATING TO 1893.

IZAAK WALTON. — On August 9, in England and many other places, was celebrated the tercentenary of 'Izaak Walton, the author of the "Compleat Angler." Of his first twenty years we know literally nothing at all; at twenty he probably was attached to the business of Henry Walton, a haberdasher in Whitechapel, London. As early as 1619 a poem was dedicated to Izaak, "The Love of Amos and Laura," by S. P. The dedication shows that Walton was himself already a versifier; nobody guessed that he was to be famous as a writer of prose, but as a poet--very far from glorious. Soon we find Walton engaged in the one delight which was as dear to him as angling—the society of the clergy. In 1624, Izaak dwelt in Fleet Street, two doors west of the end of Chancery Lane. Dr. Donne was then vicar of St. Dunstan's in the West. Through his poet-vicar, probably, Walton became the friend of Sir Henry Wotton, Hales of Eton, Dr. Henry King, and other pious and learned persons. He also knew Ben Jonson, and the river-loving poet, Drayton. Together they may have fished the Lea; there was good fishing at Hackney then, and long afterwards. In 1626 Walton married his first wife, Rachel Floud (a watery name); the lady was related to the family of Cranmer. In 1631, Donne died. Walton wrote his life, and a eulogy in verse. In 1639, Wotton writes to Izaak "about the approaching time of the fly and the cork," and this is our earliest proof that Izaak was an angler. He was better with "the cork"—that is, the float—than the fly, being a confirmed bait-fisher. Nothing else not wholly to his credit is known of Walton. The best of men have their faults; bait-fishing was Izaak's "redeeming vice." In 1640, Mrs. Walton died. She and her husband had been tried by the loss of seven children. In 1644, he retired from business, and lived as best he could through "the decay of common honesty" that attended the Great Rebellion. His only comfort was that, at least, he was no Covenanter. In 1646 Walton married again—a Mistress Ken, a kinswoman of the bishop's. His movements are now uncertain.

Probably he lived partly in Stafford, fishing Shawford Brook, which he mentions in a song; partly in London. After Worcester fight, he carried a jewel of Charles II. to Colonel Blague, a cavalier prisoner in the Tower, who made his escape and restored the gem to the King. Ashmole tells the

IZAAK WALTON,
The author of " The Compleat Angler."

story, and says that Walton is "well beloved of all good men." Among Izaak's writings, he mentions the lives of Donne, Wotton, Hooker, and Herbert. Worcester fight was in 1651; in 1653, in his sixtieth year, Walton published his "Compleat Angler." Successive editions were altered and enlarged, but 1653 is the date of the little book for which such enormous sums are paid. No man censured it save that robust salmon-fisher and Cromwellian trooper, Richard Franck. Writing in 1658, Franck calls Izaak's book "an undigested octavo," and Izaak a plagiarist. All good men have been called plagiarists. The truth is that Walton borrowed his fly-fishing lore, as he acknowledged, from Thomas Barker (1651), and that traditional ideas from Dame Juliana Berners occur in his work just as ideas of Walton's occur in all the later angling literature down to our time. A brief record of a long, charitable, kind, and pious life seems the best way of contributing to the memory of Izaak Walton. His pastoral in prose has rarely been blamed, except by Byron and Franck. The charm of peace, content, good will to men; the love of green old England, where still the milkmaids sang, despite religious and political revolution, inform that delightful work, which is like a fragrant flower in the sternest chapter of English history. Say what men will of the Church and the Crown, Nonconformity and Republicanism have never produced—can never produce—a treasure like the "Compleat Angler." A quiet mind had, in those days, its own paradise of content, whither it could withdraw and be in charity with the world. Walton lives with Bunyan, a character as gentle and loving as his own, but trained in another school. Walton, by the Itchen, is not more at ease in his heart and at peace with men than Bunyan in his prison at Bedford. But Walton had never known doubt, or stress of soul, or fear concerning the destiny which is in the hands of God. All these things had been familiar to Bunyan, and he had overcome them all. By waters more peaceful than Shawford Brook these kindred souls, on earth divided, may have met ere now, and known each other for brethren in goodness and charity. The strife of their times may have severed their sympathies on earth; in heaven they know how all things are reconciled in love.

Rev. Dr. Edward McGlynn.—The *causes célèbres* of either civil, criminal, or ecclesiastical courts usually draw their slow lengths through such long periods that, before a final decision is reached in any of them, the ordinary reader has forgotten how the case originated. This is particularly true of ecclesiastical cases, for the trial of them is conducted in a way confusing rather than enlightening to the lay mind. Every newspaper reader knows more or less of the suspension from priestly functions of the Rev. Dr. Edward McGlynn, for many years Rector of St. Stephen's Roman Catholic Church in New York, and President of the Anti-Poverty Society, of his excommunication from his Church, and, quite recently, of the removal of the ban against him and his restoration to the priesthood. In his work among the poor, Dr. McGlynn's attention was attracted by those economical questions which are vexing thinkers all over the world, and he became ambitious to assist in solving that difficult problem—the factors in which are wealth and poverty, happiness and sin. Henry George's ideas appeared to Dr. Mc-Glynn to be proper and practicable; and he became a convert to them, and favored a single tax on land. In 1886, Mr. George was a candidate for Mayor of New York as the nominee of the Labor Party, which favored single tax. Opposed to Mr. George were Mr. Abram S. Hewitt, the nominee of Tammany Hall, and Mr. Theodore Roosevelt,

REV. EDWARD McGLYNN, D.D., *Of the Anti-Poverty Society.*

the Republican candidate. Dr. McGlynn was advertised to speak in favor of Mr. George's election; and as he refused to listen to the objections of Archbishop Corrigan, who did not wish him to do so, the latter suspended him, from his priestly functions, and ultimately ejected him from his house. Dr. McGlynn went on advocating the principles enunciated in "Progress and Poverty," and there began to be rumors that his case would be reviewed at Rome. He was invited to go to Rome and submit himself to the Church. He replied that he would go to Rome if he were informed what he was to do after he got there, but that he could not appear there as a deposed priest asking clemency for sins that he knew not of. His evidence was in America, and, until he knew what he was to disprove, he could not gather it. In all that he did, he was advised by Dr. Burtsell, a man very learned in ecclesiastical law and precedents.

Satolli, the Pope's Ablegate.—When the Catholic Congress met in Baltimore about four years ago, Monsignor Satolli, Archbishop of Lepanto, came to America as the representative of the Pope. In Monsignor Satolli the Pope reposes the most implicit confidence.

Satolli was a pupil in the seminary at Peruggia when the present Pope was only Professor Pecci. When Professor Pecci became a Cardinal, Satolli was a Benedictine monk at Monte Casino. When Cardinal Pecci became Pope Leo XIII., one of his first acts was to appoint Satolli Professor of Dogmatic Theology in the Propaganda. Later, he was made Archbishop. The papal delegate to the congress in Baltimore reported to the Vatican on the general condition of the Church in America, and probably also on many special cases, and among others on the famous McGlynn case. Last autumn, when the World's Columbian Fair was to be dedicated, the Pope sent Monsignor Satolli again to America. The Apostolic delegate arrived in time to witness the Columbian celebration in New York, and also in Chicago, and then he took up his residence at the Catholic University in Washington. He heard the McGlynn case, and just before Christmas rendered his decision in favor of the deposed priest, who was restored to the communion of the Church. On Christmas Day, Dr. McGlynn celebrated mass for the first time since his excommunication. He also

MONSIGNOR SATOLLI,
Papal Ablegate to the United States.

addressed the Anti-Poverty Society. He expressed great joy at the restoration of his priestly functions, but made no apology for the actions which led to his Archbishop's disapproval, nor did he retract any of the views that he so stoutly maintained while he was outside the Church. Instead of retracting anything, he has continued to maintain his views, and in a recent address has defended them because they were in harmony with the Pope's encyclical, *Novarum Rerum*, on the condition of labor. From the encyclical he quoted, "All agree, and there can be no question whatever, that some remedy must be found, and quickly found, for the misery and wretchedness that press so heavily at this moment on the large majority of the very poor." Commenting on this, Dr. McGlynn said : "Large masses of men and women— those who have to do the hardest work—are compelled to work for the smallest possible compensation, because of the failure of our present social adjustments and laws to secure to them the right of labor and to enjoy the fruits of their labor, and they are thus left defenceless to the callousness of employers and the greed of unrestrained competition. Surely it is well worthy of Christians, and most of all of Christian ministers and priests, for the love of God and of His Christ, for the love of those who are stamped with the very image of God by nature, redeemed by Christ's blood, and in His new order of grace called to a supernatural adoption of sonship and union with God, and a closer and holier communion among themselves, to seek to right these wrongs, to denounce them in the very name of God, and to demand the remedy in the name of the law of justice, which is the holy will of God. Surely it would ill become ministers of Christ even to seem to deprecate or oppose the abolition of the poverty that flows from these wrongs, or to thwart or denounce any honest and lawful effort to abolish them." Dr. McGlynn says he is unfeignedly glad to be back in the Church, and Archbishop Corrigan has written the following for publication : " The Archbishop has learned with great pleasure the good news of the return of Dr. McGlynn to the communion of the Church. At the proper time, he will not fail to express to the Most Reverend Delegate Apostolic his thankfulness for the good offices His Excellency has rendered in the premises."

Dr. Jowett.—In October died the Rev. Benjamin Jowett, M.A., LL.D., late Vice-Chancellor of the University of Edinburgh, and Master of Balliol College, Oxford. His father, who died at Tenby in 1859, was the author of a metrical version of the Psalms. Dr. Jowett was educated at St. Paul's School, and elected to a scholarship at Balliol College in 1835. He was tutor of that college from 1842 to 1870, and was appointed Regius Professor of Greek in 1855. He received the honorary degree of LL.D. from the University of Leyden in 1875, from the

University of Edinburgh in 1884, from the University of Dublin in 1886, and from the University of Cambridge in 1890. He contributed an essay on the Interpretation of Scripture to "Essays and Reviews," and

THE LATE DR. JOWETT,
Master of Balliol College, Oxford.

wrote a commentary on the Epistles of St. Paul, and several classical books.

Edwin Booth.—In Edwin Booth, who died on June 7, passed away a notable actor and a notable man. He was the son of the well-known actor Junius Brutus Booth. To the American public the elder Booth's name is identified with the history of their stage, to the development of which he materially contributed; but on the other side of the Atlantic his chief claim to remembrance is his famous contest with Edmund Kean. Bearing a very strong personal resemblance to that great actor, he was engaged by the management of Covent Garden as a counter-attraction to Kean, who was at the height of his reputation at Drury Lane. Kean was clever enough to make his rival break his engagement and come to the opposition theatre; but there his position was soon felt to be untenable, and he returned to Covent Garden. Naturally enough, riots and a bitter paper war ensued, but Booth fairly held his own, and for a few years was a star of some magnitude in that country. In 1821 he came to America, where, with the exception of some short visits to England, he passed the rest of his professional life, dying in harness on Nov. 30, 1852. Edwin Booth—Edwin Thomas Booth, to give him his full name—was born on his father's farm in Harford County, Maryland, on Nov. 13, 1833. Although not intended by his parents for a stage career, Edwin, while still almost a child, went out with his father as companion, and, as was necessary to so wildly eccentric a personage, guide. His father seems, in a sort of moody way, to have opposed Edwin's becoming an actor, and it was by accident, almost, that he made his first appearance as *Tressel*, in "Richard III.," on Sept. 10, 1849. However, in his boundless eccentricity, the elder Booth, shortly afterwards, forced his unwilling son to play *Richard* himself. He was acting at the National Theatre, New York, in 1851, and one night flatly refused to go to the theatre, saying that he felt too unwell to play. Edwin tried all he could to move his father, but without avail; and at last exclaimed in despair: "What will they do without you, father? whom can they substitute at the last moment?" "Go; act it yourself," was the curt response. And in the end Edwin did act it, dressed in his father's clothes, which were "a world too wide," and made a great success. From this time his course was upward, though he had his struggles. It was as the chief actor of America that he appeared in London in 1861 at the Haymarket, where he made an unfortunate start, and was only beginning to be appreciated when the end of his sojourn in Britain

THE LATE EDWIN BOOTH.

came. On his return to the States, he became lessee of the Winter Garden Theatre, New York, where, in 1864, he produced "Hamlet," which had the then unheard-of run of one hundred nights. In April, 1865, occurred the terrible assassination of President Lincoln by the actor's brother, John Wilkes Booth—an event which darkened all Edwin Booth's life. He retired from the stage for nearly a year, and was with difficulty persuaded ever to return. He vowed never again to enter Washington, where the crime was committed, and he kept his vow. At the Winter Garden Theatre, he produced the "legitimate" in magnificent style; and, when the house was burnt down, rebuilt it, and continued his productions. Especially notable were "Hamlet," "Julius Cæsar," "Merchant of Venice," "Winter's Tale," and "Much Ado About Nothing." Financial disaster, unfortunately, overtook this great enterprise; but the work done in these revivals had its lasting influence on the American stage, and Edwin Booth's fame rests securely on these great achievements as manager and actor. Edwin Booth's chief characteristics were imagination, intuitive insight, spontaneous grace, intense emotional fervor, and melancholy refinement. In personal appearance, he was so far unfortunate that he was not of heroic stature; but he had a beautiful face, full of expression and power, and his voice was of magnificent quality. He was a most impressive actor; and no one who has seen can ever forget his *Hamlet*, his *King Lear*, his *Othello*, his *Richelieu*, or his *Bertuccio*.

W. S. GILBERT,
Author of "Pinafore," etc.

Gilbert and Sullivan.—Perhaps there never was a literary and musical partnership which was so well assorted as that which exists between Mr. W. S. Gilbert and Sir Arthur Sullivan. At the mention of their names, the varied scenes and words and music of their operas rise to the mind. "Pinafore," "Patience," "Iolanthe," "The Yeoman of the Guard," "The Gondoliers," and "The Mikado," are only a few of the wonderfully-spirited productions which they have introduced to a grateful public. W. S. Gilbert is fifty-eight years old, and a B.A. of Cambridge. He was educated for the law and called to the Bar, but gravitated towards dramatic literature. Sir Arthur Sullivan is fifty-two years old. His father was Principal

SIR ARTHUR SULLIVAN,
Composer of "Pinafore," etc.

Professor of Kneller Hall, the training school for British military bands. He was a chorister at the Chapel Royal, St. James', where he gained, at the age of fourteen years, the first Mendelssohn scholarship. The honorary degree of Doctor of Music was conferred upon him in 1876, and he was knighted by the Queen at Windsor in 1883.

John Ruskin.—The offering of the laureateship to John Ruskin by Mr. Gladstone was one of the events of the year which caused considerable surprise, as he never was a poet in the highest sense of the word. But as a writer of beautiful and poetical English, he is unequalled in his age. Born amid

JOHN RUSKIN.

circumstances of affluence and surroundings of refinement in 1819, he was educated privately, and at Christ Church, Oxford.

When he was twenty-four years, he wrote the first volume of his monumental work, entitled "Modern Painters," which was virtually a defence of the manner and methods of J. M. W. Turner, a landscape painter who had been exposed to much ignorant criticism. Since then, he has produced a steady stream of literature on many subjects. He has written on architecture and political economy, on churches and on people. One of the most interesting of his works is his autobiography, which he issued a year or two ago under the title of "Præterita."

J. J. Eden.—In Groningen, the northeastern province of the Kingdom of the Netherlands, beyond the Zuyder Zee and Friesland, the International Meeting of Skaters was held on Wednesday, January 11, under the direction of the "Nederlandsch Schaatsenrijdersband" and of the Groningen Ice Club. This was followed on the Friday and Saturday by a more important meeting at Amsterdam. The first meeting was on the lake of Paterswolde, a few miles from the city of Groningen. The 5,000-metres match for amateurs of all nations was won by a young Dutchman, Mr. J. J. Eden, of Haarlem, in 9 mins. 16⅔ secs. There was no English competitor. Mr. Eden won also the Netherlands amateur

J. J. EDEN,
Winner at the International Skating Tournament.

championship in the 1,500-metres race. The match for professional skaters was won by young Marten Kingma, of Grouw,

Friesland; the noted English professional, James Smart, was not present. Thousands of spectators had travelled to Groningen on skates. At the Amsterdam meeting, Norway, Sweden, and Hamburg had sent worthy representatives. There were races, or matches, at 500 metres, 1,500 metres, 5,000 metres, and 10,000 metres. To win the "Championship of the World," a man had to gain three first prizes. This was done by J. J. Eden, but he unluckily fell in the 10,000-metres race. Mr. Eden, but nineteen years of age, defeated all the English amateurs last year at Cambridge, England.

SIGNORA ELEANORA DUSE.

Eleanora Duse.—Signora Duse is a really great actress, who, during the year 1893, made a great impression in dramatic circles, both in Europe and the United States. She was bold enough to play some of Sarah Bernhardt's parts in Italian. Her performance at the Lyric Theatre, in London, constituted one of the memorable features of the dramatic year.

Emin Pasha.—The real name of Emin Pasha was Edward Schnitzler. He was born at Oppeln, in Silesia, in 1840, and was, consequently, fifty-three years old at the time of his violent death in Africa. He early displayed a great love of Natural History. He studied in the medical schools of Breslau and Berlin. He went to Constantinople in 1864, and formed one of an expedition sent out to Arabia. He was away nine years. In 1876 he went to Egypt and offered his services to General Gordon.

The two became fast friends. He was made a Bey, and appointed Governor of the Equatorial Province. In the year 1881 alone

THE LATE EMIN PASHA.

he was instrumental in liberating nearly 700 slaves; but he was at last submerged by the tide of insurrection which swept southward from the Soudan.

Bishop Brooks.—America lost her most distinguished living divine and ecclesiastic—if the latter term be altogether allowable—in Dr. Phillips Brooks, Bishop of Massachusetts, and for many years the leading figure in the

THE LATE BISHOP PHILLIPS BROOKS.

Episcopal Church in the United States, which is, of course, an offshoot of the English Establishment. Dr. Brooks' career is very largely associated with the revival of a liberal form of Anglicanism in Boston, where religious life was, up to the date of his appearance, almost completely in the hands of the Unitarians. Dr. Brooks' eloquence, personal charm, and intellectual strength broke down this monopoly, without at the same time introducing any narrow or harsh standard of theological teaching. He insisted on a more rigid historic interpretation of the Christian faith than Unitarianism allowed. But his energy and powers of speech did not run into a narrow dogmatism, and he was always ready to appear in the pulpits of other sects than his own. Dr. Brooks paid more than one visit to England, and preached before the Queen in Westminster Abbey, on the invitation of Dean Stanley. His famous church at Boston, known as Trinity Church, was burnt down in 1872, and was rebuilt at a cost of $1,100,000. During the Civil War, Dr. Brooks took a considerable part in organizing the work of the Sanitary Commission and the care of the sick and wounded. His church, indeed, was the centre of many kinds of social and intellectual activity. Dr. Brooks was a man of extremely fine presence, and of late years his position as the most notable of American preachers was easily established. His rapidity of utterance—he preached at the rate of 210 words a minute—has often been the subject of comment.

ANDREW CARNEGIE.

Andrew Carnegie.—Andrew Carnegie, the "Iron King," was born at Dunfermline, in Scotland, in 1835. His family removed, in 1845, to the United States, and settled at Pittsburg, Pa.; and two years later, when twelve years old, Andrew began his commercial career by attending to a small stationary engine. This he soon left to become a telegraph messenger, and, later, he became an operator. While clerk of the superintendent of a number of telegraph lines, he aided in the introduction of a sleeping car; and this gave him the nucleus of his present great fortune. He has spent large sums of money for educational and charitable purposes. At his native place, he erected, in 1879, commodious swimming baths, and the following year gave it $40,000 for a free library. He gave $50,000 to the Bellevue Hospital Medical College at New York. In 1885 he gave $500,000 for a public library at Pittsburg, and, in 1886, $250,000 for a music hall at Alleghany City, Pa. Edinburgh has also received $250,000 from him for a free library, and other libraries have been established by him.

Ambassador Phelps.—Hon. William Walter Phelps, American statesman and ambassador to England, was born in New York City on August 24, 1839. He graduated at Yale College in 1860, and at Columbia Law School in 1863. From 1873 to 1875 he was a representative in Congress, and from 1881 to 1882 he was American Minister in Vienna. He re-entered Congress in 1883, and remained a member of the lower branch of that body until 1889, when he was sent to represent the United States in Germany.

MR. PHELPS,
American Ambassador to England.

He was one of the American Commissioners who negotiated with Germany the Samoan treaty early in 1889.

Sergeant Davies.—The Queen's Prizeman for 1893 is a Welshman, the fortunate winner of the big event of the meeting being Sergeant Davies, of the 1st V.B., First Welsh Regiment, whose aggregate, for the three ranges, was 274. This is the first time that a Welshman has succeeded in winning the Queen's Prize, and the first time that

SERGEANT T. W. DAVIES,
Winner of the Queen's Cup.

Sergeant Davies reached the final stage in this competition. There was, of course, great rejoicing among the Welsh colony in camp, who were more numerous than anyone could have imagined. The aggregate made by Sergeant Davies, 274, is three points below that of last year's winner, Major Pollock, who also established a record by winning the silver medal at the same time, a feat that never before had been accomplished. The highest aggregate in the Queen's Prize, 281, under present conditions, was made by Sergeant Reid, of the 1st Lanark Engineers, in 1889, the highest possible being 330. It will thus be seen that Sergeant Davies made an average of little better than inners, which is certainly a very fine performance.

Sir Mortimer Durand.—Sir Mortimer Durand, who was appointed to represent Her Majesty's Indian Government in a mission to Afghanistan, left Peshawur on Sept. 16. The Ameer had consented to receive a mission, and great preparations were made throughout the country. Sir Mortimer was received at Dakka, over the frontier, by the Afghan commander-in-chief, General Sholam Hyder. Cabul was reached on Oct. 2, and the Ameer showed the greatest attention to the members of the mission, receiving them with a salute of twenty-one guns and a parade of his troops, the band playing "God Save the Queen." A first ceremonial interview with the Ameer took place on October 5, and Lieutenant McMahon delivered to him

SIR MORTIMER DURAND,
British Envoy to Afghanistan.

some valuable presents sent by the Indian Government.

Dr. G. S. Ryerson.—Dr. George Sterling Ryerson, whose portrait appears elsewhere, was born in Toronto in 1855. His father was Rev. George Ryerson, brother of the famous educationist, Dr. Egerton Ryerson. Educated at Galt Grammar School, he adopted the profession of medicine, graduating from Trinity College in 1875. After studying his profession in England and in many of the Continental schools of medicine, he returned to Toronto, assuming the Professorship of Eye and Ear Diseases in Trinity College. Appointed as surgeon to the Royal Grenadiers in 1881, he accompanied them to the Northwest on the outbreak of the rebellion in 1885; and so distinguished himself by his unremitting labors in his own field, and by his gallant behavior under fire, that he was decorated with the third class of the Order of St. John, and was recommended for special promotion to the rank of Surgeon-Major, equivalent to that of Lieutenant-Colonel. To Dr. Ryerson is due the honor of having, through his election in 1893 to represent, in the Provincial Legislature, the very important constituency of Toronto, done much to restore confidence to the Conservative party in that city, which was at the time in a state of comparative disorganization. Through his personal popularity, force of character, and unquestionable reputation for a sturdy independence of thought and action, he reconciled two conflicting factions, and solidified them once more into a disciplined phalanx. In the House itself, Dr. Ryerson has come to be a well-known figure. Whether combating what he disapproves, or initiating and promoting much-needed measures, he shines alike as an able coadjutor and as a formidable antagonist. Trenchant in style, a thorough master of the art of marshalling facts in their most effective and logical sequence, and with a keen eye for a flaw in his opponent's harness, his utterances are heard with attention by both sides of the House. That Dr. Ryerson is not content with mere academic and theoretic politics is shown by his bill regulating the sale of milk. To him it was left to point out the absurdity and danger of making penal the sale of impure milk to cheese factories, while, for household consumption, it might be introduced with impunity; and his restrictive bill on that head has been already productive of good in the improved health of the community. Among other contemplated reforms due to him may be mentioned the bill, now under consideration, for the reclamation of inebriates and narcophils; and the careful and scrupulous care with which the liberty of the subject has been safeguarded, while the best interests of humanity have been the first consideration, evidence in him the uncommon power of putting into a practical and workable shape an important social reform. In the House, he occupies the position of leader of the more advanced wing of the Conservative party.

THE LATE LORD EBURY.

Lord Ebury. Lord Ebury, who died in October, was the oldest peer of the British realm, being ninety-one years old at the time of his death. He was a good type of the old-fashioned courtly English gentleman.

M. Waddington.—The late M. William Henry Waddington, whose lamented death occurred so soon after he had presented his letters of recall to Her Majesty at Windsor,

THE LATE M. WADDINGTON,
French Ambassador in London.

was Ambassador at the Court of St. James' since July, 1883. He is the son of a naturalized Englishman who settled in France as a cotton manufacturer, and was born in Paris on December 11, 1826. He was educated at Rugby, where his knowledge of French and his good nature came to the rescue of many of his schoolfellows who were in difficulties over French exercises, and at the close of his school-life entered at Trinity College, Cambridge, where he had a distinguished career. At school he had been noted as a football player; but at Cambridge he took up rowing, joining the Second Trinity Boat Club, and rowing six in the winning Cambridge boat in the Inter-University Race on March 29, 1849. On this occasion M. Waddington scaled 11st. 10lb., and Cambridge won easily in twenty-two minutes. He also won the University Pairs in 1845 and 1847. In 1849, besides rowing in the Boat Race, he came out Second Classic, was bracketed a Chancellor's Medallist, and was third in the Senior Optimes. Up to this time he had been all an Englishman should be; but, on coming of age, he had chosen the French nationality, and, in returning to France, devoted himself to archæology and the study of antiquities, being especially noted as a Hellenist. He then went to the East, and spent some time travelling in Asia Minor, Syria, and Cyprus, in pursuit of his favorite studies, and, in 1865, was elected a member of the Academy of Inscriptions et Belles Lettres.

In early life, M. Waddington, though he took little or no part in French politics, was known to be in favor of constitutional monarchy, but, on the fall of the Empire, he had so far modified his earlier views as to become a supporter of the conservative Republic, which was then instituted, as to enrol himself as a follower of M. Thiers. In February, 1871, he was returned by Aisne to the National Assembly, and on May 19, 1873, was appointed by M. Thiers Minister of Public Instruction—a post which, however, he only held for a very short time. In 1876 he was elevated to the Senate as Member for the Department of the Aisne, a position which he held till 1885. In 1876 he joined the Ministry of M. Jules Simon, and again held the Portfolio of Minister of Public Instruction until 1877, when, on the fall of M. Jules Simon, he entered the Cabinet formed by M. Dufaure as Minister for Foreign Affairs. In 1878 M. Waddington was appointed French Plenipotentiary at the Berlin Congress, where he represented France with much credit to himself and the Ministry. In the following year, he became President of the Council. He was M. Grévy's first Prime Minister, and succeeded M. Dufaure on February 1 on the fall of Marshal MacMahon, but there were only four actual changes in the Cabinet, the most important newcomers being M. Jules Ferry as Minister of Public Instruction, and Admiral Jaureguiberry as Minister of Marine. The result of the crisis and the election of the new Ministry gave general satisfaction, but, before long, the Cabinet began to be the object of attacks in the Chamber; and on December 21 M. Waddington resigned, after having held office nearly eleven months, and was replaced by M. de Freycinet. In 1880 he was offered, and refused, the post of Ambassador to England; but in July, 1883, he accepted it, and succeeded M. Tissot in London. M. Waddington was French Ambassador in England for nearly ten years, and he retired from his post with the respect, and to the regret, of not only all classes of Englishmen, but also of the French community in London, whose welfare he had always done his utmost to promote, and at whose social gatherings he had always been a kindly representative of the French Government. During his term of office in London he had to deal with three Foreign Ministers—Earl Granville, the Marquis of Salisbury, and the Earl of Rosebery, for Lord Iddesleigh's tenure of that post was so short as only to amount to an episode in M. Waddington's career.

WILLIAM SMITH, M.P.—VICOMTE FERDINAND DE LESSEPS.

Mr. William Smith, M.P., of Columbus, Ont., is a native Canadian, born on the farm where he now resides on the 16th of November, 1847. His parents came from Morayshire, in Scotland, when the forest still held

WILLIAM SMITH, M.P.

dominion in the country where they settled. He was educated in the public schools of Ontario, and, like many of the leaders in the affairs of our land, took a course at Upper Canada College in Toronto. Mr. Smith has an innate love for everything pertaining to agriculture, and his efforts as a practical farmer have been crowned with success, as is evidenced by a visit to his splendid farm near Columbus.

He has filled the offices of president of the county agricultural society and reeve of his own township, East Whitby, and was elected to represent South Ontario in the House of Commons in 1887. In the general elections of 1891 he was defeated by a narrow majority by Mr. J. I. Davidson, who was unseated for bribery by agents, and in the bye-election held in February, 1892, Mr. Smith carried the county again by a majority of 161.

Ferdinand de Lesseps.—Born Nov. 19, 1805, the son of a diplomatic servant of the Empire under Napoleon I., was appointed, in 1828, Attaché to the French Consulate at Lisbon, and became Consul at Barcelona in 1842. He had, with his father, in Egypt, gained some knowledge of the schemes of Mohammed Ali for the aggrandizement of that province of the Turkish Empire. Among these was the project of the Suez Canal, always favored by France. In 1854, Ferdinand de Lesseps proposed that undertaking to Said Pasha. By the influence of Napoleon III., a firman sanctioning the enterprise was obtained from the Sultan at Constantinople; and in January, 1856, the Viceroy of Egypt granted the concession to the Suez Canal Company, taking also for himself a large number of shares. The works, commenced in 1859, were, to a great extent, carried on by forced native labor, and the Egyptian Government aided them by vast expenditure, to which the beginning of its financial difficulties may justly be ascribed. In August, 1869, the waters of the Red Sea mingled with those of the Mediterranean; and on Nov. 17 of that year the canal was formally opened. M. de Lesseps was created a Vicomte, received the Grand Cross of the Legion of Honor, and obtained many other honors, including that of Grand Commander of the Star of India from our Queen. The

VICOMTE FERDINAND DE LESSEPS.

Panama Canal scheme, which he was persuaded to take up about twelve years ago, was based on engineering surveys and reports made by supposed experts to more than one International Congress.

Retreat of Matabele Warriors after an Engagement.

CANADIAN CHURCHES.

STATEMENTS AS TO THE POSITION AND WORK OF VARIOUS RELIGIOUS BODIES IN 1893.

The following tabulated statements afford interesting information as to the extent of the labors carried on by several of the more important religious bodies in Canada. An endeavor has been made to show their position in 1893.

THE METHODIST CHURCH.

Conferences.	Membership.	Ministers.	Superannuated Do.	Supernumerary Do.	Probationers.	Local Preachers.	Exhorters.	Class Leaders.	Steward's Representatives.	Sunday School Superintendents.	Epworth League Presidents.	Missionary Fund.	Superannuation Fund.	Educational Fund.	Sabbath School Aid Fund.	Sustentation Fund.	Contingent Fund.	Woman's Mission Fund.
Toronto	33,829	144	49	10	40	370	94	958	1,064	377	115	$35,680 11	$9,859 95	$3,664 37	$444 80	$892 06	$1,076 17	$4,223 13
London	28,725	117	34	1	20	180	*60	*970	1,650	320	115	18,066 33	6,408 30	2,166 27	260 42	772 63	658 53	3,410 57
Niagara	28,731	107	31	4	32	183	64	994	1,681	270	77	27,023 90	7,386 73	2,451 61	262 68	621 52	681 14	4,895 48
Guelph	29,873	132	26	5	19	309	93	989	2,012	331	125	19,883 56	6,769 48	2,447 10	297 08	582 99	654 05	2,298 68
Bay of Quinte	37,506	155	25	5	26	307	94	1,089	2,233	483	118	23,514 96	7,706 65	1,708 34	381 62	503 22	638 43	4,990 23
Montreal	36,126	170	23	1	54	294	156	802	2,499	468	85	38,311 03	10,097 87	3,631 08	398 72	1,989 84	958 69	4,683 20
Nova Scotia	13,882	83	18	..	24	44	48	282	1,005	228	60	11,632 10	1,373 39	693 42	157 92	1,332 26	328 64	3,941 17
New Brunswick	13,511	76	13	..	13	82	80	302	1,078	236	34	7,897 31	1,237 83	1,070 22	167 39	1,655 21	297 35	4,751 97
Newfoundland	10,834	41	2	..	20	51	286	665	367	172	12	7,103 28	302 01	280 44	112 71	695 73	228 36	188 52
Manitoba	14,271	75	6	8	53	228	67	355	1,393	194	50	9,754 62	4,093 11	688 43	216 48	....	392 05	538 10
British Columbia	4,255	27	1	..	22	121	67	145	330	54	28	3,427 40	1,484 70	185 85	68 30	1,038 25	113 10	567 58
	†251,743	1127	228	34	323	2,169	1,109	7,551	16,202	3,133	819	$202,294 60	$56,714 02	$18,987 13	$2,768 12	$10,083 71	$6,026 51	$34,488 63

* These figures are only approximate. The London Conference furnished no statistics on these points. † These are members only. Adherents would be in the proportion of 3½ to 1, or about 880,000.

ANGLICAN CHURCH.

Rural Deaneries	No. of Churches	No. of Stations	Church Population	Communicants	No. of Schools	No. of Teachers and Officers	No. of Scholars	Average Attendance	Contributions	Clerical Stipends	Parochial	Extra Parochial	Total Church Collections	Domestic Missions	Diocesan Missions	Foreign Missions	Clergy Trust Fund
Toronto	45	2	45,783	9,111	42	1,159	11,283	7,977	$6,711 80	$38,135 29	$69,998 92	$23,089 53	$22,449 42				
Peel	15	2	2,842	739	14	104	754	462	191 94	3,157 00	2,898 47	944 59	1,024 49				
West York	18	2	2,613	791	15	104	667	480	221 48	3,270 98	2,762 86	652 46	634 58				
East York	21	4	3,417	761	14	113	831	563	215 24	4,730 12	3,787 57	920 15	904 66				
South Simcoe	31	4	4,894	937	29	166	1,240	859	196 96	4,910 16	2,836 71	1,046 99	1,328 62				
West Simcoe	20	4	3,947	850	14	138	942	666	419 97	4,044 47	3,137 57	1,322 03	876 15				
East Simcoe	11	8	2,597	497	7	64	484	351	312 05	2,619 34	3,873 87	831 10	3,193 60				
Durham	30	8	6,743	1,296	23	194	1,582	1,122	431 23	5,677 14	9,303 23	3,231 23	2,344 84				
Northumberland	20	8	5,407	1,422	18	168	1,350	1,017	648 43	5,676 12	7,407 68	2,338 80	151 50				
Haliburton	11	17	1,602	227	10	30	315	179	...	378 50	124 65	156 10	83				
Totals	222	51	79,845	16,631	186	2,240	19,448	13,676	$9,349 86	$72,599 12	$106,131 53	$34,532 98	$33,932	$12,066 89	$12,909 73	$3,761 76	$24,358 81

PRESBYTERIAN CHURCH.

Synods	No. of Churches and Stations Supplied	No. of Families connected with Congregation	No. of Communicants on Roll	Elders	Office Bearers	No. in Sunday School and Bible Class	No. engaged in S. S. Work, including Superintendent and other Officers	Contributions for strictly Congregational purposes	Payments to College Fund, Special	Payments to College Fund, Ordinary	Payments to Home Mission Fund	Payments to Augmentation of Stipend Fund	Payments to French Evangelization Fund	Payments to Foreign Mission Fund	Payments to Aged and Infirm Ministers' Fund	Payments to Widows' and Orphans' Fund	Payments to Expenses. Assembly Fund	Total Payments to Schemes of the Church	Total Payments for all Purposes	Superannuated Ministers
Maritime Provinces	550	21554	34533	1417	1774	29336	3599	$277,677	$3,695	$3,544	$8,454	$8,042	$4,222	$18,496	$1,037	$ 420	$ 625	$48,566	$348,321	...
Montreal and Ottawa	248	14244	28460	981	1553	21433	2352	284,801	6,017	8,204	11,594	7,317	6,545	17,502	3,395	1,486	756	62,726	381,872	...
Toronto and Kingston	416	23551	51258	1764	2959	41785	4657	495,783	3,390	7,007	18,594	10,412	8,259	30,831	10,352	2,138	1,428	92,843	624,831	...
Hamilton and London	...	20824	44316	1503	2547	34367	4037	383,152	2,404	4,482	15,232	5,958	7,189	27,537	4,387	1,589	1,216	70,148	475,384	...
Manitoba and N.W.T.	427	6717	10735	322	1053	10067	1042	129,142	5,373	2,721	3,723	1,518	591	3,131	292	241	185	17,806	153,990	...
British Columbia	146	2694	3382	109	313	3321	369	75,341	90	314	1,052	497	272	824	143	130	63	3,386	91,743	...

CANADIAN CHURCHES.

BAPTIST CHURCH.

ASSOCIATIONS	Membership.	Pastors.	Number of Sunday Schools.	Number of Scholars on Roll.	FINANCES.			
					Pastoral Support.	Home Missions.	Foreign Missions.	Grand Ligne (French Evangelization).
Amherstburg	583	3	..	....				
Brant	2,409	12	20	2,194	$9,332 12	$1,851 45	$2,216 94	$509 57
Canada (Central)	1,823	17	22	925	8,225 00	742 96	815 07	299 53
Eastern	1,741	14	16	1,756	8,593 37	1,117 55	1,350 49	1,233 38
Elgin	2,049	14	21	1,355	6,638 04	995 36	963 27	.: 96 52
Grand Ligne (French)	276	15	..	....				
Hamilton	1,195	11	8	1,123	3,635 15	494 43	498 34	82 45
Middlesex and London	2,628	26	26	2,351	11,478 60	1,247 83	1,275 73	346 81
Midland	2,191	20	21	1,825	10,481 82	829 82	1,042 93	321 79
Niagara	1,647	15	21	1,350	6,601 31	598 57	799 74	123 70
Norfolk	2,722	27	33	2,535	7,966 49	481 66	447 72	80 75
Northern	1,055	9	21	1,053	5,352 11	417 34	385 39	108 97
Northwestern B.C.	2,465	26	..	....				
Ottawa	2,505	22	26	1,403	10,761 34	1,209 49	1,487 26	909 45
Owen Sound	1,317	21	24	697	5,118 31	393 40	383 65	128 40
Peterborough	1,417	18	22	1,380	6,546 10	702 17	775 77	200 42
Toronto	4,831	15	34	6,270	18,249 40	5,021 11	4,253 64	1,226 80
Walkerton	1,257	15	19	1,031	5,697 95	699 29	457 93	51 44
Western	1,867	21	28	2,120	6,652 26	435 60	457 72	73 92
Whitby and Lindsay	1,264	17	24	1,175	6,338 50	1,018 44	1,506 85	163 35
Woodstock	2,183	12	21	1,704	8,646 46	758 29	755 85	310 66
Totals	39,425	350	407	32,620	$148,414 33	$19,015 76	$17,824 16	$6,268 11

FROM THE OLD WORLD TO THE NEW: FASTNET LIGHTHOUSE.

EXHIBITIONS AND FAIRS.

SOME OF THE PRINCIPAL CANADIAN MEETINGS FOR SHOW PURPOSES.

HE Toronto Exhibition for 1893 was a good deal better, in many respects, than some of its best friends had previously ventured to hope. The directors say in their annual report:

"The year 1893 was perhaps one of the most critical, yet at the same time the most important, in the history of the Industrial Exhibition Association. In the first place, the holding of the great World's Fair at Chicago would, it was feared by many, seriously interfere with the success of the Industrial for that year, and the time had arrived when it was imperatively necessary that a large sum of money should be expended in the erection of new stables, cattle sheds, etc., the formation of new roadways, the completion of the system of drainage, and a great deal of grading, etc. With regard to the World's Fair, it was a pleasure and gratification to your directors to be able to say that its effect on the Toronto Exhibition was scarcely perceptible, either favorably or unfavorably, unless the very slight diminution in the attendance of visitors under the previous year can be attributed to this cause; but this was more probably due to the general depression in business that prevailed throughout the country at that time than from any other cause."

The following statement of receipts and expenditure was given, the receipts being $1,000 less than in 1892:

REVENUE.

Admission fees, general	$65,324 90	
Admission fees, exhibitors' tickets	300 50	
Admission fees, dog show	1,794 30	
		$67,419 70
Subscription account, general	$587 00	
Subscription account, dog show	160 00	
		747 00
Museum, gross receipts	$1,577 80	
Congress of Nations	2,776 15	
Manitoba animals	188 40	
		4,542 35
Entry fees, general	$3,506 45	
Entry fees, dog show	1,250 00	
		4,756 45

Booths, dining hall, and refreshment privileges	6,110 00	
Special rights of sale	3,671 80	
Total		$87,247 30

EXPENSE.

Prize account, general	$31,232 13	
Prize account, judges' fees	1,350 00	
		$32,582 13
Proprietor of museum, proportion of receipts	$1,229 23	
Proprietor of Congress of Nations, proportion of receipts	2,168 51	
Proprietor of Manitoba animals, proportion of receipts	94 20	
		3,491 94
Interest		1,669 11
General expense.—		
Manager and Secretary's Department	$4,423 10	
Treasurer's Department	1,089 00	
Printing and stationery	4,139 54	
Advertising and postage, reduced by $500 received from the city	4,362 08	
Electric lighting	2,120 50	
Fireworks and illuminations	7,433 38	
Special attractions	13,479 15	
Music, etc.	2,067 00	
Dog show expenses	664 64	
General wages	5,799 28	
General expenses	2,709 82	
		48,287 49
Balance, being profits of exhibition of 1893, carried to general account		1,216 63
Total		$87,247 30

The Montreal Exhibition was held for one week only instead of for ten days, as on the two previous occasions, it being considered that it would be more in the public interest to have the entire Exhibition open at one time, the former Exhibitions having proved that during the first three days, when the live stock was not on the grounds, the attendance was very small. Owing to the unfavorable weather, the fact that there was rain on two days of the week, and from other causes, the attendance this year was very disappointing, and much less than might have been expected. The number of exhibitors and entries in the various departments were as follows:

EXHIBITIONS AND FAIRS.

Departments.	Number of Exhibitors.	Number of Entries.
Horse	133	525
Cattle	66	540
Sheep	22	275
Swine	29	306
Poultry	86	1,263
Dairy Products	92	166
Agricultural Products	59	558
Horticultural	75	1,332
Machinery	22	26
Agricultural Implements	19	109
Carriage	18	86
Natural History	6	8
Honey and Apiary Supplies	12	54
Ladies' and Children's	126	688
Miscellaneous Manufactures	107	139
Totals	872	6,075

SUMMARY.		
Live Stock	250	1,646
Poultry	86	1,263
Industrial and Machinery	292	1,048
Natural History and Honey	18	62
Agricultural and Dairy	151	724
Horticultural	75	1,332
Totals	872	6,075

This year, owing to the courtesy of the Honorable Commissioner of Agriculture, there was a Working Dairy in operation, and the various improved methods of butter-making were fully explained and illustrated by competent experts from the college at St. Hyacinthe. Great interest was shown by the numerous visitors to this department, and the intelligent observations of the audience proved the utility and success of the arrangements. The number of exhibitors in the Main Building was less than in the previous year, owing to absence of many of the smaller exhibits. The individual displays this year were much larger and more attractive, and several leading houses exhibited for the first time.

The Horticultural Department was managed by the officers of the Montreal Agricultural Society, to whom the best thanks of the company are due. The building presented a handsome appearance; the beautiful plants and flowers were elegantly and artistically arranged, and, in connection with the sweet strains of the "Hungarian Gypsy Band," proved an admirable feature of the Exhibition. The Poultry Building was well filled, the new coops giving it a most attractive appearance. Subjoined is a table showing the daily receipts:

Date.	Day.	Amount.
4th September	Monday	$3,228 65
5th "	Tuesday	1,352 15
6th "	Wednesday	5,374 25
7th "	Thursday	1,623 65
8th "	Friday	3,869 65
9th "	Saturday	1,263 90
Total receipts		$16,712 25

The following is the Treasurer's statement:

RECEIPTS.

Dec. 31, 1892. Balance on hand		$ 994 64
1893. Third Call on Stock		9,770 00
" Corporation of Montreal		10,000 00
" Interest on Deposits		127 18
" Rental of Grounds		1,145 50
" Entries		1,396 00
" Privileges		1,270 65
" Space		235 00
" Restaurants		2,140 95
" Sale of Old Boiler		420 00
" Horticultural Society		1,006 60
" Admissions:		
Gate Money	$14,484 40	
Grand Stand	2,428 25	
Special Attractions	160 60	
		17,073 25
" Special Prizes:		
Wells & Richardson Co	$ 50 00	
Homing Pigeon Association	20 00	
Montreal Street Railway Co	100 00	
		170 00
" Sundries		293 20
		$46,042 97

EXPENDITURE.

Outstanding Accounts, 1892	$ 2,781 15
Real Estate	28 80
Legal Expenses	380 60
Prizes $11,433 64	
" Horticultural 1,758 25	
	13,191 89
Trades and Labor Council	322 87
Printing	2,198 89
Advertising	1,946 08
Postage and Stationery	254 11
Petty Expenses	102 37
Wages	7,166 64
Entries and Privileges refunded	31 45
General Expenses	2,661 14
Special Attractions and Bands	4,607 35
Judges' Fees	296 95
Expenses of Travelling Agents, etc.	695 55
Poultry Feed and Bedding for Stock	431 13
Construction and Repairs	6,382 03
Plant	528 63
Insurance Premiums	519 00
Interest	1,435 00
	$45,961 63
Balance on hand	81 34
	$46,042 97
Balance in Bank	81 34

The Western Fair, held at London on September 14 to 23, was not so successful as that of 1892. The total receipts from gate and stands were $17,278.28. About 40,000 people attended during the week.

The Peterborough Central Fair was held September 25 to 27. It was opened by Sir Charles H. Tupper, and was a most successful show.

The North Ontario Fair was held at Uxbridge, and was opened by Lieutenant-Governor Kirkpatrick.

EXHIBITIONS AND FAIRS.

The Central Exhibition at Ottawa was opened by the Governor-General, Lord Aberdeen.

The North Oxford Fair at Woodstock was opened by the Minister of Agriculture, and was an unprecedented success.

The Newmarket Fair was a successful meeting. The total receipts from all sources, including Government and municipal grants, were $2,810, against $2,526 in 1892. Total entries were 2,000, against 2,345 in 1892.

The Brantford Fair, September 28, was a signal success.

The following is the list of fall fairs in 1893:

Industrial	Toronto	Sept. 4-16
Western	London	Sept. 14-23
Alexandria	Alexandria	Sept. 18-19
Culross	Teeswater	Sept. 19-20
Wellesley	Wellesley	Sept. 19-20
Renfrew, South	Renfrew	Sept. 19-20
Bentinck	Hanover	Sept. 19-20
Dundas		Sept. 19-20
Central	Guelph	Sept. 19-21
Ontario-Durham	Whitby	Sept. 19-21
Lanark, South	Perth	Sept. 19-21
Bay of Quinte	Belleville	Sept. 19-22
Bayham	Staffordville	Sept. 20
Sidney	Frankford	Sept. 20-21
Northwestern	Goderich	Sept. 20-22
Bruce, South	Mildmay	Sept. 21
Clarksburg	Clarksburg	Sept. 21-22
Addington	Harrowsmith	Sept. 22
Central	Ottawa	Sept. 22-30
London Township	Ilderton	Sept. 25
Elden	Woodville	Sept. 25-26
Lambton, East	Watford	Sept. 25-26
Huron, South	Exeter	Sept. 25-26
Tavistock		Sept. 25-26
Central	Peterborough	Sept. 25-27
Lincoln	St. Catharines	Sept. 25-27
Simcoe	Barrie	Sept. 25-27
Midland Central	Kingston	Sept. 25-29
Oxford, North	Woodstock	Sept. 26-27
Mornington	Milverton	Sept. 26-27
Grey, South	Durham	Sept. 26-27
Bruce, Centre	Paisley	Sept. 26-27
Mitchell	Mitchell	Sept. 26-27
Huron, Centre	Clinton	Sept. 26-27
Ontario, North	Uxbridge	Sept. 26-27
Bowmanville	Bowmanville	Sept. 26-27
York, North	Newmarket	Sept. 26-27
Huron Township	Ripley	Sept. 26-27
Northwestern	Wingham	Sept. 26-27
Muskoka, E	Huntsville	Sept. 26-27
Central	Walter's Falls	Sept. 26-27
Netherby		Sept. 26-27
Esquesing	Georgetown	Sept. 26-27
Southern	Brantford	Sept. 26-28
Northern	Walkerton	Sept. 26-28
Waterloo, N	Berlin	Sept. 26-28
Elgin	St. Thomas	Sept. 26-28
Grenville, S	Prescott	Sept. 26-28
Northern	Collingwood	Sept. 26-29
Middlesex, W	Strathroy	Sept. 27-28
Wellington, W	Harriston	Sept. 27-28
Nipissing, W	Sturgeon Falls	Sept. 27-28
Frankville	Frankville	Sept. 27-28
Tilbury, E	Tilbury Centre	Sept. 27-28
Niagara		Sept. 27-28
Orillia	Orillia	Sept. 27-28
Central	Lindsay	Sept. 27-29
Ross and Bromley	Cobden	Sept. 28
Horticultural	Hespeler	Sept. 28-29
Cannington	Cannington	Sept. 28-29
Welland	Welland	Sept. 28-29
Peel	Brampton	Sept. 28-29
Dereham	Tilsonburg	Sept. 28-29
Perth, N	Stratford	Sept. 28-29
Muskoka	Bracebridge	Sept. 28-29
Wawanosh	Belgrave	Sept. 28-29
Bruce, North	Port Elgin	Sept. 28-29
Dufferin	Orangeville	Sept. 28-29
Plympton	Wyoming	Sept. 29
Garafraxa, W	Belwood	Sept. 29
Romney	Wheatley	Sept. 29-30
Gainsboro'		Sept. 29-30
Horticultural	Palmerston	Sept. 29-30
North Norwich	Norwich	Sept. 29-30
Tyendinaga	Shannonville	Sept. 30
Dunnville		Sept. 30 / Oct. 1
Iona	Iona	Oct. 2
Tilbury, W	Comber	Oct. 2-3
Kent, E	Thamesville	Oct. 2-3
Malahide	Aylmer	Oct. 2-4
Lincoln	St. Catharines	Oct. 2-4
Puslinch	Aberfoyle	Oct. 3
Humberstone		Oct. 3
Middlesex, N	Ailsa Craig	Oct. 3-4
Acton Hort	Acton	Oct. 3-4
Fenelon	Fenelon Falls	Oct. 3-4
Normanby	Neustadt	Oct. 3-4
Oxford	Ingersoll	Oct. 3-4
Glenelg	Markdale	Oct. 3-4
Haldimand	Cayuga	Oct. 3-4
Brant	Paris	Oct. 3-4
Northeastern	Midland	Oct. 3-4
Arthur Township	Arthur	Oct. 3-4
Simcoe, N	Stayner	Oct. 3-4
Northumberland, W	Cobourg	Oct. 3-4
Lennox	Napanee	Oct. 3-4
Horticultural	Wroxeter	Oct. 3-4
Manvers	Bethany	Oct. 3-4
Algoma, East	Sault Ste. Marie	Oct. 3-4
Himsworth	Powassan	Oct. 4
Lanark, North	Almonte	Oct. 3-5
G. Southwestern	Essex	Oct. 3-5
Peninsular	Chatham	Oct. 3-5
Thorold	Thorold	Oct. 4-5
Whitchurch	Stouffville	Oct. 4-5
Algoma, West	Thessalon	Oct. 4-5
Brook	Alvinston	Oct. 4-5
Wellandport		Oct. 4-5
York, East	Markham	Oct. 4-6
Euphrasia	Rocklyn	Oct. 5
Zorra, West	Embro	Oct. 5
McLean	Baysville	Oct. 5
Bertie Township		Oct. 5
Trafalgar	Oakville	Oct. 5-6
Blanshard	Kirkton	Oct. 5-6
Wellington, C	Elora	Oct. 5-6
Wallacetown	Wallacetown	Oct. 5-6
Renfrew, North	Beachburg	Oct. 5-6
Northumberland, E	Warkworth	Oct. 5-6
Elgin, West	Wallacetown	Oct. 5-6
Huron, East	Brussels	Oct. 5-6
Waterloo, South	Galt	Oct. 5-6
Wellington, C	Fergus	Oct. 5-6
Pelham		Oct. 5-6
Durham, East	Millbrook	Oct. 5-6
Caledon	Charleston	Oct. 5-6
Nassagaweya	Brookville	Oct. 6
Nissouri, East	Kintore	Oct. 6
Greenock	Pinkerton	Oct. 6
Springfield	Springfield	Oct. 6-7
Norwich, South	Otterville	Oct. 6-7
Howick	Gorrie	Oct. 7
Hensall	Hensall	Oct. 7-8
Glencoe	Glencoe	Oct. 9-10
Grimsby, South	Smithville	Oct. 9-10

INDEX.

	PAGE
Abbott, Sir John	63
" " Political Career of	63
" " Death of	23, 135
Aberdeen, Countess of	30
" Earl and Countess of	135
Allan, A., Death of	119
Anarchists	162
Anglican Church Synod	132-4
Annexation Meeting	119
Australian Matters	169
Barley	40
Beauport Asylum	25
Behring Sea Arbitration	18
Bishop of British Columbia, Appointment of	120
Blake, Edward, First Speech of, in the Imperial Parliament	122
Booth, Edwin	175
Bowell's Australian Commission	23
Boyd, Ex-Governor, Death of	136
Brazilian Revolution	169
British Soldiers, Parade of	131
Brooks, Bishop Phillips	178
Buffalo Robes	116
CANADIAN CHURCHES	184
Methodist	184
Anglican	185
Presbyterian	185
Baptist	186
Canada Revue and *Echo*	25
Canadian Magazine, Appearance of	122
Cape Breton Coal Mines	119
Carnegie, Andrew	178
Caron, Sir Adolphe	15
Cathedral in New York	168
Cattle Disease	60, 122
Children, Protection of	26
Children's Charter	26
" Aid Society	33
"Chippewa" Steamer	123, 9
Cholera, Apprehension of	120
Christian Endeavor Convention	126
"City of Collingwood" Steamer	123
Claimant, A, of Toronto	122
Coal Mining Contracts in Nova Scotia	23
Confederation Life Building Opened	123
Creameries' Association	60
Dairy Products	58
" Association	119
Davies, Sergeant	179

	PAGE
Defaulting Accountant	124
Derby's, Earl of, Farewell	128
Dominion Day at the World's Fair	125
" Parliament	6
Dragoons, Royal Canadian	131
Dryden, Hon. J.	55
Durand, Sir Mortimer	179
Duse, Eleanora	177
Eastern Extension Railway	23
Ebury, Lord	180
Eden, Champion Skater	177
Edison's, Mr., Opinion on Niagara Falls Power	122
Editor Sent to Jail	22
Electric Railroad, Niagara	126
Emin Pasha	177
Exhibitions and Fairs	188
Experimental Farm, Ottawa	46
Farmers' Institute, West York	118
Farming Interests	45
Fishing and Canning	42
Fleet of Columbus	125
France and Germany	162
French Treaty	16
Galt, Sir A. T., Death of	23
Gilbert and Sullivan	176
Governor-General, A New	29
" Staff of	30
" Installation of	30
" at Canada Central Fair	31
" at Board of Trade Banquet, Montreal	31
Governor-General's Reception at Montreal	31
" " Toronto	33
Grand Orange Lodge	129
Guelph Agricultural College and Farm	54
Halifax, Sham Fight at	135
Hawaiian Revolution	168
Hay, Export of	38
Honey	60
Hooper, John R., Charged with Murder	134
Howland, W. H., Death of	136
India, New Governor for	169
Jowett, Dr.	174
June Weather	125
Lachine Bridge Scandal	21
Lambton and Bruce Elections	27
Laurier, Hon. Wilfrid	131

INDEX.

	PAGE
Lesseps	182
Liberal Convention	20
Life-Boat	123
Liquor Plebiscite	27
" Traffic Commission	120
Lumber	40
Macdonald, Sir John A., Statue of	135
Mackenzie, Mrs., Death of	123
Mammoth Cheese	58
Manitoba School Legislation	7
Marter, M.P.	27
Metropolitan, Election of	120
Millers' Association	130
Minerals, Ontario	66
Mowat, Lady, Death of	123
Murder of a Farmer in Quebec	123
" " Police Constable	120
" at Port Credit	136
" Trial of Luckey	135
McCarthy, D'Alton	5
McGlynn, Dr.	173
McGreevy-Connolly Scandal	22, 136
Nansen's Trip to the Pole	165
National Council of Women	33
" Rifle Association	126
Nelson, Hugh, Death of	123
" Monument, Attempt on	136
New Brunswick Governorship	22
Newfoundland	6, 42
New York Cathedral	168
Northwest Governorship	22
" Products of the	39
" Schools	24
Nova Scotia Coal	17
Observatory, Toronto	119
Ontario Agriculture and Arts Association	45
" and Quebec	23
" Legislature	26
Orange Order	178
Panama Canal	162
Papineau, Mr., Conversion of	26
P.P.A.	27
Parliament Buildings	123
Patrons of Industry	13, 27
Phelps, American Ambassador	179
Polar Exploration	165
Pork	40
Presbyterian and Congregationalist Conference	118
Prince Edward Island Elections	24
" and Princess of Wales	140
" of Wales and Yacht Racing	142

	PAGE
Prof. John Campbell, Alleged Heresy of	128
Prohibition Commission	135
Prorogation of Parliament	17
Quebec Legislature	136
Queen, The, at Florence	138
" " at Imperial Institute	138
Robbery by Daylight	120, 122-3
Robertson, Prof., Return of	120
Ruskin, John	176
Ryerson, Dr.	180
" Election of	26
Satolli, Papal Ablegate	173
Servia, Revolution in	163
Shipping in the Maritime Provinces	43
Speech from the Throne	6
Sports, 1893	69
Yachting	69
Aquatics	75
Football	75
Cricket	81
Lacrosse	85
Baseball	87
Cycling	87
Bowling	93
Billiards	95
Curling	95
Athletics	96
Stallion Show	45
Storm in Toronto and Neighborhood	136
St. Paul's Bazaar	118
Sunday Street Cars, Vote on	131
Tariff Changes	9
Thompson, Sir John, at Glencoe	134
Trade and Commerce	35
" with Great Britain	35
Tupper, Hon. C. H., Knighted	131-2
United States	166
"Victoria" Disaster	171, 182
Waddington, M., The Late	181
Wallace, Hon. N. C.	13
Walton, Izaak	130, 172
Water Supply, Toronto	119
Welland Canal	7
Wheat Product of the World	53
Woman Suffrage	27
World's Fair	97
Yarmouth, N.S.	40-1
York, Duke of	138-144

List of Illustrations.

	PAGE
Her Majesty the Queen	Frontispiece
Sir John Thompson	6
Hon. Wilfrid Laurier	7
Hon. Mackenzie Bowell	8
Hon. G. E. Foster	9
Hon. John Haggart	10
Hon. J. A. Ouimet	11
Sir John Carling	12
Sir Oliver Mowat	13
Hon. John Costigan	14
Hon. David Mills	15
Hon. T. M. Daly	16
Hon. G. W. Ross	17
Hon. Edward Blake	18
Sir Charles H. Tupper	19
Hon. J. C. Patterson	20
Honore Mercier, M.P.	21
Sir Adolphe Caron	22
Hon. W. B. Ives	23
W. R. Meredith	24
Col. O'Brien, M.P.	25
Dr. Ryerson, M.P.P.	26
D'Alton McCarthy, M.P.	27
Hon. Lieutenant-Governor Kirkpatrick	27
Doorway, Toronto University	28
Earl of Aberdeen	30
Countess of Aberdeen	32
Horticultural Gardens and Pavilion, Toronto	34
Scott Street, Toronto	36
Main Entrance, Parliament Buildings, Toronto	38
Doorway of Victoria College, Toronto	39
Toronto University Library	41
Huron Street, Brantford—Christmas, 1893	43
Among the Rockies	44
Hon. John Dryden	46
William Saunders	47
President Mills	48
Leauchoil Mountains and the Chancellor Rockies	50
James W. Robertson	54
J. Fletcher	56
William Rennie	57
On the Grand River, near Elora	59
Entrance to the Whirlpool, Niagara River	62
Sir John Abbott	64
Dam on Grand River	65
Steam Yacht "Cleopatra"	67
"Adagio"	68
Yacht "Zelma"	70
"Here They Come!"	72
A.C.A. Races	74
Queen's University Rugby Football Team	76
"Gone!"	78
"Check"	80
The International Eleven	82
"Found"	84
Cobourg Baseball Club	86
Toronto Wanderers' Racing Team	88
Toronto B.C. Racing Team	90
Half-Moon Bay	92
Jarvis Street, Toronto	94
Castle Rest	96
CHICAGO EXPOSITION :	
Hon. Lyman J. Gage	97
Bird's-Eye View, World's Fair	99
Thomas B. Bryan	100
Anthony F. Seeberger	101
Illumination of the Art Building at Night	103
Ontario Department	106
Mrs. B. H. Palmer	108
Harlow N. Higinbotham	109
Administration Building by Night	111
Thomas W. Palmer	113
Col. Geo. R. Davis	114
Buffalo Robes	116
Group of British Soldiers	117
Central Prison Grounds, Toronto	121
The "Nina" Skiff	124
Church of the Gesu, Montreal	127
Imperial Institute, British American Conference Room	130
Mount Pleasant, North Toronto	133
Most Rev. Archbishop Machray	135
The Late W. H. Howland	136
St. Catherine Street, Montreal	137
"Victoria" Disaster	139
Prince George of Wales	141
Princess May of Teck	143
Lord Roberts	144
Duke and Duchess of Edinburgh	145
Lord Rosebery	146
Lord Houghton	146
Lord Salisbury Speaking	147
Mr. Gladstone Speaking	147
Lord Rosebery Speaking	148
Colonel Saunderson "Making a Point"	148

LIST OF ILLUSTRATIONS.

Illustration	Page
Poets' Corner, Westminster Abbey	150
Pope Leo XIII.	152
Marshal MacMahon	154
Battleship H.M.S. "Revenge"	155
Abbas Pasha, Khedive of Egypt	156
Lord Cromer	156
Admiral Humann	157
King of Siam	157
Queen of Siam	158
M. Pavie, French Minister at Siam	158
Fortified Island near Bangkok	159
King Lobengula	160
Map of South Africa	161
Panama Canal	162
King Alexander of Servia	163
Ex-King of Servia	163
Ex-Queen Natalie of Servia	163
Great Mosque at Wazan	164
Departure of Dr. Nansen in the "Fram"	165
Dr. Nansen	165
Cathedral of St. John, New York	166
Cleveland and His Cabinet	167
Bishop Potter, of New York	168
President Peixoto	168
Admiral Mello	168
Liliuokalani	169
Entrance to Rio de Janeiro	170
Rival Religions in Bombay	171
Izaak Walton	172
Dr. Edward McGlynn	173
Monsignor Satolli	174
Dr. Jowett	175
Edwin Booth	175
Gilbert and Sullivan	176
John Ruskin	176
J. J. Eden, Champion Skater	177
Signora Eleanora Duse	177
Emin Pasha	178
Bishop Phillips Brooks	178
Andrew Carnegie	178
American Ambassador Phelps	179
Sergeant T. W. Davies	179
Sir Mortimer Durand	180
The Late Lord Ebury	180
The Late M. Waddington	181
Mr. William Smith, M.P.	182
Ferdinand Lesseps	182
Matabeles in Retreat	183
Fastnet Lighthouse	186
Sandwich Island Girls	187

www.ingramcontent.com/pod-product-compliance
Lightning Source LLC
Chambersburg PA
CBHW032136160426
43197CB00008B/659